Religion in America

ADVISORY EDITOR

Edwin S. Gaustad

New Themes

for the

Protestant Clergy

Stephen Colwell

ARNO PRESS & THE NEW YORK TIMES

New York 1969

Reprint edition 1969 by Arno Press, Inc.

*

Library of Congress Catalog Card No. 71-83417

*

Reprinted from a copy in the
Princeton University Library

*

Manufactured in the United States of America

NEW THEMES

FOR THE

PROTESTANT CLERGY

NEW THEMES

FOR THE

PROTESTANT CLERGY:

CREEDS WITHOUT CHARITY,

THEOLOGY WITHOUT HUMANITY,

AND

PROTESTANTISM WITHOUT CHRISTIANITY:

With Notes by the Editor

ON THE

LITERATURE OF CHARITY, POPULATION, PAUPERISM,
POLITICAL ECONOMY, AND PROTESTANTISM.

PHILADELPHIA:

LIPPINCOTT, GRAMBO & CO.

No. 14 NORTH FOURTH STREET,

1851.

Printed by T. K. & P. G. Collins.
Stereotyped by L. Johnson & Co., Philadelphia.

CONTENTS.

Notes, Bibliographical and General.

PREFACE.

In offering the following pages to the public, we furnish no formal or complete treatise upon any of the topics embraced. We have reflected long and earnestly upon them, as they arose incessantly in the course of kindred studies, until we became painfully convinced that they were neglected, and that the time had arrived when the public attention should be specially invoked. This labour is devoted to that purpose. We have poured forth our feelings, and, with scarcely a pretence of method, sketched an outline of our thoughts. We would thus provoke others to more elaborate performances. If this work is unworthy of the subject, let its imperfections stimulate those of more leisure, better training, and greater ability to undertake the task we have only indicated. We ask attention to the *subject*, as of sufficient interest and novelty to arrest the thoughts of the reader, despite all our deficiencies : let no one, therefore, who desires the progress of Christianity or the promotion of humanity refuse to hear the feeblest voice which is raised in their behalf.

Let it not be thought that, whilst dwelling so emphatically upon Charity, we have violated its dictates by undue severity of remark. We have intended no censures upon individuals, even when severe upon the class to which they belong. We regard the faults of individuals, whether priests, clergy, ministers, or laymen, as being the faults of their age or their station, or as the results of education or training,—circumstances all beyond their control; and whilst we do not abate a jot from the responsibility which belongs to wrong-doing, we admit, human nature being ever prone to err, that men placed in similar circumstances will be likely to transgress in similar paths. We believe there are few instances in which one class of men can, in the sight of God, glory over others: if any are better, they have more light and better opportunities, and will be held to a stricter account. Many of our expressions doubtless require qualification, but we trust that the reader who is earnestly in quest of truth will readily perceive our scope, and follow the channel of our thoughts until he is fully embarked in the subject; he will then perceive there is "ample room and verge enough" for the mind, without aiming censure at any one. We denounce none: we ask the serious consideration and co-operation of all. We insist that Protestants have long overlooked and neglected charity—that it has not been, and is not, a feature in their creeds; that, while Protestantism has gone far before the world in liberality, it is almost a stranger to that charity which the Author of our faith preached and exemplified. We plead the cause of the poor, the suffering, the friendless, before those who claim pre-eminence in Christianity: we ask whether, as Protestants, enjoying the highest Christian privileges which have fallen to the lot of men, we have, in the matter of human welfare, done that which it was our duty to do? We may not postpone this inquiry without suffering in public estimation and in our ability to do good;—we cannot postpone it

without danger of being put on our defence as recreant
- to the cause of humanity. The world now believes
that the religion, announced by the Author and Finisher
of our faith, embraces HUMANITY as well as DIVINITY
in its range. We must meet the great questions now
raised in behalf of humanity, and not be overtaken by
them. Let us unite in the effort to adjust the claims of
charity and justice; and let us not wait until they are
settled without our aid or our consent—we being thrust
aside as unworthy a voice in the matter. Human weal
and human wo cannot as subjects be postponed. The
duties we owe to our fellow-men, long passed by in the
Gospels, are being brought to light. Theology must
soon sink to its subordinate position, and charity—the
law of kindness—must soon be exalted to its proper rank.

The value of kindness, as a remedy for the ills of life,
is beginning to be appreciated. It is now the established
specific for insanity : it is the only mitigation of madness.
Where a spark of reason is left to the raving maniac,
though invisible to every other human eye, it is fanned
into life, and soon perceived by the messenger of mercy.
It is but a few years since the most atrocious cruelties
were perpetrated by good people against those bereft of
reason. The age of cruelty is giving way to that of mercy.
Kindness is known to be a specific for many forms of
disease, and kind nursing for many more. Christ's whole
ministry was one of personal kindness. Charity is the
great lever of Christianity : by it the messengers of the
gospel can open the eyes of pagan blindness : by it the
ears of the most obstinate and hardened can be unstopped :
by it reason can be restored and life saved : by it every
human ill can be alleviated : by it all obstacles to the pro-

1

gress of Christianity can be removed or diminished. Men are selfish, unfeeling, and prone to the abuse of power and wealth; yet, where charity appears in her simplest garb, she is hailed as a heavenly visitant, and the message which accompanies her deeds of kindness is received as the voice of Heaven.

It is time the virtue of this remedy were tried in the name of Christianity upon the whole mass of humanity: try it upon the poor, upon paupers, upon prisoners, soldiers, sailors, servants, labourers; try it upon infidels, socialists, reforming zealots, revolutionists; try it upon all men—and the result will be happy beyond all our present conceptions.

BY THE EDITOR.

Let no one cast aside this little volume, as the work of a crude and unfurnished mind; or as the product of a captious grumbler, ignorant of the theology he underrates and incapable of grasping his subject; or as the sickly dreams of a diseased imagination. If any are so dead to the interests of humanity as to be insensible to the considerations here presented, it is time they were awakened; if any are alive to them, but inactive, it is time they were put on the alert. Few, it is hoped, can follow the train of reflection here suggested, without experiencing a feeling that there is a lamentable omission in our Protestantism, and without a desire to understand the subject better. It will be found there is a wide range for the mind in the topics here touched, and that a reformation remains to be effected greater than any yet conceived.

We have added to the text extended bibliographical notices and catalogues, in the hope of tempting the studious and humane into this field of research, and of facilitating the labours of those who may be willing to devote their thoughts to the service of humanity.

October 20th, 1851.

WHY HAS CHRISTIANITY MADE SO LITTLE PROGRESS?

WHAT impedes the progress of Christianity? This inquiry must very often arise in the mind of every thoughtful Christian, and no one can over-estimate the importance of a right answer. Apart from its Divine origin, and its vital personal consequence to every human being, the triumphs of Christianity over all other religious systems assert its claims to the support of all lovers of order, of civilization, of industry, of art, of science, of literature and social well-being. Its triumphs are, however, thus far, greater in kind than in extent. The Christian world is distinguished immeasurably above all the rest in all these respects; but the Mohammedan and Pagan world yet greatly exceeds it in extent

and population. Eighteen centuries have
been sufficient to establish Christianity over
but a small portion of the earth; and even
many of the conquests once made are now
lost! Both Mohammedism and Paganism
prevail now where Christians once dwelt. If
the question were only—Why are not the advantages of Europe and America extended to
Asia and Africa?—it would be of unspeakable
importance to find a solution : but the solution
is of infinitely more importance than this
would imply. How many in Christian lands
are really Christians? Less, perhaps, than a
tenth, or a fourth, or a third. The inquiry
then arises,—What restricts Christianity to
this small proportion? How comes it, that
among the enlightened, upon whom the truths
of the Gospel are urged from God's own word,
where eternal blessedness is placed in the alternative with eternal misery, so few make
their election to be on the safe side?—Whatever circumlocution may be indulged on this
subject, the plain truth is, that men who neg-

lect to seek eternal happiness, do not believe the message of the Gospel. There is not a sane man in existence, who, if he believed that an eternal existence of happiness or misery awaited him, as he made his peace with God or not in this world, that would lose one moment in turning his face heaven-ward. They do not believe in Christ who do not seek his favour. It is a vain waste of words to distinguish between the tenets of him who openly denies the message of God to men, and of him who constantly refuses submission to his will. The one but denies by words what the other denies as fully by his acts, whatever may be his words. The people of Christendom are, therefore, properly classified into believers and unbelievers.

But why this appalling disproportion under the full light of the truth? The fault cannot be with Him who offers this grand alterna-tive. No doubt every individual must answer for himself to God, and each must bear the penalty of his own impenitence and unbelief;

yet it is certain that, in the order of Providence, human means are employed in the propagation of Christianity. Why then are the means so ineffective? How much of this reproach belongs to the professed followers of Christ, to whom the duty of proclaiming the truth is committed? Do they suppose they have discharged their whole duty in this respect? Are their skirts clear of the blood of those who are perishing by millions? No inquiry can be so important to Christians as that, whether, next to their own salvation, they have done what they could for the salvation of others. It is the work of Christians— all the means are committed to them.

It is true that men are, by nature, blind to their eternal interests, and unwilling to obey, or even hear, the truth: but the power of the truth is sufficient to subdue the most obdurate; and God is always ready to bless every proper effort. Where, then, lies the difficulty—the obstacle—the barrier to the progress of Christianity? There can be only one reply—that, aside from the accountability of each individual for himself, the responsibility for the slow progress of Christianity lies at the door of those who profess to be the friends of Christ.

It may not be easy to say, in what precise manner they are liable to this heavy charge; but it is clear that it lies nowhere else, and that they are bound to examine themselves and see what it is they have done, or what they have left undone, which subjects them to the accusation of obstructing the progress of their Master's cause.

We propose to enter a little upon this examination, not with the hardihood of expecting to offer any solution of the difficulty, but merely to make a few suggestions—to mark out a line of thought, which, followed up by others more capable, may lead to profitable results.

What, then, is the mission upon which Christ came into this world, and which, upon leaving it, he committed to his followers?—

To state this it is not necessary to enter into a history of the Jews, nor even to notice the prophecies which heralded his approach. The mission of Christ is explicit and intelligible. He came to redeem the perishing; to offer terms of reconciliation to rebels; to accomplish a sacrifice, being himself the victim, and thus to become a Saviour through whom all that believe should inherit eternal life. He came to fulfil and satisfy the law which men had not kept, that no jot or tittle might pass unfulfilled; he came in the fulness of time with a new dispensation of mercy, and a new commandment, comprehending all the moral obligations of the old law, and embracing, in a few words, every duty of man to God, and to his fellow man—"Thou shalt love the Lord thy God with all thy heart, and all thy soul, and with all thy strength, and with all thy mind; and thy neighbour as thyself."* This is the sum of human duty; this is the

---

* Luke x. 27.

law which Christ has given us; this law, received from him, is Christianity. Its comprehensiveness and purity proclaim its divine origin. No such law, nor such doctrine, nor such philosophy ever fell from mere human lips or human pen. No other religion embraces such requirements. The expositions of this law, given by Christ in the course of his ministry, leave no doubt of its comprehensiveness and the nature of its application— of its stringency, and its searching obligation. " A *new commandment* I give unto you, That ye love one another; as I have loved you, that you love one another." He frequently employs the terms " my commandment," showing that there is something special and peculiar in the precepts thus announced.

For the sake of distinctness and convenient reference, we here place in conjunction some of the more special teachings of Christ on the subject to which we desire more especially to draw the attention of the reader.

And he opened his mouth, and taught them, saying, Blessed are the poor in spirit: for theirs is the kingdom of heaven. Blessed are they that mourn: for they shall be comforted. Blessed are the meek: for they shall inherit the earth. Blessed are they which do hunger and thirst after righteousness: for they shall be filled. Blessed are the merciful: for they shall obtain mercy. Blessed are the pure in heart: for they shall see God. Blessed are the peace-makers: for they shall be called the children of God. Blessed are they which are persecuted for righteousness' sake: for theirs is the kingdom of heaven. Blessed are ye when men shall revile you, and persecute you, and shall say all manner of evil against you falsely, for my sake.—*Matt.* v. 2—11.

Ye have heard that it was said by them of old time, Thou shalt not kill; and whosoever shall kill, shall be in danger of the judgment: but I say unto you, That whosoever is angry with his brother without a cause, shall be in danger of the judgment: and whosoever shall say to his brother, Raca, shall be in danger of the council: but whosoever shall say, Thou fool, shall be in danger of hell-fire. Therefore, if thou bring thy gift to the altar, and there rememberest that thy brother hath aught against thee, leave there thy gift before the altar, and go thy way; first be reconciled to thy brother, and then come and offer thy gift.—*Matt.* v. 21—24.

Ye have heard that it hath been said, An eye for an eye, and a tooth for a tooth. But I say unto you, That ye resist not evil: but whosoever shall smite thee on thy right cheek, turn to him the other also.   And if any man will sue thee at the law, and take away thy coat, let him have thy cloak also.   And whosoever shall compel thee to go a mile, go with him twain.   Give to him that asketh thee, and from him that would borrow of thee turn not thou away.

Ye have heard that it hath been said, Thou shalt love thy neighbour, and hate thine enemy: but I say unto you, Love your enemies, bless them that curse you, do good to them that hate you, and pray for them which despitefully use you and persecute you; that ye may be the children of your Father which is in heaven: for he maketh his sun to rise on the evil and on the good, and sendeth rain on the just and on the unjust.   For if ye love them which love you, what reward have ye? do not even the publicans the same?—*Matt.* v. 38—46.

Take heed that ye do not your alms before men, to be seen of them: otherwise ye have no reward of your Father which is in heaven.   Therefore, when thou doest thine alms, do not sound a trumpet before thee, as the hypocrites do, in the synagogues, and in the streets, that they may have glory of men.   Verily I say unto you, They have their reward.   But when thou doest alms, let not thy left hand know what thy right hand doeth; that thine alms may be in secret: and thy Father which seeth in secret, himself shall reward thee openly.—*Matt.* vi. 1—4.

And forgive us our debts, as we forgive our debtors.— *Matt.* vi. 12.

2

For if ye forgive men their trespasses, your heavenly Father will also forgive you : but if ye forgive not men their trespasses, neither will your Father forgive your trespasses.—*Matt.* vi. 14, 15.

Lay not up for yourselves treasures upon earth, where moth and rust doth corrupt, and where thieves break through and steal : but lay up for yourselves treasures in heaven, where neither moth nor rust doth corruupt, and where thieves do not break through nor steal. For where your treasure is, there will your heart be also.—*Matt.* vi. 19—21.

Therefore I say unto you, Take no thought for your life, what ye shall eat, or what ye shall drink ; nor yet for your body, what ye shall put on. Is not the life more than meat, and the body than raiment? Behold the fowls of the air; for they sow not, neither do they reap, nor gather into barns; yet your heavenly Father feedeth them. Are ye not much better than they? Which of you by taking thought can add one cubit unto his stature ? And why take ye thought for raiment? Consider the lilies of the field how they grow; they toil **not,** neither do they spin; and yet I say unto you, That even Solomon in all his glory was not arrayed like.one of these. Wherefore, if God so clothe the grass of the field, which to-day is, and to-morrow is cast into the oven, shall he not much more clothe you, O ye of little faith? Therefore take no thought, saying, What shall we eat? or, What shall we drink ? or, Wherewithal shall we be clothed ? (For after all these things do the Gentiles seek :) for your heavenly Father knoweth that ye have need of all these things. But seek ye first the kingdom of God, and his righteousness, and all these things shall be added unto you. Take therefore no thought for the morrow: for the morrow shall take thought for the things of itself. Sufficient unto the day is the evil thereof.—*Matt.* vi. 25—34.

Judge not, that ye be not judged. For with what judgment ye judge, ye shall be judged: and with what measure ye mete, it shall be measured to you again. And why beholdest thou the mote that is in thy brother's eye, but considerest not the beam that is in thine own eye? Or how wilt thou say to thy brother, Let me pull out the mote out of thine eye; and behold, a beam is in thine own eye? Thou hypocrite, first cast out the beam out of thine own eye; and then shalt thou see clearly to cast out the mote out of thy brother's eye.

Give not that which is holy unto the dogs, neither cast ye your pearls before swine, lest they trample them under their feet, and turn again and rend you.

Ask, and it shall be given you; seek, and ye shall find; knock, and it shall be opened unto you: for every one that asketh, receiveth; and he that seeketh, findeth; and to him that knocketh, it shall be opened. Or what man is there of you, whom if his son ask bread, will he give him a stone? Or if he ask a fish, will he give him a serpent? If ye then being evil know how to give good gifts unto your children, how much more shall your Father which is in heaven give good things to them that ask him? Therefore all things whatsoever ye would that men should

do to you, do ye even so to them : for this is the law and
the prophets.—*Matt.* vii. 1—12.

Not every one that saith unto me, Lord, Lord, shall
enter into the kingdom of heaven; but he that doeth the
will of my Father which is in heaven. Many will say to
me in that day, Lord, Lord, have we not prophesied in
thy name? and in thy name have cast out devils? and in
thy name done many wonderful works? And then will I
profess unto them, I'never knew you: depart from me,
ye that work iniquity.—*Matt.* vii. 21—23.

And when he had called unto him his twelve disciples,
he gave them power against unclean spirits, to cast them
out, and to heal all manner of sickness, and all manner
of disease.—*Matt.* x. 1.

And as ye go, preach, saying, The kingdom of heaven
is at hand. " Heal the sick, cleanse the lepers, raise the
dead, cast out devils : freely ye have received, freely give.
Provide neither gold, nor silver, nor brass in your purses;
nor scrip for your journey, neither two coats, neither
shoes, nor yet staves : (for the workman is worthy of his
meat.) And into whatsoever city or town ye shall enter,
inquire who in it is worthy; and there abide till ye go
thence. And when ye come into a house, salute it. And
if the house be worthy, let your peace come upon it : but
if it be not worthy, let your peace return to you.—*Matt.*
x. 7—13.

And whosoever shall give to drink unto one of these
little ones, a cup of cold water only, in the name of a dis-

ciple, verily I say unto you, he shall in no wise lose his reward.—*Matt.* x. 42.

And Jesus called a little child unto him, and set him in the midst of them, and said, Verily I say unto you, Except ye be converted, and become as little children, ye shall not enter into the kingdom of heaven. Whosoever therefore shall humble himself as this little child, the same is greatest in the kingdom of heaven. And whoso shall receive one such little child in my name, receiveth me. But, whoso shall offend one of these little ones which believe in me, it were better for him that a millstone were hanged about his neck, and that he were drowned in the depth of the sea.—*Matt.* xviii. 2—6.

Moreover, if thy brother shall trespass against thee, go and tell him his fault between thee and him alone: if he shall hear thee, thou hast gained thy brother. But if he will not hear thee, then take with thee one or two more, that in the mouth of two or three witnesses every word may be established. And if he shall neglect to hear them, tell it unto the church: but if he neglect to hear the church, let him be unto thee as an heathen man and a publican.—*Matt.* xviii. 15—17.

Then came Peter to him, and said, Lord, how oft shall my brother sin against me, and I forgive him? till seven times? Jesus saith unto him, I say not unto thee, Until seven times: but, Until seventy times seven.

Therefore is the kingdom of heaven likened unto a certain king which would take account of his servants. And when he had begun to reckon, one was brought unto him

which owed him ten thousand talents. But forasmuch as
he had not to pay, his lord commanded him to be sold,
and his wife and children, and all that he had, and payment to be made. The servant therefore fell down, and
worshipped him, saying, Lord, have patience with me, and
I will pay thee all. Then the lord of that servant was
moved with compassion, and loosed him, and forgave him
the debt. But the same servant went out, and found one
of his fellow-servants, which owed him an hundred pence:
and he laid hands on him, and took him by the throat,
saying, Pay me that thou owest. And his fellow-servant
fell down at his feet, and besought him, saying, Have patience with me, and I will pay thee all. And he would
not: but went and cast him into prison, till he should pay
the debt. So when his fellow-servants saw what was done,
they were very sorry, and came and told unto their lord
all that was done. Then his lord, after that he had called
him, said unto him, O thou wicked servant, I forgave thee
all that debt, because thou desiredst me: shouldest not
thou also have had compassion on thy fellow-servant, even
as I had pity on thee? And his lord was wroth, and delivered him to the tormentors, till he should pay all that
was due unto him. So likewise shall my heavenly Father
do also unto you, if ye from your hearts forgive not every
one his brother their trespasses.—*Matt.* xviii. 21—35.

Jesus said, Thou shalt do no murder; Thou shalt not
commit adultery; Thou shalt not steal; Thou shalt not
bear false witness; Honour thy father and thy mother:
and, Thou shalt love thy neighbour as thyself. The young
man saith unto him, All these things have I kept from
my youth up: what lack I yet? Jesus said unto him,

If thou wilt be perfect, go and sell that thou hast, and give to the poor, and thou shalt have treasure in heaven : and come and follow me.—*Matt.* xix. 18—21.

Jesus said unto him, Thou shalt love the Lord thy God with all thy heart, and with all thy soul, and with all thy mind. This is the first and great commandment. And the second is like unto it, Thou shalt love thy neighbour as thyself.—*Matt.* xxii. 37—39.

When the Son of man shall come in his glory, and all the holy angels with him, then shall he sit upon the throne of his glory; and before him shall be gathered all nations : and he shall separate them one from another, as a shepherd divideth his sheep from the goats : and he shall set the sheep on his right hand, but the goats on the left. Then shall the King say unto them on his right hand, Come, ye blessed of my Father, inherit the kingdom prepared for you from the foundation of the world : for I was an hungered, and ye gave me meat : I was thirsty, and ye gave me drink : I was a stranger, and ye took me in : naked, and ye clothed me : I was sick, and ye visited me : I was in prison, and ye came unto me. Then shall the righteous answer him, saying, Lord, when saw we thee an hungered and fed thee? or thirsty, and gave thee drink? When saw we thee a stranger, and took thee in? or naked, and clothed thee ? Or when saw we thee sick, or in prison, and came unto thee? And the King shall answer and say unto them, Verily I say unto you, Inasmuch as ye have done it unto one of the least of these my brethren, ye have done it unto me. Then shall he say also unto them on the left hand, Depart from me, ye

cursed, into everlasting fire, prepared for the devil and
his angels: for I was an hungered and ye gave me no
meat: I was thirsty, and ye gave me no drink: I was a
stranger, and ye took me not in: naked, and ye clothed
me not: sick, and in prison, and ye visited me not. Then
shall they also answer him, saying, Lord, when saw we
thee an hungered, or athirst, or a stranger, or naked, or
sick, or in prison, and did not minister unto thee? Then
shall he answer them, saying, Verily I say unto you, Inasmuch as ye did it not to one of the least of these, ye did
it not to me.   And these shall go away into everlasting
punishment: but the righteous into life eternal.—*Matt.*
xxv. 31—46.

For whosoever shall give you a cup of water to drink
in my name, because ye belong to Christ, verily I say
unto you, he shall not lose his reward.   And whosoever
shall offend one of these little ones that believe in me, it
is, better for him that a millstone were hanged about his
neck, and he were cast into the sea.—*Mark* ix. 41, 42.

And they brought young children to him, that he should
touch them; and his disciples rebuked those that brought
them.   But when Jesus saw it, he was much displeased,
and said unto them, Suffer the little children to come unto
me, and forbid them not: for of such is the kingdom of
God.   Verily I say unto you, Whosoever shall not receive the kingdom of God as a little child, he shall not
enter therein.   And he took them up in his arms, put
his hands upon them, and blessed them.

And when he was gone forth into the way, there came

one running, and kneeled to him, and asked him, Good Master, what shall I do that I may inherit eternal life? And Jesus said unto him, Why callest thou me good? there is none good but one, that is God. Thou knowest the commandments, Do not commit adultery, Do not kill, Do not steal, Do not bear false witness, Defraud not, Honour thy father and mother. And he answered and said unto him, Master, all these have I observed from my youth. Then Jesus beholding him loved him, and said unto him, One thing thou lackest: go thy way, sell whatsoever thou hast, and give to the poor, and thou shalt have treasure in heaven; and come, take up the cross, and follow me. And he was sad at that saying, and went away grieved; for he had great possessions.

And Jesus looked round about, and saith unto his disciples, How hardly shall they that have riches enter into the kingdom of God! And the disciples were astonished at his words. But Jesus answereth again, and saith unto them, Children, how hard is it for them that trust in riches to enter into the kingdom of God! It is easier for a camel to go through the eye of a needle, than for a rich man to enter into the kingdom of God. And they were astonished out of measure, saying among themselves, Who then can be saved? And Jesus looking upon them, saith, With men it is impossible, but not with God: for with God all things are possible.—*Mark* x. 13—27.

But I say unto you which hear, Love your enemies, do good to them which hate you, bless them that curse you, and pray for them which despitefully use you. And unto him that smiteth thee on the one cheek, offer also the

other; and him that taketh away thy cloak, forbid not to
take thy coat also. Give to every man that asketh of thee;
and of him that taketh away thy goods, ask them not
again. And as ye would that men should do to you, do
ye also to them likewise. For if ye love them which love
you, what thank have ye? for sinners also love those that
love them. And if ye do good to them which do good
to you, what thank have ye? for sinners also do even the
same. And if ye lend to them of whom ye hope to receive, what thank have ye? for sinners also lend to sinners, to receive as much again. But love ye your enemies, and do good, and lend, hoping for nothing again;
and your reward shall be great, and ye shall be the children of the Highest: for he is kind unto the unthankful
and to the evil. Be ye therefore merciful, as your Father
also is merciful.   Judge not, and ye shall not be judged:
condemn not, and ye shall not be condemned: forgive,
and ye shall be forgiven: give, and it shall be given unto
you; good measure, pressed down, and shaken together,
and running over, shall men give into your bosom.   For
with the same measure that ye mete withal, it shall be
measured to you again.—*Luke* vi. 27—38.

And why call ye me Lord, Lord, and do not the things
which I say?—*Luke* vi. 46.

And behold, a certain lawyer stood up, and tempted him,
saying, Master, what shall I do to inherit eternal life? He
said unto him, What is written in the law? how readest thou?
And he answering said, Thou shalt love the Lord thy God
with all thy heart, and with all thy soul, and with all thy

strength, and with all thy mind; and thy neighbour as thyself. And he said unto him, Thou hast answered right: this do, and thou shalt live. But he, willing to justify himself, said unto Jesus, And who is my neighbour? And Jesus answering, said, A certain man went down from Jerusalem to Jericho, and fell among thieves, which stripped him of his raiment, and wounded him, and departed, leaving him half dead. And by chance there came down a certain priest that way; and when he saw him, he passed by on the other side. And likewise a Levite, when he was at the place, came and looked on him, and passed by on the other side. But a certain Samaritan, as he journeyed, came where he was: and when he saw him, he had compassion on him, and went to him, and bound up his wounds, pouring in oil and wine, and sat him on his own beast, and brought him to an inn, and took care of him. And on the morrow, when he departed, he took out two pence, and gave them to the host, and said unto him, Take care of him: and whatsoever thou spendest more, when I come again, I will repay thee. Which now of these three, thinkest thou, was neighbour unto him that fell among the thieves? And he said, He that showed mercy on him. Then said Jesus unto him, Go, and do thou likewise.—*Luke* x. 25—37.

Then said he also to him that bade him, When thou makest a dinner or a supper, call not thy friends, nor thy brethren, neither thy kinsmen, nor thy rich neighbours; lest they also bid thee again, and a recompense be made thee. But when thou makest a feast, call the poor, the maimed, the lame, the blind; and thou shalt be blessed : for they cannot recompense thee : for thou shalt be recompensed at the resurrection of the just.

And when one of them that sat at meat with him heard these things, he said unto him, Blessed is he that shall eat bread in the kingdom of God. Then said he unto him, A certain man made a great supper and bade many : and sent his servant at supper-time, to say to them that were bidden, Come, for all things are now ready. And they all with one consent began to make excuse. The first said unto him, I have bought a piece of ground, and I must needs go and see it : I pray thee have me excused. And another said, I have bought five yoke of oxen, and I go to prove them : I pray thee have me excused. And another said, I have married a wife : and therefore I cannot come. So that servant came, and showed his lord these things. Then the master of the house being angry, said to his servant, Go out quickly into the streets and lanes of the city, and bring in hither the poor, and the maimed, and the halt, and the blind. And the servant said, Lord, it is done as thou hast commanded, and yet there is room. And the lord said unto the servant, Go out into the highways and hedges, and compel them to come in, that my house may be filled. For I say unto you, that none of those men which were bidden shall taste of my supper.— *Luke* xiv. 12—24.

And he spake this parable unto certain which trusted in themselves that they were righteous, and despised others : Two men went up into the temple to pray ; the one a Pharisee and the other a publican. The Pharisee stood and prayed thus with himself, God, I thank thee that I am not as other men are, extortioners, unjust, adulterers, or even as this publican. I fast twice in the week, I give tithes of all that I possess. And the publican, standing afar off, would not lift up so much as his eyes unto heaven, but smote upon his breast, saying, God be merciful to me a sinner. I tell you, this man went down to his house justified rather than the other: for every one that exalteth himself shall be abased; and he that humbleth himself shall be exalted.—*Luke* xviii. 9—14.

And Zaccheus stood, and said unto the Lord; Behold, Lord, the half of my goods I give to the poor; and if I have taken any thing from any man by false accusation, I restore him four-fold.—*Luke* xix. 8.

And the scribes and Pharisees brought unto him a woman taken in adultery: and when they had set her in the midst, they say unto him, Master, this woman was taken in adultery, in the very act. Now Moses in the law commanded us, that such should be stoned: but what sayest thou? This they said, tempting him, that they might have to accuse him. But Jesus stooped down, and with his finger wrote on the ground, as though he heard them not. So when they continued asking him, he lifted up himself, and said unto them, He that is without sin among you, let him first cast a stone at her.—*John* viii. 3—7.

After that, he poureth water into a basin, and began to wash the disciples' feet, and to wipe them with the towel wherewith he was girded. Then cometh he to Simon Peter: and Peter saith unto him, Lord, dost thou wash my feet? Jesus answered and said unto him, What I do thou knowest not now; but thou shalt know hereafter. Peter saith unto him, Thou shalt never wash my feet. Jesus answered him, If I wash thee not, thou hast no part with me. Simon Peter saith unto him, Lord, not my feet only, but also my hands and my head. Jesus saith to him, He that is washed needeth not save to wash his feet, but is clean every whit: and ye are clean, but not all. For he knew who should betray him: therefore said he, Ye are not all clean. So after he had washed their feet, and had taken his garments, and was set down again, he said unto them, Know ye what I have done to you? Ye call me Master, and Lord: and ye say well; for so I am. If I then, your Lord and Master, have washed your feet, ye also ought to wash one another's feet. For I have given you an example, that ye should do as I have done to you.—*John* xiii. 5—15.

A new commandment I give unto you, That ye love one another; as I have loved you, that ye also love one another. By this shall all men know that ye are my disciples, if ye have love one to another.—*John* xiii. 34, 35.

This is my commandment, That ye love one another, as I have loved you.—*John* xv. 12.

Ye are my friends if ye do whatsoever I command you.—*John* xv. 14.

These things I command you, that ye love one another.—*John* xv. 17.

CAN any believer in Christ deliberately think upon these and other similar teachings, and not be apprehensive that a great reformation remains to be effected among his followers : a reformation not less important than that which rescued us from the errors of the Romish church ? How does our Protestantism compare with these precepts of our Divine Master ? May we not be indulging our complacency a little too far since our escape from Rome ? Have we not stopped the progress of a reformation which had far to conduct us before we adorned these doctrines of our Lord and Master ? Where is yet the exemplification of Christianity, even as it may be looked for on Earth ? There is reason to fear, that while, as Protestants, we deny the infallibility of the Pope, we are setting up one of our own. There is no greater enemy to the progress of truth than self-sufficiency. Spiritual arrogance is not rare among Protestants. " We are right, and you are wrong," are assertions dealt out with unsparing frequency and energy.

But, in the present condition of Christianity, should not Christians qualify their opinions with—" Lord, I believe; help thou mine unbelief!" When we are divinely taught that if we had " faith as a grain of mustard-seed," we could perform miracles, there is surely meaning enough in this expression to warn the followers of Christ not to be of those who " trust in themselves that they are righteous, and despise others."

The precepts of Christ—how striking their point, their power, their purity, their simplicity, and their vast comprehensiveness!— These exhibit Christianity; but where is its exemplification? Where are the Christians of whom it may be said, " By this shall all men know that ye are my disciples, if ye have love to one another,"—such love as Christ himself prescribes and characterizes? If no such exemplification, and no approach to it, can be found, may we not fear that this is the barrier which now stays the progress of Christianity? The world needs to be convinced through other avenues than the ears. When the men of the heathen world look upon the Christian world, what do they behold? Christianity?—No! Civilization:—civilized men indebted to Christianity, but not repaying the obligation. They behold the evidences of science on every side; but illustrations of the pure teachings of Christ they find nowhere.

We shall not now dwell on this topic, but merely inquire, in passing, where we shall find any adequate exposition of the teachings of Christ. In Protestant religious literature, where is that treatise upon the Love of God, which does justice to the magnitude of the subject? Or in what system of divinity, or work upon theology, does this subject occupy the place it deserves? It would appear as if theology should be developed from that point.

We may inquire, in like manner, where has the rule of our Saviour, " Whatsoever ye would that men should do to you, do you even so to them," received that full exposition its im-

3*

portance requires? It covers the whole ground
of man's duty to man; yet what space does it
occupy in our religious literature? There are
scores of thousands of theological works of
Protestant origin, yet how few of these treat
of Love to God, or, Love to Man! Where
shall we find any adequate application of the
command that we should "love our neighbour
as ourself," to the constitution of society, as
now existing in Christendom? If these commands are as broad and obligatory as their
terms imply, they constitute the basis of
the Christian system, and of all true social
economy. No theology can be rightly framed,
and no system of morals or politics can be
rightly constructed, which have not this foundation, and of which the superstructure is not
cemented by the same material. Yet, where
is the system of theology which takes the love
of God as its starting point, and the love of
man as a chief element? This question is
merely thrown out here : the subject will be
resumed before we close.

THE MISSION OF CHRIST IN HIS OWN WORDS.

WE have glanced at the teachings of our
Saviour.   Let us also examine his own practical exposition of these teachings.   He came
into the world, not only to save, and to teach,
but to exemplify his precepts.   If his human
lineage was noble, his birth was lowly in the
extreme.   His parents were not only poor and
in humble life, but residents of a district
despised by the rich and the great.   He not
only did not appear in the world as a noble or
a king, but he did not come as a priest or a
Levite.   His ministry, which did not commence until he reached a ripened manhood,
can be fitly characterized only in his own
words.   When John sent two of his disciples
to Christ, to inquire, "Art thou He that
should come, or do we look for another?"   The
reply was not an exposition of his title to the

Messiahship; not a summary of his doctrine;
neither a creed nor a sermon; but,—" Go and
show John those things which ye do hear and
see: the blind receive their sight, and the lame
walk; the lepers are cleansed, and the deaf
hear; the dead are raised up, and the poor
have the gospel preached to them."*   He announced a mission to the poor, to the infirm,
the diseased, and the dying; and yet the missionary was so poor himself, he had not where
to lay his head.   Of this world's goods it does
not appear that he had any.   The chosen assistants of his ministry were selected not only
from among the poor, but from among those
engaged in the humblest and most despised
employments.   They were ignorant and un-
learned men, and were even readily recognised
to be such after the resurrection of Christ.†
That they had high qualifications or aptness
for the duties to which they were called, we
cannot doubt, for they were chosen by that

---

* Matt. xi. 3, 4, 5.   † Acts iv. 13.

discrimination which never errs: and yet that fitness did not consist in clearness of apprehension nor powers of intellect; for it is apparent that some of these disciples did not comprehend many of their Master's plainest teachings until after his crucifixion. Under these instructions they made almost no progress in theology : their labours, like those of their master, were works of exhortation and charity. The personal efforts of Christ being chiefly among the poor, his instruments were chosen for that purpose. The Love of God, and the Love of Man, are the keys of all his doctrines, and the text of his life and labours. He came to the poor, because they were the most numerous, the most suffering, the most humble, the most helpless, and the most ignorant. He regarded the poor as the most hopeful, because least wedded to this world. Not only so, but he taught that the door of poverty was the safest way to heaven. "How hardly shall they that have riches enter into the kingdom of God! It is easier for a camel to

go through the eye of a needle, than for a rich
man to enter the kingdom of God."* He taught
that those who trust in riches must give up that
trust, which is selfishness, and become " poor
in spirit," before they can enter the kingdom
of heaven. He never wearied in affording
succour, consolation, and instruction to the
poor. He exhorted them to lay up for themselves treasures in heaven, and not upon earth.
He encouraged them—" Are not five sparrows
sold for two farthings, and not one of them is
forgotten before God? But even the very
hairs of your head are all numbered. Fear
not, therefore: ye are of more value than
many sparrows."† He taught that the
widow's mite was more than all the offerings of the rich. How beautifully did his
life illustrate this lesson!—" Take no thought
for your life, what ye shall eat, neither for the
body, what ye shall put on. Consider the
ravens: for they neither sow nor reap: which

---

* Mark x. 23—25.   † Luke xii. 6, 7.

have neither store-house nor barn; and God feedeth them. How much more are ye better than the fowls?"—"Consider the lilies how they grow: they toil not, they spin not; and yet I say unto you, that Solomon in all his glory was not arrayed like one of these. If then God so clothe the grass, which is to-day in the field, and to-morrow is cast into the oven; how much more will he clothe you, O ye of little faith."*

His miraculous power was chiefly exerted in behalf of the poor, in healing diseases, casting out devils, in feeding the hungry, in calming the tempest. His parables of the Prodigal Son, and the Good Samaritan, touchingly enforce our duty to the destitute and forsaken. But whilst his mission and ministrations were chiefly among the poor, the rich and the great were not forgotten, but were also objects of solicitude. His warnings to them are solemn and awful. For their sakes his parable of Lazarus the beggar, who died in the street,

* Luke xii. 22—28.

covered with sores, and went to Abraham's bosom, institutes a dialogue between an inhabitant of heaven, and one in the regions of eternal despair, in which the rich are plainly told, that if they will not believe Moses and the prophets, neither would they believe though one rise from the dead to warn them. To the rich ruler, who had kept all the commandments from his youth up, Christ said, "Yet lackest thou one thing: sell all that thou hast, and distribute unto the poor, and thou shalt have treasure in heaven: and come, follow me."* Our Lord did not by this teach that there should be no individual property, or that goods should be in common. The special instruction was for the particular man. His general doctrine is, "How hardly shall they that trust in riches enter into the kingdom of God! But what is impossible with man, is possible with God." He that trusts in riches cannot enter into the kingdom of God. Every disciple of Christ must be God's steward,

---

* Luke xviii. 22. Mark x. 21.

and hold his riches, if he hold them at all, for Him whose servant he is. To one the command may be, " Sell all thou hast, give to the poor, and come and follow me ;" because he can be saved only in that way. To another the command may be, " Occupy till I come ;" administer what I have given thee under the law—" Love thy neighbour as thyself," until I call thee to account. He to whom riches prove a snare and a temptation too great for his strength, must give them up; whilst he who can hold them as instruments of good, becomes the servant of God.

Christ took the institutions of men as he found them, and seemed to require that they should be changed only as the hearts of those who lived under them changed. He knew that no change could be permanent unless founded in the hearts and minds of the people. He did not require that the rich and poor should change places, nor that all men should be lifted above the state of poverty; for he said, " The poor always ye have with

4

you."* He did not require that the master
should give up his slave, nor that the slave
should quit or resist his master. He did not
offer resistance to the laws or public authorities, or in any manner teach that his kingdom was of this world. He simply taught
that men should love their neighbours as
themselves, and left that great law of human
conduct to accomplish all the changes and
revolutions necessary for the progress of his
doctrines and the best interests of men. He
utterly refused to take any authority or administration in temporal matters. To him
who asked him to interfere in the division of
an inheritance, he replied, " Man, who made
me a judge, or a divider over you ?"† When
the woman taken in adultery was brought to
him for judgment, he said, " He that is without sin among you, let him first cast a stone

---

* John xii. 8.

† Luke xii. 14.—This is somewhat in contrast with the course
of the Bishops of the Established Church of England, who have
taken charge of the administration of estates, and have become
judges and dividers over their fellow-men.

at her." And when her accusers had slunk
away, he said to the woman, "Neither do I
condemn thee. Go, and sin no more."* He
did not require him whom he exhorted to sell
his goods, to bring the proceeds to him for distribution, but to give to the poor himself. To
those who tempted him in regard to paying
tribute to the Roman emperors, he replied,
"Render unto Cæsar the things that are
Cæsar's, and unto God the things that are
God's."† To Pilate he said, "My kingdom
is not of this world."‡

The most striking illustration of our Saviour's life and doctrines is to be found in his
exemplification or parable of the last judgment. When all nations are gathered before
the final Judge, and when the blessed are
placed on his right hand, and the guilty
on his left,—"Then shall the King say unto
them on his right hand, Come ye blessed of
my Father, inherit the kingdom prepared for
you from the foundation of the world: for I

---

* John viii. 7, 11.   † Matt. xxii. 21.   ‡ John xviii. 36.

was an hungered, and ye gave me meat: I
was thirsty, and ye gave me drink: I was a
stranger, and ye took me in: naked, and ye
clothed me: sick, and ye visited me; I was
in prison, and ye came unto me." And to
the question of the righteous, when had they
done these things, the reply is, "Verily, I
say unto you, Inasmuch as ye have done it
unto one of the least of these my brethren,
ye have done it unto me."* The condemnation of the wicked is placed upon the ground
that "Inasmuch as ye did it not unto one of
the least of these, ye did it not to me."† There
is here nothing about churches, creeds, confessions, catechisms, prayer-books; nothing
of theology, faith, or doctrine; and yet this
is the *last judgment*, characterized by the final
Judge Himself.

Can it be more strongly enforced that the
mission of the disciples of Christ on earth is
one of charity and mercy? If the tree bear

---

* Matthew xxv. 31.   † Ibid. xxv. 45.

not these fruits, it is none of his planting.
There cannot be a doubt that he who loves
God supremely, and his neighbour as himself,
cannot err fatally in his theology.   He may
require for his profit, encouragement, and
spiritual sustenance, all the means of grace
and instructions within his reach; but no
amount of this sort of work constitutes Christianity, nor insures salvation.   There must,
in the infinite variety of minds, be an infinite
variety in the way of regarding these subjects; and every one is bound, under the
instructions given in the word of God, to
think for himself.   These instructions are not
so detailed but that every believer must in
very many things be left to his own discretion : he is a steward, bound to execute his
Lord's will, but with a large discretion as to
the mode of performance.   Those servants
who received the talents from their master, to
be employed by them in his absence, used
their own discretion in the manner of it, and
he who buried his in a napkin was con-

demned, because he had refused to exercise
that discretion.   It is abundantly clear that
those who love God and their fellow-men,
with all their hearts and minds, have the gift
of spiritual perception, and can, as they
walk through life, unlock all the treasures
they find, comprehending them with as much
certainty as is consistent with the limited
intellects and many infirmities of human
nature.   We are far from asserting that it is
immaterial what men believe, so they are
honest in their belief; we say that men may
greatly err in doctrine and theology, and yet
be safe.   They are not excusable for remaining in error, when they have the means
to escape from it.   Every man, with the Scriptures in his hands, is bound to search them
anxiously, carefully, and with an honest desire after the truth: it is his duty to supply
himself with all the help he can, both from
books and living teachers; but in the last resort
he must believe for himself, and not by another; his belief must be built on his own

convictions, and not on those of another. A
man's religious mind, the state of his soul in
its relations with religious truths, must be
made up from its own investigations, decisions,
and exercises, and not those of another. He
is bound to perfect himself in belief and
practice, to the utmost extent of his capacity;
and no doubt all men fall short of their duty
in this respect. It is obviously absurd to bind
men by creeds and confessions, and expect
them to keep together and be uniform in faith
or speculation. Such efforts can only produce a seeming uniformity, and exert a decided
influence towards hypocrisy or want of can-
dour. Happy are we indeed, that there is a
way of salvation equally efficacious for errors
of judgment as well as errors of life. No
human scrutiny nor discrimination dare draw
the line of doctrine or conduct which bounds
the mercy of God in Christ.

Let every man, therefore, examine himself,
upon his eternal peril, and see whether he
has made that progress in truth of which he

is capable, and whether he may not be entertaining errors in doctrine, for which it is no
excuse for him that others entertain them.
And let all religious teachers take heed to
their teaching, and not think they have done
their duty by aiming at an apparent conformity
of faith, to be maintained by church discipline,
public opinion, and other external influences :
let them remember that their hearers are to
be made free in Christ, and not to have yokes
laid upon them.   They are bound to instruct
them in the truth, but they cannot command
their assent.   The Reformation let in a flood
of light, and set multitudes free from the
bondage of error; their minds rioted in religious truth, and, as a necessary consequence,
diversities of opinion arose, and diversities of
conviction resulted in a variety of sects.   This
was unavoidable; not only so, but freedom
of religious thought not merely begets this
variety of sects,—it must produce an equal
diversity of opinion in the bosom of each
sect: nay more, in the mind of every active

Christian there is much diversity. And it must be so, because it is clearly a part of God's mode of dealing with men, that they must be continually struggling between good and evil; continually deciding between truth and falsehood, between right and wrong; continually exercising patience, practising self-denial, resisting temptations, and undergoing an infinity of trials of greater or less magnitude,—all which constitute the school in which souls take their form and character, which determine their capacity for everlasting happiness, or fix their destiny for unending misery. Men who by long and patient study acquire great knowledge, and by continual exercise strengthen their intellect, attain to a capacity for intellectual enjoyment not only great, but capable of indefinite enlargement. So those who exercise their religious affections, capacities, and graces, to their utmost power here, are the better fitted to enter upon the pure joys of the heavenly state, whenever called to a separation from the body. From this preparation, in the infinity of these various exercises and experiences, operating on individual minds, there must necessarily be evolved an endless variety of thought, of character, and of opinions; a diversity as great as the number of individuals. As from these differences are constituted many sects, not agreeing in all things, but in many things which consist with harmony of action; it does not comport with God's government that these diversities of opinion should be obliterated or smoothed away. The cords which bind his disciples together should not be composed of opinions, nor doctrines, nor creeds: the cords provided for this unity are love to God and love to man; the ties of the affections are the real bonds of peace with God and man. If the bonds of love be made strong enough, and drawn close enough, differences in theology will be little remarked and sectarian asperity will find no soil in which to grow. The struggle among sects will then be not to injure each other, not to surpass in numbers and power, but to surpass each other in efforts to promote the interests of the Redeemer's kingdom, by labouring for the best interests of men temporal and eternal.

THE MINISTRY AND TEACHING OF THE APOSTLES.

WHILST the words of Christ were yet sounding in the ears of his disciples, they commenced their ministry at Jerusalem. They followed their Master's example of preaching the gospel to the poor, of healing the sick, the lame, the blind, and deaf, and of raising the dead. "Silver and gold have I none," said Peter to the man lame from his birth; "but such as I have give I thee: in the name of Jesus Christ of Nazareth, rise up and walk."* One of the earliest results of their ministry and teaching is thus recorded: "And all that believed were together, and

---

* Acts iii. 6.

had all things common: and sold their possessions and goods, and parted them to all
men, as every man had need."* "And the
multitude of them that believed were of one
heart and of one soul: neither said any of them
that aught of the things which he possessed
was his own, but they had all things common." "Neither was there any among them
that lacked: for as many as were possessors
of lands or houses sold them, and brought
the prices of the things that were sold, and laid
them down at the apostles' feet, and distribution was made unto every man according as
he had need."† The distribution of the proceeds of these benefactions among the needy
soon absorbed so much of the time and attention of the apostles, as to draw them unduly
from their peculiar duties of preaching the gospel, and made it necessary to select and appoint
men to this special business.‡ Frequent mention is made, throughout the Acts of the Apos-

---

* Acts ii. 44, 45.   † Acts iv. 32, 34, 35.   ‡ Acts vi. 1—3.

tles and the Epistles, of the great liberality
and hospitality of the early Christians; but
it is obvious that within the space permitted
to these writings, few details of the private life
of the converts could be included. We can
refer to what the apostles taught, as some
evidence of what the first Christians practised.

And all that believed were together, and had all things
common; and sold their possessions and goods, and parted
them to all men, as every man had need.—*Acts* ii. 44, 45.

And the multitude of them that believed were of one
heart, and of one soul: neither said any of them that
aught of the things which he possessed was his own: but
they had all things common. And with great power gave
the apostles witness of the resurrection of the Lord Jesus:
and great grace was upon them all. Neither was there
any among them that lacked: for as many as were possessors of lands or houses sold them, and brought the
prices of the things that were sold, and laid them down
at the apostles' feet: and distribution was made unto every
man according as he had need.—*Acts* iv. 32—35.

He that giveth, let him do it with simplicity: he that
ruleth, with diligence; he that showeth mercy, with cheer-
fulness. Let love be without dissimulation. Abhor that
which is evil; cleave to that which is good. Be kindly
affectioned one to another with brotherly love; in honour
preferring one another.—*Rom.* xii. 8—10.

5

Distributing to the necessity of saints; given to hospitality. Bless them which persecute you; bless, and curse not. Rejoice with them that do rejoice, and weep with them that weep. Be of the same mind one toward another. Mind not high things, but condescend to men of low estate. Be not wise in your own conceits. Recompense to no man evil for evil. Provide things honest in the sight of all men. If it be possible, as much as lieth in you, live peaceably with all men.. Dearly beloved, avenge not yourselves, but rather give place unto wrath: for it is written, Vengeance is mine; I will repay, saith the Lord. Therefore, if thine enemy hunger, feed him; if he thirst, give him drink: for in so doing thou shalt heap coals of fire on his head. Be not overcome of evil, but overcome evil with good.—*Rom.* xii. 13—21.

Owe no man any thing, but to love one another: for he that loveth another hath fulfilled the law.—*Rom.* xiii. 8.

Love worketh no ill to his neighbour: therefore love is the fulfilling of the law.—*Rom.* xiii. 10.

For none of us liveth to himself, and no man dieth to himself.—*Rom.* xiv. 7.

But why dost thou judge thy brother? or why dost thou set at nought thy brother? for we shall all stand before the judgment-seat of Christ.—*Rom.* xiv. 10.

Let us not therefore judge one another any more: but judge this rather, that no man put a stumbling-block, or an occasion to fall, in his brother's way.—*Rom.* xiv. 13.

We then that are strong ought to bear the infirmities

of the weak, and not to please ourselves. Let every one of us please his neighbour for his good to edification.—*Rom.* xv. 1, 2.

Now the God of patience and consolation grant you to be likeminded one toward another according to Christ Jesus.—*Rom.* xv. 5.

Wherefore receive ye one another, as Christ also received us, to the glory of God.—*Rom.* xv. 7.

Now I beseech you, brethren, by the name of our Lord Jesus Christ, that ye all speak the same thing, and that there be no divisions among you; but that ye be perfectly joined together in the same mind, and in the same judgment.—1 *Cor.* i. 10.

Now therefore there is utterly a fault among you, because ye go to law one with another. Why do ye not rather take wrong? why do ye not rather suffer yourselves to be defrauded? Nay, ye do wrong, and defraud, and that your brethren.—1 *Cor.* vi. 7, 8.

Though I speak with the tongues of men and of angels, and have not charity, I am become as sounding brass, or a tinkling cymbal. And though I have the gift of prophecy, and understand all mysteries, and all knowledge; and though I have all faith, so that I could remove mountains, and have not charity, I am nothing. And though I bestow all my goods to feed the poor, and though I give my body to be burned, and have not charity, it profiteth me nothing. Charity suffereth long, and is kind; charity envieth not; charity vaunteth not itself, is not puffed up, doth not behave itself unseemly, seeketh not her own, is not easily provoked, thinketh no evil; rejoiceth not in iniquity, but rejoiceth in the truth; beareth all things, believeth all things, hopeth all things, endureth all things. Charity never faileth: but whether there be prophecies, they shall fail; whether there be tongues, they shall cease; whether there be knowledge, it shall vanish away.— 1 *Cor.* xiii. 1—8.

And now abideth faith, hope, charity, these three; but the greatest of these is charity.—1 *Cor.* xiii. 13.

Let all your things be done with charity.—1 *Cor.* xvi. 14.

For to their power, I bear record, yea, and beyond their power, they were willing of themselves; praying us with much entreaty, that we would receive the gift, and take upon us the fellowship of the ministering to the saints.— 2 *Cor.* viii. 3, 4.

Only they would that we should remember the poor; the same which I also was forward to do.—*Gal.* ii. 10.

For all the law is fulfilled in one word, even in this, Thou shalt love thy neighbour as thyself.—*Gal.* v. 14.

But the fruit of the Spirit is love, joy, peace, long-suffering, gentleness, goodness, faith.—*Gal.* v. 22.

Bear ye one another's burdens, and so fulfil the law of Christ.—*Gal.* vi. 2.

As we have therefore opportunity, let us do good unto

all men, especially unto them who are of the household of faith.—*Gal.* vi. 10.

With all lowliness and meekness, with long-suffering, forbearing one another in love.—*Eph.* iv. 2.

Wherefore putting away lying, speak every man truth with his neighbour : for we are members one of another. Be ye angry, and sin not : let not the sun go down upon your wrath.—*Eph.* iv. 25, 26.

Let all bitterness, and wrath, and anger, and clamour, and evil-speaking, be put away from you, with all malice : and be ye kind one to another, tender-hearted, forgiving one another, even as God for Christ's sake hath forgiven you.—*Eph.* iv. 31, 32.

If there be therefore any consolation in Christ, if any comfort of love, if any fellowship of the Spirit, if any bowels and mercies, fulfil ye my joy, that ye be like-minded, having the same love, being of one accord, of one mind.   Let nothing be done through strife or vain-glory; but in lowliness of mind let each esteem other better than themselves.   Look not every man on his own things, but every man also on the things of others.—*Phil.* ii. 1—4.

Put on therefore, as the elect of God, holy and beloved, bowels of mercies, kindness, humbleness of mind, meek-ness, long-suffering; forbearing one another, and forgiv-ing one another, if any man have a quarrel against any : even as Christ forgave you, so also do ye. And above all these things put on charity, which is the bond of perfect-ness.— *Col.* iii. 12—14.

5*

And the Lord make you to increase and abound in love one toward another, and toward all men, even as we do toward you.—1 *Thes.* iii. 12.

But as touching brotherly love ye need not that I write unto you: for ye yourselves are taught of God to love one another.—1 *Thes.* iv. 9.

And be at peace among yourselves. Now we exhort you, brethren, warn them that are unruly, comfort the feeble-minded, support the weak, be patient toward all men. See that none render evil for evil unto any man; but ever follow that which is good, both among yourselves, and to all men.—1 *Thes.* v. 13—15.

Yet count him not as an enemy, but admonish him as a brother.—2 *Thes.* iii. 15.

Now the end of the commandment is charity out of a pure heart, and of a good conscience, and of faith unfeigned.—1 *Tim.* i. 5.

If ye fulfil the royal law according to the scripture, Thou shalt love thy neighbour as thyself, ye do well.— *James* ii. 8.

If a brother or sister be naked, and destitute of daily food, and one of you say unto them, Depart in peace, be ye warmed and filled; notwithstanding ye give them not those things which are needful to the body; what doth it profit?—*James* ii. 15, 16.

But the wisdom that is from above is first pure, then

peaceable, gentle, and easy to be entreated, full of mercy and good fruits, without partiality, and without hypocrisy.—*James* iii. 17.

Behold, the hire of the labourers who have reaped down your fields, which is of you kept back by fraud, crieth; and the cries of them which have reaped are entered into the ears of the Lord of Sabaoth. —*James* v. 4.

Seeing ye have purified your souls in obeying the truth through the Spirit unto unfeigned love of the brethren, see that ye love one another with a pure heart fervently.— 1 *Pet.* i. 22.

Honour all men. Love the brotherhood. Fear God. Honour the king.—1 *Pet.* ii. 17.

Finally, be ye all of one mind, having compassion one of another; love as brethren, be pitiful, be courteous : not rendering evil for evil, or railing for railing : but contrariwise, blessing; knowing that ye are thereunto called, that ye should inherit a blessing. For he that will love life, and see good days, let him refrain his tongue from evil, and his lips that they speak no guile.—1 *Pet.* iii. 8—10.

And above all things have fervent charity among yourselves : for charity shall cover the multitude of sins. Use hospitality one to another without grudging. As every man hath received the gift, even so minister the same one to another, as good stewards of the manifold grace of God.—1 *Pet.* iv. 8—10.

And besides this, giving all diligence, add to your faith, virtue; and to virtue, knowledge; and to knowledge, temperance; and to temperance, patience; and to patience, godliness; and to godliness, brotherly-kindness; and to brotherly-kindness, charity.—2 *Pet.* i. 5—7.

He that saith he is in the light, and hateth his brother, is in darkness even until now. He that loveth his brother abideth in the light, and there is none occasion of stumbling in him. But he that hateth his brother is in darkness, and walketh in darkness, and knoweth not whither he goeth, because that darkness hath blinded his eyes.—1 *John* ii. 9—11.

For this is the message that ye heard from the beginning, that we should love one another.—1 *John* iii. 11.

We know that we have passed from death unto life, because we love the brethren. He that loveth not his brother, abideth in death.—1 *John* iii. 14.

But whoso hath this world's good, and seeth his brother have need, and shutteth up his bowels of compassion from him, how dwelleth the love of God in him. My little children, let us not love in word, neither in tongue, but in deed and in truth.—1 *John* iii. 17, 18.

And this is his commandment; That we should believe on the name of his Son Jesus Christ, and love one another, as he gave us commandment.—1 *John* iii. 23.

Beloved, let us love one another: for love is of God;

and every one that loveth is born of God, and knoweth God. He that loveth not, knoweth not God; for God is love.—1 *John* iv. 7, 8.

Beloved, if God so loved us, we ought also to love one another. No man hath seen God at any time. If we love one another, God dwelleth in us, and his love is perfected in us.—1 *John* iv. 11, 12.

And we have known and believed the love that God hath to us. God is love: and he that dwelleth in love, dwelleth in God, and God in him.—1 *John* iv. 16.

If a man say, I love God, and hateth his brother, he is a liar. For he that loveth not his brother, whom he hath seen, how can he love God, whom he hath not seen? And this commandment have we from him, That he who loveth God, love his brother also.—1 *John* iv. 20, 21.

By this we know that we love the children of God, when we love God, and keep his commandments. For this is the love of God, that we keep his commandments; and his commandments are not grievous.—1 *John* v. 2, 3.

We trust that these quotations, which are only a portion of what can be adduced to the same purport, have not proved tedious.*

---

* We have deemed it right to place these passages before the reader, in place of sending him to the sacred volume whence they are taken, as they can be read in less time than their places can be found.

Should not these passages, taken in gross
and in detail, awaken inquiries of vital import? Where is the Christianity which they
prescribe? Where are the Christians who
receive these instructions and obey them?
Where are those people whose charity is
greater than that faith which could remove
mountains—more liberal than that bounty
which bestows all its goods to feed the poor,
and more self-sacrificing than his devotion
who gives his body to martyrdom?—Whose
charity never fails—bearing all things, believing all things, hoping all things, enduring
all things; whose love is without dissimulation; in honour preferring one another; who
bless them which persecute—bless and curse
not; who feed their enemies; who bear one
another's burdens; who let not the sun go
down upon their wrath; who put away all
bitterness and wrath, and clamour, and evil
speaking, with all malice? Where are those
Christians who, having this world's goods,
never shut up their bowels of compassion

when they see their brothers have need ? The sufferings and utter destitution of the millions upon millions of the poor throughout rich Christendom; the strife, and clamour, and evil speaking, ambition, jealousy, bitterness, malice, oppression, wars, and perpetual struggles for power, wealth, and precedence, furnish a reply to these inquiries.

What do we see, then, in Christendom? Civilization, arts, sciences, knowledge; a vast complication of church machinery to keep men in the traces of sectarianism; a vast accumulation of duties to be performed; of things to be said and done; of yokes to be carried; of doctrines to be understood and believed; of traditions, glosses, comments, explanations: a vast array of biblical learning and criticism, in which every word is examined, weighed, and defined. We have creeds, confessions, liturgies, prayer-books, catechisms, forms and platforms of faith and discipline. We have councils, conventions, synods, and assemblies, and other ecclesiastical bodies without number. We have sacraments, ordinances, ceremonies, observances without limit. We have bishops, priests, ministers, preachers, and teachers. We have congregations, schools, colleges, and seminaries. We have costly temples and palaces built for Him who dwelleth not in temples made with men's hands. We have assemblages of infinite variety for religious purposes. We have thousands upon thousands of volumes of religious books; but where is our Christianity? for all these things do not constitute us followers of Christ. Where is the exemplification of that charity without which all these things are mere sounding brass and tinkling cymbals? In what city is the "gospel preached to the poor?" In what country are the poor such special object of care and attention on the part of Christians, as is contemplated by the teachings of Christ and his disciples? This is not merely feeding and clothing the poor; for if you give all your goods for this purpose, it does not meet the requirements of Christian charity. All such exterior manifestations of Christianity as are above enumerated are, in the best sense, merely means to an end. Where, we ask, are the results of this immense and costly paraphernalia of Christianity? Is there not reason to inquire if the essence of true religion has not been crushed, repelled, and sometimes wholly extinguished, under this load? Compare all this mass of Christian machinery with the extreme simplicity of that example in practice and teaching which is left for our instruction by Him who could "speak as never man spake." While we adhere so closely to the letter, let us not be in danger of perishing in the letter. Knowledge will not save us: while we rely on the Bible as an instructor, let us not trust in it as a Saviour.

While one portion of nominal Christians have busied themselves with forms and ceremonies, and observances, with pictures, images, and processions; others have given to doc-

trines the supremacy, and have busied themselves in laying down the lines by which to
enforce human belief,—lines of interpretation,
by which to control human opinion,—lines
of discipline and restraint, by which to bring
human minds to uniformity of faith and
action; they have formed creeds and catechisms,—they have spread themselves over
the whole field of the sacred writings, and
scratched up all the surface,—they have gathered all the straws and turned over all the
pebbles, and detected the colour and determined the outline of every stone and tree and
shrub; they have dwelt with rapture upon
all that was beautiful and sublime, but they
have trampled over mines of golden wisdom,
of surpassing richness and depth, almost
without a thought, and almost without an
effort to fathom these priceless treasures,
much less to take possession of them.

In what part of Christendom is Christian
charity occupying that space in the teachings
of the schools or churches, or in the works of

the people, which we perceive to be occupied
by other things in the two classes above-men-
tioned?   Where are men found as anxiously
bent on fulfilling the duties of loving God
and loving their neighbour as they are in
other things pertaining in their estimation to
religion?   We hear far more of the sufferings
of Christ, of the redemption wrought out for
us, of the atonement, of the vicarious sacrifice, of the law fulfilled in our behalf, of his
righteousness in which we are exhorted to
clothe ourselves, of his blood shed for us in
which we are to wash and be clean; of the
cross at the foot of which we must lie until
we are purified by the sacrifice there accomplished for us, than we do of all the precepts
and all the example of Christ.   To have
faith in Christ implies not only belief in his
atonement, in his redemption, in his fulfilment of the law, in the shedding of his blood,
in his personal sufferings, but in his ministry,
teaching, and example.   It is not enough to
say, Lord, Lord; we are not his followers

unless we walk in his footsteps; we are not his believers if we do not believe what he taught and imitate what he did. He came into this world and assumed our nature, not merely to accomplish his various offices, but to be the bearer of a message the most benign and pure which has ever greeted the ears of man. Can we claim the benefit of his expiatory sacrifice while we forget his message or treat it with contempt? Can we be saved by the offices of Christ, if we receive not the instructions of Christ?

We must refrain from entering further into this branch of the subject until we have completed our historical survey. We have noticed the instructions of Christ and his apostles, and also their example: it may be worth while to notice, however slightly, the usages of Christians in the early and middle ages of Christianity under these instructions, before we come to compare them with the practices of the present day.

A HISTORY of Christian charity in the first ages of Christianity is deserving of volumes: it is possible now merely to sketch a few prominent features. Our Saviour found slavery an established institution in the world. Inconsistent as that relation may appear with his teachings, he utters not one syllable of reproach against it, or against slaveholders as such. He publishes the law of love; he lays down the rule of doing unto others as we would have others do unto us; both which are as binding on the slave as on the master. Upon the operation of these Christian principles he relies for the abolition of slavery. Before the advent of Christianity, no axe had ever been laid at the root of slavery; no philosopher had denounced it, and it does not appear to have been considered by any as an

6*

evil to be repressed. Nor did the apostles
teach differently, but distinctly laid down
rules for the conduct of master and slave;
thereby clearly recognising the relation, without denouncing it as in itself sinful. Their
Master's instructions were intended to make
men what they should be, and then every
institution, every law, and every practice
inconsistent with that state, would fall before
it. If a community of slaveholders, under
Christian instruction, were gradually tending
to the point of general emancipation, both
masters and slaves would gradually be fitting
for so great a change in their relative condition. It would be a subject of great interest
to trace, in the early ages of Christianity, its
influences upon the institution of slavery,
so much in contrast with the movements or
influences of paganism. During the first four
or five centuries of the Christian era, emancipation of slaves by converts to Christianity
took place upon a large and progressively
increasing scale, and continued until the

occurrence of political events, the invasion of barbarians, and other causes, agitated the whole Christian world and shook the very foundations of the social systems in which Christianity had made most progress. When Christianity sank into the darkness of the middle ages, the progress of emancipation ceased, because the influence which produced it ceased during that period to operate. The annals of emancipation in these primitive ages, if materials were extant for a full narrative, would be of extraordinary interest, and would fully reveal the effects of our Saviour's precepts when brought to bear upon the hearts of men in their true spirit, even where the letter did not apply. Under paganism, slavery could never come to an end: under the continual light of Christianity, it hastens to an inevitable end, but by that progress and in that mode which is best both for master and slave; both being bound to love each other until the door of emancipation is fully open without injury to either.

The ranks of the slaves, in the early period
in review, were constantly replenished by
captives taken in the continual wars of that
time.   One of the marked characteristics of
Christian kindness is seen in the liberality
exercised in ransoming from slavery its constant recruits.   In many cases, whole communities were impoverished by their efforts
in this way, and instances are not wanting
in which men sold themselves into slavery
to procure the means of redeeming others.[*]
When Genseric took and pillaged Rome, he
carried off a host of its best citizens as captives, and landed them at Carthage, in Africa,
where, husbands being separated from wives,
and parents from children, they were sold
into bondage.   Christians at Rome sent after
their unhappy brethren all the means they
could command towards their redemption
and relief; but the prisoners found Christians
in Africa.   Deogratias, bishop of Carthage,

---

[*] Epistle of Clement to the Corinthians.

gave himself at once to the work of succour-
ing these slaves of Vandals and Moors.   To
prevent separation of families, he purchased
a large number of them.   The churches of
Carthage were fitted up with beds and furni-
ture, and became the habitations and hospitals
of those who were the descendants of. the
former enemies of that city.   To meet this
great expense, the gold and silver ornaments
and vessels of the churches were sold.   Medical attendance and nursing were liberally
bestowed upon the numerous sick.   The good
bishop day and night gave his personal super-
intendence and aid to this great and good
work, and this under the weight of a feeble
old age.*

The origin of the monastic system was
charity.   Many of those who felt impelled
by the Saviour's injunction, "Go sell that
thou hast and give to the poor," united themselves for facility of support, and formed

_____

* A. D. 455.

houses of charity for each other, and for all
whom they could help.   Their doors were
open to all strangers, to the sick, and to all
who asked their aid.   Many carried their
worldly possessions to these establishments,
and there they were dispensed for the general
object of the association.

The more these institutions were managed
in the spirit of true Christian charity, the
more popular they became; and large gifts
and bequests were poured upon them to assist
in their charitable enterprises.   The value of
such gifts for charitable uses made in these
early times cannot now be told; and if they
could, the amount would be deemed incredible.   The administrators of these houses
of charity, who in their origin laboured
with their own hands in their communities
for their support and for the means of suc-
couring others, were in the end overwhelmed
by the amount of those benefactions which
the zeal of Christians for charity showered
upon them.   It is but little from the mark to

say, that all the property held by the Roman
church and her ecclesiastics, if we except her
temples, was given purely for charitable purposes. It was given to feed the hungry, to
clothe the naked, to redeem the captive, to
aid in the cure and care of the sick, the
infirm, the halt and the blind, and for the support of a generous hospitality. Where these
houses were found, and they were once densely
strewed through Christendom, the poor were
never without a resource for every want, and
the stranger never at a loss for a home. The
history of these houses, in the days of their
purity, is greatly needed as a practical exposition of charity by the first Christians.

When the plague raged in Alexandria, in
the time of the Emperor Gallianus, Christians
distinguished themselves, in contrast with the
pagan population, by their undaunted courage
and persevering care for the sick, dying, and
dead. They omitted no duty and fled from
no contact in the care of those labouring
under the frightful malady, in closing the

eyes of the expiring, in cleansing the bodies
of the dead, ånd in carrying them to their
graves; and as fast as the ranks of those
thus exposed were thinned by death, others
stepped in to fill their places. These sacrifices were made not only for Christian brethren,
but for the heathen, who were deserted by
their own families, and left to die without a
single attendant, in the street as well as in
the houses, and their bodies to go unhearsed
and unburied.

Hospitals were, in those early ages, made
an appendage of Christian churches. There
cannot be a doubt that Christians fully relieved all their own poor, and very many of
the pagan poor besides. There is on record
the testimony of an enemy, to the fact. The
Emperor Julian, one of the bitterest enemies
of Christianity, provoked by the good works
of Christians, thus instructs one of his
pagan priests: "Establish hospitals in every
town, for the care of the sick and the entertainment of strangers, and for extending the

cares of humanity to all that are poor. I will
furnish the means. For it is a shame for us
that no Jew ever begs, and that the impious
Galileans should not only keep their own
poor, but even many of ours, whom we leave
to suffer." To another he writes thus: "The
impious Galileans, having observed that our
priests neglect the poor, have applied themselves to that work: and like those who
would steal our children to sell them, they
attract them by offering cakes; and so they
have led our faithful ones into infidelity, by
commencing with charity, hospitality, and
the service of tables, for they have many
names for these works, which they practise
abundantly." This testimony is of great
value in showing the customs of Christians
in those days, and the nature of that teaching
by example, which not only commanded the
admiration of an enemy, but compelled an
emperor to follow it, in pure defence, lest the
hearts of his subjects should be stolen from
him. Very many proofs of this charity could

7

be adduced from the conduct of Christians in different parts of the world; but the evidence of Julian is ample enough for his day.

The Emperor Constantine followed this good example, not from rivalry, but because he was a Christian. "He poured out his alms liberally both upon Christian and Pagan. To the public beggars he gave both food and clothing; he assisted generously those who had fallen from a better condition; giving to some, pensions; to others, lucrative offices. He took especial care of widows and orphans, giving their daughters in marriage to rich men, known by himself to be worthy."*

The Empress Flacilla, wife of Theodosius, made the care of the poor her chief occupation, to serve whom she undertook any office, however degrading. A letter from an eminent Christian to King Clovis contains this passage:—"Be the father and protector of your people; lighten their burdens as much as is consistent with the necessary wants of

* Eusebius, Life of Constantine.

your government. Console and relieve the poor; nourish orphans; take care of widows; permit no oppression. Let the door of your palace be ever open, that every one of your subjects may be able to claim justice at your hands."

A better idea cannot, perhaps, be given of the sentiments of early Christians on this subject, than is furnished by an incident which occurred in Rome. The liberality shown to the poor had led a Roman officer, in the days of persecution, to believe that Christians had great treasures at their command. Laurentius, one of the deacons or guardians of the poor, was commanded by the Roman Prefect to deliver up the treasures of the church. He demanded three days to comply with the requisition. In that time he collected from the whole city all the poor taken care of by Christian benevolence, and having assembled, in the courts and porches of one of their churches, the immense multitude of the aged, infirm, lame, blind, diseased, destitute poor who received constant aid from the hands of Christians, he called upon the prefect and said, "Come see the treasures of our God; you shall see a great court full of vessels of gold, and talents are heaped up in porches." The Prefect followed, and was shown the assembled poor. "Behold the treasures I promised you. I add to these the widows and orphans; they are our pearls and precious stones, the crown of the church. Take this wealth for Rome, for the emperor, and for yourself."*

These few incidents speak far from adequately, but still strongly, the opinion of primitive Christianity on the subject of practical charity. We cannot reach our own time, however, without traversing a period during mediæval ages, when, by a slow but sure process of corruption, Christianity, overcome by forms, ceremonies, and superstitions, sank,

---

* These incidents are taken from Histoire de la Charité pendant les quatre premiers Siècles de l'ère Chrétienne, par Martin-Doisy. The subject of the charity of early Christians is treated in some detail, in Cave's Primitive Christianity, part 3, chap. 2.

gradually, into all the abuses of Roman Papacy. Priestly power and dignity usurped the place of apostolic simplicity and teaching; political sway and ambition were substituted for ministerial labours devoted mainly to the spiritual welfare of men's souls. Those who claimed to be successors of Peter, the fisherman of Galilee, who followed a master who had not where to lay his head, grasped a kingly rule and swayed a spiritual sceptre : those who claimed to be the special delegates of the meek and lowly Jesus, who had neither house nor home, nor bishopric, nor church, who refused all participation in temporal affairs, who would neither punish the guilty woman, nor assume the distribution of an inheritance, nor be judge nor ruler over any one, but who enjoined submission to the civil authorities, claimed and exercised lordship over kings and emperors, and gave themselves out as the source of all power in Christendom.

Herein lies the explanation of the sad declension of Christianity in this unhappy pe-

7*

riod. The purity of the early Christian ministry inspired confidence : confidence led many
to commit important trusts to them, as the
most worthy and the most enlightened : the
execution of these trusts gave power and
patronage : the exercise of power and patronage proved a source of corruption and ruin.
The most dangerous foes of Christianity are
wealth and power : the human heart is so
little proof against these enemies, that it has
always yielded to their influence. Christianity
was founded in poverty and worldly weakness ; it cannot be reared nor flourish in
worldly splendour or in regal rule. He who
taught that it was easier for a camel to pass
through the eye of a needle than for a rich
man to enter into the kingdom of God, meant
what he said—that no rich man, in his own
strength, can turn from his riches and become his disciple. Riches are so many grap-
ples which hold men to this world ; and grap-
ples they are which the men who have forged
them cannot break without aid from on high.

Yet Christian ministers absorbed and brought under their administration during the middle ages a large proportion of the wealth of the world. Christ said, " Sell that thou hast, and give to the poor;" these ministers of his said, " Bring in your offerings to us, and we will feed the poor." Under this stimulus, the offerings of the people poured in upon the priesthood in a profusion which proved how deeply Christian charity had taken hold of the minds of men. Christian ministers were not long proof under the corrupting tendencies of this fatal error, and Christianity sank into a degradation of more than a thousand years, and into a neglect of charity visible in all subsequent history.

No doubt, Christians as a church, or in their special organizations, are bound to administer wisely and faithfully such charities as are committed to them; but they should regard such trusts as dangerous to the welfare of churches, and they should not encourage individuals in their creation, but endeavour to dif-

fuse that light and spirit which enables every
individual Christian to become a faithful
steward of that which is in his hands, under
the great law of charity.   Even when individuals have done all in their power to carry
out Christian duties, much must still devolve
upon some public administration.   This will
be as much as human weakness can perform
with safety and success.   That the papal
practice of making the church the grand
almoner of all its members is radically wrong,
is plain from all past results; it is clearly
wrong, because human virtue cannot be proof
against the temptations incident to such an
administration; it is clearly wrong, because
not according to the teachings of Christ, who
undertook no such offices.   It is very apparent in many of the passages above quoted,
that Christ's plan in the exercise of charity,
contemplates more the spiritual good of him
who exercises charity than of him who is its
object.   The poor are the objects of many
promises and of much providential care and

bounty: they have little to tie them to this world, and therefore are the more readily induced to fix their affections upon things above, and to look to the future world as a final home and place of rest. They are more likely to be " poor in spirit," to " mourn," to be " meek," to " hunger and thirst after righteousness," to be " merciful," to be " pure in heart," to be " peacemakers," to be " persecuted for righteousness' sake," to be " reviled, and to have all manner of evil spoken of them falsely;" and they are, of course, the more likely to enjoy the blessings promised to such. The rich in this world's goods must look upon the poor and the suffering as the special objects of their stewardship: poverty and pain are the fields in which they must labour, and in which their graces must be exercised, and their Christian characters formed. It is not enough to found hospitals, build churches, establish monasteries—to feed, lodge, and clothe the poor; but to cultivate that " charity, without which, if men bestow all their goods to feed the poor and give their bodies to be burned, it profiteth nothing." The inheritance of the kingdom prepared for the blessed from the foundation of the world, is given to those who give meat to the hungry, drink to the thirsty; who receive strangers, clothe the naked, visit the sick, and go unto those who are in prison. This blessedness is not proffered to those who perform this duty by proxy. . It is not promised to the church, but to individuals who perform these offices for even the humblest of the human family.

Papal Rome did not cease to inculcate charity, and extol it as the highest of Christian virtues; but this she did, not that she cared for the poor, but because "she was a thief, and had the bag, and bare what was put therein."* Like Judas, whose apparent zeal for the poor exceeded that of the other disciples, his zeal to fill his bag having increased with the avarice which the bearing of that bag had engendered, the papacy preached charity with in-

---

* John xii. 6.

creasing earnestness when avarice had become the motive. The experience of the Romish church proved that where there is a bag of money to be held, or large sums to be administered, a Judas will creep into the office. It was a fatal error of that church to expose her officers to such manifold temptations. Having assumed the charge of such vast wealth and the administration of such immense power, virtue in priests and bishops and popes became nearly impossible. Religious houses and charitable institutions became the scenes of frightful abuse and perversion. No wickedness of this world has much exceeded that which these abuses have exhibited.

The history of the world proves that such power and such wealth cannot safely be confided to human agencies. Even if the virtues of those whose purity of life has commanded unlimited confidence, being strengthened from above, hold out, their positions will be coveted, and eventually seized by those whom no scruples restrain. The true theory is, to reduce temptation to the lowest practicable point, in social, political, and religious life : enough will still remain to tax all the energies of human virtue and endurance.

When Rome had assumed the government of all Christendom, and had put forth every device which cunning and wickedness could contrive to increase her power and to extract money from her votaries, she preached charity unceasingly, as the great feature and characteristic of the Christian religion. Charity was proclaimed as the highest of graces and the most pressing of duties. Whilst the main object was to become the administrators of charity, and to absorb the alms of the faithful, it happily fell out, that all the givers did not select the church as the medium of their bounty, and that many actually practised that charity which was chiefly enforced from interested motives. St. Paul says that some, even in his day, "preached Christ of envy and strife."—" What then ?—whether in pre-

tence or in truth, Christ is preached.* So
charity was inculcated during a long series of
ages, from interested motives, and continues
so to be enforced.   Yet we have much reason
to rejoice over this teaching. During the long
night of the dark ages, the duties of alms-
giving and liberality to the church for the
sake of the poor being urged with all the zeal
of self-interest, was thus kept before the minds
and in the hearts of men, in a period when
almost every other semblance of Christianity
disappeared.

When the annals of Charity shall be fully
written, it will be found that this dark period
furnishes, under the influence of Romish
teachings, many as bright and beautiful examples of lives devoted to charity as any the
world has ever beheld.   The invention of
works of supererogation contributed, no doubt,
to form such characters, and to stimulate that
perseverance in good works which should have
sprung from a clear comprehension of the true

---

* Phil. i. 16, 18.
8

plan of salvation. The corruptions and abuses of the Romish church assumed in this period a form in which the priesthood, in. all its grades, must naturally become ambitious, corrupt, and tyrannical; the mass of the people ignorant, superstitious, and enslaved. A few, from peculiar temperament or accidental advantages, might stand forth in the exercise of Christian graces of the highest degree, but not unfrequently mingled with forbidding austerities and stoical virtues more pagan than Christian. The dark ages added many saints to the Roman calendar, and the church, which could not make these men available for selfish ends while they lived, canonized them and used them efficiently after they left this world. It was this interested devotion to the subject of charity which constituted the salt by which, humanly speaking, Christianity was preserved from utter suspension during this lapse of ages. This was at least the spark which kept it alive in the Romish communion, which, by the worship of saints and images, had made a long step back into paganism. He who could have looked upon this church in this period, and compared its immense complications of power and wealth, and wickedness, with the practices and teachings of the great Head of Christianity, would have perceived nothing in common between the two systems but these gleams of charity shooting athwart the vision in the vast mass of papal gloom.

During this corrupt period the charitable institutions, which had multiplied without number in the primitive ages of Christianity, under an infinity of names and organization, were, to a great extent, perverted from their true design and the objects of the founders. Monasteries, hospitals, religious houses of every name became nests of lazy drones, consuming and wasting the bounty of the charitable—the patrimony of the poor. Many associations, which had their origin in a plan of joint labour for the poor, became sinks, swallowing the benefactions attracted to their institutions by the purity and industry

of the early associates.   The richly endowed
establishments which were to feed the poor
and take care of the sick, to ransom the captive, far and wide around them, ceased to be
dispensers of alms, and consumed within
their own walls those streams of plenty
which should have watered a wide region.
It is true, these houses seldom wholly shut
their doors against the poor who were able
to reach them, but the inmates ceased to
furnish the cup of cold water to those who
could not apply, to visit the sick and those
who were in prison. These duties were left
to the charity of individuals.   Not only were
these ancient establishments thus perverted
and abused, but innumerable others were
founded, and, in like manner, abused.   The
mass of these perversions and corruptions,
became so great finally, as to draw the attention of all who had minds even partially free
from the bondage of the church.   They became an offence to all such in Christendom.
The streams which fed the abuses began to

fail, and charity itself to fall into discredit.
But though alms-giving to the begging poor
was never given up among any Catholic population, that liberality which sustained in idleness and debauchery a lazy priesthood was
sensibly checked. This led at last, to the
incredibly wicked device of selling indulgences to sin, an impiety without parallel in
any other form of religion, among any other
people, or in any age of the world. The
abuses of the divine grace of charity had
opened the eyes of many to the corruptions
of the church : this sale of indulgences so
roused their indignation, that they shook off
the chains of superstition, and, becoming free
in thought, soon determined to be free in action. A very slight examination, in this frame
of mind, betrayed the depths from which they
had emerged, and spread before them the
vast mass of benighted humanity held in the
grasp of papal power ;—that power which
bound all its·subjects to believe as it dictated,
to bow to its decision in faith as well as in

8*

practice; which forbade all freedom of thought
or speech, and denied the word of God to those
whose salvation it was intended to secure;
which extinguished all thirst for knowledge
and all independence of thought; which
robbed God of his government and made
men slaves of the Church.   The long abuse
of charity and its institutions had made
them a stench in the nostrils of those who
became awakened to papal usurpation.   The
church for nearly a thousand years had
merely been telling her people what to do:
the men who now, after a thousand years
of oblivion, had taken up that rejected book,
the Bible, and received it as the word of God,
began to inquire almost exclusively, as they
emerged from darkness, what they should
believe.   The intellect, set free after this long
inaction, exerted itself with immense vigour.
The truths of Holy Writ evolved with great
rapidity, were seized with avidity by multitudes sighing for emancipation from mental

bondage. A wide field of inquiry was thus
thrown open, and hosts of eager inquirers
soon thronged the area. The absurdities and
enormities of the papacy were exposed without mercy, and the doctrines of the gospel
were proclaimed as far as voice and press
could reach. It was soon experienced that
freedom of thought did not produce uniformity of belief. Strong minds differed in the
interpretation of the gospel; sharpened by the
excitements of a new liberty, and impatient of
control, differences of opinion gave rise to
animated controversies, which only confirmed
the disputants in the sides they had taken.
Papal power could enforce a seeming uniformity of practice, but the power of the Reformation could establish no uniformity of faith.
These differences, which sprang up in the
sixteenth century, being magnified in importance by the special circumstances of the Reformation, being widened by protracted discussions, remain unsettled to this day; they
gave origin to various sects, which maintain

their several views with a rigid obstinacy,
which often engenders most unchristian
strife. This diversity of belief and interpretation is an inevitable incident of free inquiry; but the evils of diversity were early
felt, and strong efforts were made, by the
adoption of creeds, platforms, confessions
of faith, catechisms, and other devices, to
secure that unity of opinion which appeared
to be wanting to the reformers. These efforts,
whatever success may be due to them, did
not put an end to sectarian controversies.
From the era of the Reformation until the
present time, the question has still been, What
is the true doctrine? what shall we believe?
and if the disputants have been sects and
not merely individuals, it has rendered the
various sects only more watchful in maintaining their special tenets, and in keeping their
several followers to the line of their various
creeds. The eyes of Protestants have been
long and intently fixed upon these sectarian
lines of demarcation. They are jealous

of their infringement in proportion to the
heat of controversy, rather than in proportion to their importance. They have become
far less zealous of the great substantial truths
in which they agree, than in those matters
of interpretation and speculation in which
they differ. A large region is given them to
cultivate, and they quarrel about their several
boundaries, while the land on each side runs
to waste. It is clear that opinions have, by
these contests, been magnified into undue
importance, and these disputes have absorbed
time and attention which belonged to other
subjects. They have given a harshness and
severity of outline to sectarian differences, at
once forbidding and unchristian. So long as
the Word of God is taken as the rule of life,
and so long as men are permitted to think
for themselves, so long there must be diversities of opinion; but if the love of God and
the love of our fellow-men, about which there
can be no dispute, be allowed to exercise their
due sway, all these differences will fade into

insignificance, compared with the duties to God and man which invoke to active effort on every side. It is no more the province of any Protestant denomination to claim infallibility for its opinions, than for the Bishop of Rome; and Protestants will no more yield this claim to each other than to the papal chair. If we examine the articles, confessions of faith, creeds and catechisms of Protestants; if we look into their controversies, if we attend their convocations, conferences, conventions, and assemblies, we find that the burden of the whole has been doctrines, theology, and church government. In aid of these discussions, the Scriptures are searched unceasingly; every book, chapter, verse, and word* have been put to the test of severe examination: and no bounds are placed to the industry with which they are read and taught, but with results far beneath what such efforts should seem to promise. May not this study

* Some have even counted the letters in all the words of the Bible.

of the Scriptures have been made too sub-
servient to sectarian opinions, and too little
conducive to the active duties of Christian
love? It should be matter of inquiry how
far the instructions of Christ have been made
the basis of reformed theology and religious
teaching. His precepts do not enter largely
into creeds nor confessions, catechisms nor
articles, nor are they prominent in theology
or religious literature. There may be reasons
for this, which we do not perceive; but the
main reasons we take to be, those already
indicated in the abuses of charity and its institutions, by the Romish Church, and in
the controversies growing out of the Reformation, which naturally took the form of disputes about what we should believe, rather
than what we should practise as Christians.
Besides the abuses which led to the Reformation, the disruption itself, the wars which
followed, and the disputes among the reformers
were all unsuitable soil for the growth of that

mutual love and forbearance inculcated by
our Saviour as the manner of life which
characterizes his disciples.

PROTESTANT ERRORS AND OMISSIONS.

WE shall not attempt further to vindicate
the omissions of Protestant religious instruction : it is a subject too vast for us to conceive,
much less to execute. That there are great
omissions, it would be claiming too much for
human imperfection to doubt; that they are
of vital consequence to the progress of true
religion, the present state of Christendom and
of the world demonstrates. We cannot attempt this great task, although we lament
deeply that Christianity is suffering for want
of a vindication which shall clearly separate
the divine from the human. All the errors
of Romanism were not left behind by those
who came out of that church. The idea of a

great mysterious organization, a heaven-or-
dained corporation, which is the medium of
communication between Christ and his followers, still clings to the minds of many. The
disposition to judaize, to "tithe mint and
rue, and pass over judgment and the love of
God,"* has not been exhausted, but has been
visible in every age since the days of the
apostles. "Lading men with burdens grievous
to be borne,"† "putting yokes upon the neck
of disciples,"‡ has been done in modern times,
and continues to be done, and will probably
continue to be done, until a further reformation takes place, or until men become too enlightened to be fit subjects for such spiritual
domination.

To step in between the soul of man and
his Creator, Redeemer, and Sanctifier, to assume the office of mediator between them, or
of arbiter and absolute interpreter, is an act
of usurpation so daring and impious as to be
incredible, if our knowledge rested on less evi-

---

* Luke xi. 42.   † Luke xi. 46.   ‡ Acts xv. 10.

dence than our own eyes and ears. This intervention of man between God and his creatures, is not all confined to members of the
papal church. The assumption is not strange
in the Protestant world. The gospel is to be
preached to every creature; instruction is to be
given to every extent that is practicable; those
for whom it is intended are to receive it humbly and teachably, exercising all their faculties to understand and digest: but the opinions
then formed, the faith then built up, and the
working of the affections then excited, the
union between God and the soul then formed,
are operations wholly between God and his
subject man, in which no church or other ecclesiastical agency or office can have any
share. The sooner men are made to feel, individually and as masses, the great fact that
their eternal salvation depends not upon any
church or form of religious organization, but
upon their individual reception of the truth—
not upon their union with any religious denomination, nor upon their observance of any

forms or ceremonies, or modes of worship, but upon their individual union with God in Christ, the sooner will Christianity acquire a new progress and surmount the barriers which now retard its movements. When men fully comprehend that the basis of saving truth lies in the teachings of Christ, and that all forms of worship and religious observance are merely means of grace, without any intrinsic saving power, they will begin to look upward at once to Him with whom their peace is to be made, and then to their fellow men of various Christian organizations for aid, for instruction, for encouragement, for discipline, in their struggle to maintain a Christian life.

THE THIRST OF POWER ALWAYS HATEFUL, STILL MORE IN MATTERS OF RELIGION.

THERE is no craving of the human heart more strongly written in human history, than that after power.   It is no more strongly written in political than in ecclesiastical history : but its exhibitions, hateful and mischievous everywhere, are still more so in whatever concerns religion. It is the tendency of human nature, exhibited in every religious denomination, to obtain all the power and influence it can. This tendency in the primitive churches led to their ruin and to the rise of the papal power. Every minister and teacher and church-officer felt that if he had more power he could do more good, not remembering his own weakness, and the corrupting influences of power; not calling to mind that "God hath chosen the foolish things of the world to confound the wise, and the weak things of the world to confound the things which are mighty."* God works by human agencies, but He gives no right, and takes away all pretence, of these agencies, or any "flesh to glory in his presence."

The thirst for power, the rage to govern, infects more or less the mass and the indi-

---

* 1 Cor. i. 27—31.

viduals of every religious denomination; it reaches towards every thing in men's conduct, and every thing in their opinions. Thus men, themselves weak, fallible, and the prey of temptation, strive after a power which does not belong to them, which they have not wisdom to wield, and which, if obtained, saps their morals and ruins their souls. How little countenance is given to church domination by any thing contained in the lives or teachings of Christ and his apostles! How little to forms and ceremonies! The Jewish religion had been one of forms and ceremonies in detail without number; nearly all power was in the priesthood. All this had been perverted and abused to the very utmost extent of human wickedness. The Christian dispensation came and swept off every vestige of these forms and ceremonies and the whole framework of priestly power; it re-enacted the whole moral law, in terms so comprehensive and so simple as apparently to leave no escape to the evasive ingenuity of erring man. It

9*

laid down no long array of man's duties to
God; but commanded him to love God with
all his heart, and all his soul, and all his mind;
and, instead of a long line of man's duties to
his fellow, he is simply enjoined to love his
neighbour as himself. "On these two commandments" are made to "hang all the law
and the prophets." There is no form of church-
government implied in these commands,
which clearly import that man's great duty
to God and his fellow-man can only be discharged by a personal performance. All that
is contained in the writings of the apostles
[in the teachings of Christ there is nothing]
is so dim and shadowy in outline, we are
forced to the conclusion it was not intended
to set up authoritatively any form of church
government, nor to convey the impression
that the subject was of any vital import. If
the form adopted by the apostles and thus
slightly traced be deemed obligatory, certainly
the manner in which it is handed down to
us by its authors admonishes that we should

not magnify the importance of that which is
so little dwelt upon by those who framed it.
It was because Christ appeared in the garb
of poverty, and without any of the power or
pomp or riches of this world, that the Jews
rejected him with such disdain: being wedded
to these things, they could not believe in the
reality of His mission who condemned and
denounced them. This spirit, manifested so
strongly by the Jews, is not extinct to this
day, but has been equally visible in every
age of the Christian era. It was with great
difficulty the first converts at Jerusalem could
believe the gospel was to be preached to the
Gentiles,—that they could be brought to give
up the practice of circumcision, the observance of days and feasts, and other Jewish
forms and regulations, and bring themselves
to the simple requirements of a purely spiritual
worship. In reality, nothing was left of Jewish
forms, for this spirit to feed upon; and to remove every pretext in regard to days,—as,
otherwise, there would seem to be a great

propriety in adopting the seventh day of the
week as the day of Christian worship,—even
that was changed, lest it should come to be regarded rather as a continuance of the Jewish
Sabbath than as a day appointed by Christians for rest from labour and for religious
services. The necessity of that change is
made plain enough by the whole history
of Christianity : even now, many enforce the
observance of the first day of the week, in
the same terms and under the same sanctions
as those which are applied in the Old Testament to the seventh day. It would be incredible, if the like were not seen upon all sides,
and more or less in every form of Christianity, how this spirit of clogging its pure
system with excrescences which in few instances have been of any use, and, in very
many, of incalculable injury—this putting new
wine into old bottles—has prevailed from the
days of the apostles down to this moment.
It is a spirit which may be losing some of its
strength, but which yet exerts its power with

extraordinary vigour: having its root in some of the worst vices of the human heart, it cannot readily be extirpated. The more numerous these excrescences upon the Christian system, the more numerous are the pretexts for human agencies, and for the exercise of spiritual power. They were piled on for ages by the Romish church. Protestants have not only failed to cast off all these accumulations, but adopt many of their own invention or selection. It is in regard to the adoption or rejection of these, that some of the most violent religious controversies have been carried on, and in regard to which the greatest religious animosity and uncharitableness have been displayed. The Lord's supper, an institution of the simplest possible kind, was the subject of rank abuse in the days of the apostles, and has ever since, in various ways, been the subject of singular perversion. The simple emblem of purification in baptism has been the subject of like abuse; and because a man may simply wash his face or hands or feet, or may bathe his whole body in the water, in either of which cases the emblem is equally significant, a controversy is waged with heat, not only whether baptism implies washing or bathing, but whether it carries with it regeneration. The ceremony of washing the feet has been observed among Romanists, in a manner which is a perfect mockery of that humility its appointment was intended to promote and signify: among Protestants it is wholly neglected. The fondness for ceremony and outward forms does not reach so low as this act of humility, which is as clearly enjoined as the Lord's supper.

The beautiful and sublime simplicity of the Christian religion is thus continually sacrificed by attempts to improve—to build upon it; its progress is continually impeded by loading its movements with innumerable additions of man's invention. It asks none of these aids or accompaniments. It can live through all these abuses; it can save many of those who are unwittingly guilty of them. It requires no

superstructure of man's devising, no adorn-
ment or trickery of his wisdom : it asks its
votaries to give their affections to God, and
their services to their fellow-men : it asks an
exemplification of its purity and power in
their lives and conversation.

HOW THE GREAT LAW OF CHARITY HAS BEEN
CARRIED OUT BY PROTESTANTS.

WE have already adverted to the fact that
the reformers of the sixteenth century addressed themselves mainly to the task of res-
cuing Holy Writ from the utter disuse to
which it had been doomed, and the truth
from that mire of traditions, superstitions, and
unmeaning ceremonies in which it had been
for so many ages sunk and lost. Their first
inquiries, as we have seen, were, since we discard this mass of error and priestly trash
which has so long been heaping up in the

church of Rome, what shall we believe, and
what shall constitute the outline of reformed
doctrines ? The whole subject of charity had
become odious to those who had long been
contemplating the abuses of their church, and
especially the frauds and atrocities perpetrated
under the cloak of that Christian grace. Many
heavy yokes had been placed upon the necks
of the people by that church, and by no means
the lightest were those imposed under the
specious pretences of charity. The reformers,
in carrying out their work, in the ardour of a
conflict in which none but men of surpassing
energy could engage, soon forgot every consideration and dropped every semblance of
charity—a virtue so long distorted before their
eyes. Their cry was for freedom of opinion
and worship, for truth, for sound doctrine.
They may have supposed that, the truth once
re-established and freely proclaimed, the practical duties of religion would be fulfilled, not
only with increase of intelligence, but of zeal.
They carried on their great work until Pro-

testantism stood up clearly revealed and defined before the world. The contest by which this was accomplished, both physical and intellectual, was one of the most remarkable for interest, fierceness, and endurance, which the world has ever witnessed. Rome did not permit this affront to her supremacy without exerting all her power and all the unscrupulous wickedness of interested dignitaries. The vigour of youthful liberty and free opinions overpowered a church in its dotage. In this contest charity had no part. Unhappily, the reformers not only scouted the Romish abuse of charity, but they neglected to give this divine grace that place in their system which it occupies in the New Testament, which it claims in every Christian's heart, and without which all forms of religion must be incomplete, if not false. In none of the formulas of the Reformation, in none of its creeds, confessions, catechisms, did the subject of charity figure according to that precedency which is given to it in the teachings of Christ and his

apostles; and in many instances it was lost
sight of altogether. The doctrine of human depravity, imputed righteousness, justification
by faith, repentance; regeneration, the headship of Christ, the freeness of God's grace,
among very many others, were brought to
light and vindicated as truths of the gospel:
innumerable errors of Romish doctrine and
belief were singled out, refuted, and held up
to ridicule or public detestation. All this was
done; but all reformers have found it more
easy to pull down than to build up. Men can
seldom glory over their own work. They
dragged Romanism from the horse, and in attempting to mount, they went clear over to
the other side. The priests of Rome preached
charity as a mode of enriching the church;
and while streams of charity flowed from their
people to the poor, many of the rich continued
to make the church and its officers the depo-
sitaries of their wealth, in confidence that it
would be applied to the relief of the needy.
These streams of bounty they swelled with all

the skill and all the means in their power. The subject was never forgotten, but kept constantly before the minds of the people. However unfaithful the priest, the bishop, or the monk may have been to their trust, yet how many were moved, by such constant appeals to their kindness, to the regular and faithful distribution of alms! How many were in consequence visited in prison! how many of the naked were clothed! how many of the sick were visited! to how many of the thirsty was the cup of cold water administered. True, many did all this without any clear conception of scriptural charity; but the exercise of such kindness must more or less cultivate the true grace it represents.

The reformers took the Bible in their hands, reared the standard of truth, swept off the rubbish of Romanism, and erected the fabric of Protestantism, but overlooked, in their readings of the New Testament, its imperative injunctions of brotherly kindness. Their building was massy, of noble and severe outline : its frame-work of truth was of impregnable strength, yet was it cold, forbidding, and uncomfortable; it was neither warmed nor lighted by charity. The men of the Reformation were men of truth, not of charity. It was an age which called into action all the stern energies of the man, the warrior, and the defender of truth. When every nerve of mental and physical exertion was strung to its utmost intensity, the milder graces of charity were forgotten amid scenes in which there appeared so little occasion for their exercise. Look into the theology of the Reformation and see if it be not subject to this reproach. It is a form of Christianity with charity left out; and yet if this form implied a strength of faith which "could remove mountains," it would be "nothing." It is a monstrous technicality; it is sculptured marble, white and beautiful, but rigid and unfeeling.

This takes away none of the real merits of the Reformation. The Bible was rescued from oblivion and placed in the hands of the people, as the rule of their faith—a lamp for their feet, and a light to their path. It would be very wrong to assert that those who had thus newly placed their hands upon the word of God must be the safest expositors of its injunctions. They executed a task as great as any men ever achieved, but they should not continue to be our sole spiritual teachers. We are bound to search the Scriptures for ourselves, and all who faithfully study the teachings of Christ will find a mine of instruction which is not prominent in the writings of reformers. Romanism is like a man full of all manner of disease, immersed in ignorance and mental darkness, in slavish subjection to the power of the church, but with a hand often open to succour the poor. Protestantism is a giant of bone and sinew and iron nerve; full of enterprise, energy, and action; ready to defend the right and to do justice, and armed to battle for the truth; but with a hand more ready to *discipline* than relieve the beggar. It is very clear that true Christians are

10*

not made so by any virtue in Romanism, nor by any virtue in Protestantism. Both these forms of religion are of man's construction, and, however great the difference in their merit, they both partake of human frailty. Our only safe guide is the word of God in our own hands, the teachings of which in their main scope are so plain that the humblest intellect may find the words of eternal life.

THE BENEFITS OF THE REFORMATION NO REASON FOR PERPETUATING ITS ERRORS.

WHILST it is true that the errors of the reformers were such as belonged to the period, the occasion, and the kind of men who were called to do the work; and whilst it is equally true that in some sense the reformation is a work continued to this day—for the contest with Romish error is far from being ended,—yet the sins, omissions, and mistakes

of the early reformation should be as carefully
rectified and avoided as any other errors or
transgressions. The success of the reformers,
in the first instance, was remarkable; but they
were far from seizing and presenting the whole
scope and spirit of Christianity. Error mingles in all human doings : the reformation exhibits its share. It has been the duty of Protestants ever since, not only to vindicate
constantly the great truths brought out at the
Reformation, but constantly to extend and purify their knowledge; and, whilst thus holding up the truth, to aim at a better fulfilment
of the duties of Christianity. It is to be feared
that what was a necessary feature of the
early reformation has been too exclusive a
characteristic ever since of Protestantism—a
devotion to Christian truth far exceeding our
devotion to Christian duty. Our preaching
and our teaching have been carried on with
wonderful zeal and diligence; many run to and
fro, and knowledge is increased; the means
of grace are spread abroad and resorted to with

a perseverance that evinces a just appreciation of Christian truth; but it is too little felt
that all this comes far short of practical Christianity.

No attendance upon the preaching of the
gospel, nor upon the ordinances of any
church or congregation, nor upon any ministrations—no zeal nor industry in Bible classes
nor catechetical teaching—no liberality in
sustaining the ministry, nor any of the enterprises of the churches, can dispense us from
the obligation to love our neighbour as ourselves—from doing unto others as we would
have them do unto us; nor from any of those
duties of charity which are so strongly enjoined by Christ himself as the chief of our
duties. Truth cannot save us; even that
faith which can remove mountains is insufficient without charity. No zeal for prayers,
or liturgy, or church service, nor creed, nor
confessions, nor for the Bible itself, can re-
place the duties of brotherly kindness. It is
all vain to call Lord, Lord, if we do not the

things which our Lord says.* "But whoso
hath this world's good, and seeth his brother
have need, and shutteth up his bowels of compassion from him, how dwelleth the love of
God in him? My little children, let us not
love in word, neither in tongue, but in deed
and in truth."†

CHARACTERISTICS OF PROTESTANTISM DEVE-
LOPED IN ITS GROWTH.

PROTESTANTISM does not, however, owe all
its distinguishing features to the events of the
Reformation nor to the peculiarities of the
reformers. The church of Rome having
long held men in temporal and spiritual
bondage, the truths which the Reformation
brought to light constituted a real emancipation. Before that time, men's minds and
estates were claimed by the church, and the
claim was enforced to an extent which checked

---

* Luke vi. 46.   † 1 John iii. 17, 18.

energy, enterprise, and industrial progress.
All Europe and the world soon felt the activity and life infused into business by Protestant energy. This was the natural result of that mental freedom which permitted men to determine their course of life, free from the bonds of superstition and priestly rule. Science, literature, industry, and commerce, all felt the new impulse, and commenced the great career which has brought the world to its present advanced position; the fetters being removed which had bound men for a thousand years to miserable inaction and mental sloth. Galileo and Copernicus could safely have announced their discoveries under the protection of Luther. Newton would have been treated like them, had he lived in their days, under papal rule. At the time this Protestant energy began to display its power, the treasures of the New World were pouring into Europe, and doubtless aided to stimulate that movement which was then so remarkable, and which has continued until it

exhibits in the results of three centuries' progress a greater advance than in all the previous history of the world. To trace this progress in its connection with reformed Christianity, would be a topic worthy of volumes. We do not speak of this as progress in Christianity; we do not claim it as a Christian conquest. It has sprung from that freedom of mind which is essential to Christianity, but it has in a large degree been achieved in defiance or neglect of the great law of charity.

The most remarkable developments of human energy which have ever been exhibited have taken place in connection with the enjoyment of more than ordinary personal or national liberty. Thus was manifested the military energy of Greece and Rome; thus the commercial energy of the Italian republics, the Hanse towns; but no human energy has ever equalled that which has been displayed under the liberty conferred by Protestantism. This has been exerted equally in peace, in science, in arts, in industrial production, and in commerce. It would not be just to claim for Protestantism all that has been accomplished, yet it may be safely asserted that Protestants have led the way in this great advance of knowledge, art, and industry. Many Catholic countries have remained almost stationary: witness Italy, Spain, Portugal, Ireland, Mexico, and the countries of South America. German Catholics have had the aid and have been stimulated by the example of German Protestants. France once had a large infusion of Protestants, who were notoriously the most enlightened and the most industrious of her people: when they were cruelly massacred or driven abroad, they carried with them the best manufacturing skill of their country. How much the progress of France was retarded by this insane and wicked persecution can never be told; it may be conjectured from the advance made since that revolution in which the whole nation rose in mass and shook off the thraldom of the papacy. If France had then become Protestant, her social progress would have responded to the greatness of her efforts and sacrifices; but having made the attempt to cast off all religion, she easily fell back into the arms of the Priesthood, never again, we may hope, to relapse into the darkness of papal superstition. The Romish religions of France and Spain are far from being identical in their power over the people.

But we cannot by any means claim this Protestant superiority as any triumph for Christianity. The energy which has achieved so much in Great Britain and the United States, and other Protestant countries, has not always been controlled by the pure motives of Christianity. No, far from it! Human faculties and energies, set free from bondage, spiritual and temporal, would not naturally engage in the service of the Redeemer. Rome, where she had or has the power, holds her subjects to the service of the church: Protestantism can only offer

11

to those by whom she is surrounded, the invitations of the gospel on the one hand; whilst the world, with all its allurements, presents its inducements on the other. In this struggle, every human effort has been employed. The Protestant ministry have armed themselves with all the learning of the world; they have built up a great science of theology; they have formed themselves into a variety of camps, holding every variety of opinion which free minds can draw from the study of their acknowledged rule of life, the Scriptures; and they have unitedly exerted an amount of labour and zeal in their work, which has seldom been surpassed in any department of life, by any class of men. These efforts, continued now through two centuries, have not been without results. Yet the full benefits of Christianity have been brought home to a few only of those who have enjoyed all these advantages. It may be feared that not a tenth of the people of any Protestant country can be truly claimed as having been unfeigned disciples of Christ, taking their ministers as judges. This is a small triumph, indeed, if we regard the efforts made, and the means employed. But if few have been saved, many have been brought within the influences of the gospel, to submit to many of its requirements, to contribute to its support, to acknowledge its worth, to conform to its morality; and thus characteristics have been imparted to the population of Protestant countries which are peculiarly their own. While the zeal and labours of Christian ministers were thus applied to draw converts from the multitude, the men of the world were not less energetically employed. Whilst they, for the most part, were constrained by the force of public opinion to preserve an outward appearance of respect for religion, all their plans and labours were dictated and carried on under motives of consideration purely human. In this play of the human faculties, under no powerful constraint, their powers for good and evil have been more signally developed

and displayed than in any age of the world.
A new race of men has sprung up, and intellectual power is more widely spread among
the masses than ever heretofore. Human
nature has asserted its evil tendencies in the
most striking forms; but in no way so remarkable as in the form of that intense selfishness which is manifested in the pursuit
of wealth and power. Whilst we might dwell
upon many triumphs of science, art, and industry, in Protestant countries, as these do not lie
within the scope of our subject, we feel bound
to say that too great devotion to the pursuit
of riches, to the increase of production and
the extension of commerce, has been their
chief characteristic. It is not to be wondered
that where human nature had full scope, it
should spend itself in a direction, so much
in accordance with its dictates. Men no longer
feared the deprivation of their wealth under
the fearful terrors of the inquisition or the
powerful suction of the church. They regarded only the laws of the land. Under these

circumstances, the business of the world took a start, which left far in the shade any example in its previous history. The energies and the talents of men grew with their unwonted exercise, and strengthened from generation to generation. It became a great struggle, in which the most powerful intellects, the greatest talents, the largest experience, the deepest skill, or the most consummate cunning, gained the victory. In this contest every possible human effort was exerted. Emulation and competition became controlling elements in this pursuit of wealth. The excitements of the gambler were often added to the other motives of those engaged in this struggle, by the unavoidable complications and uncertainties which attended many of the best laid schemes. The minds of men became thus absorbed to a degree which would be incredible if we were not daily witnesses. In the midst of all this turmoil, there arose a business morality, exhibiting a punctuality, an adherence to contracts, an honesty

11*

in the execution of trusts, a faithfulness to promises—far exceeding what the world had ever known. It was in fact, a necessity of business, without which by mutual consent, the immense transactions of which it was the bond, could never have been carried on. It borrowed some of its maxims from Christianity, and the whole of this vast movement had a tinge of Christian colouring thrown over it, gilding many of its deformities, but not sanctifying them.

It is but too plain that the Protestant ministry, not being able to stem the tide of this resistless stream of human selfishness, mingled too much with it. As the early Roman priesthood compromised. with that paganism which they became less and less able to overcome as they became more corrupt, and adopted many of its customs and practices, as a fit amalgamation with the papacy, we have too much reason to believe that a gradual compromise took place between the devotees of mammon and the ministers of

Christ. Protestantism was strong enough and pure enough to command respect, to establish a public opinion, and by this means to enforce a seeming submission to some of the external requirements of Christianity. The men of this world conceded so much, and are received into Protestant congregations, not as Christians, but as the material upon which the teaching and preaching is to be expended. They become hearers of the word, and large contributors to the maintenance of ministers and teachers. They are officers in the temporal affairs of the congregations, and exercise no small control in all their concerns. In the Romish church, the priesthood hold in their hands not only all its spiritual affairs, but all its property and business of every kind. Among the Protestants are two classes—the real Christians, members of the church; and the mere hearers, spectators, members of the congregations. Among the Romanists, all are alike members of the church, whatever difference there may be in their respective attention to its requirements : all are members who are not excommunicated. The men of the world have, then, a strong position in Protestant churches, and exercise a visible influence. The whole expenditure of Protestant congregations of almost every denomination, for every purpose, religious and philanthropic, is derived, in a large degree, from those who are not acknowledged to be real disciples of Christ.

Those who thus contribute may be, and are, frequently, patterns of business morality; they may be kind neighbours, good friends, and praiseworthy in all the relations of this life; but they are regarded as more devoted to this world than to the world to come. We undertake not to say how much of good or of evil may be in all this; but we ask if there be not some danger in this commingling of the men of the world and the disciples of Christ in the business of the churches? Will not the former exercise an influence proportionate to their contributions? And are not their con-

tributions frequently the largest? Can we
not, in fact, readily point out some of the results of this hybrid system? One of these is,
that the spirit of business, which rules in the
affairs of the world, has largely invaded the
churches. In many Protestant countries,
others being the judges, religion has become
merely an affair of state, or a matter of business. But we may pass over these large exemplifications, in which political control aided
the evil result, and regard only the purest and
best of their churches. In these, even, religion
has assumed many of the maxims and practices of business. Buildings are erected for
the worship of God where men are found to
pay for them; ministers preach where men
are found to pay them; congregations assem-
ble in costly temples which they have contributed to build, or the services of which they
contribute to maintain; ministers and missionaries are trained up and go forth where
there is money provided to educate and maintain them; associations are created to promote

every form of philanthropy where money can
be had to sustain them. Every manner of
good work is accomplished where money can
be had to pay for it. A division of labour is
established in religion and good works. Some
furnish the head, some the heart, some the
hands, and some the money. In these processes, the riches of this world become a ruling
element, a foundation of all the system, and
the cause of all the success. It would be impossible to distinguish in all this work, what
share is taken by those of whom it is said,
" It is easier for a camel to go through the
eye of a needle, than for a rich man to enter
into the kingdom of God;" but it is well
known they partake largely and wield an important influence. Money, in too strong a
sense, is the mainspring of a large portion of this
activity; remove this spring, and the machinery would stop. Whence comes this money?
It is not the voluntary offerings of crowds
who come up cheerfully and pour their contributions into the treasury of the churches.

It is levied, nay even exacted, by a system and under influences which do not permit denial; under such penalties as the givers are afraid to incur. It has become a great business to raise money for religious and benevolent purposes. A man may live in the house of another, if he pays the rent; he may own real estate in any country, if he pays the taxes; so he may have a seat in the house of God if he pays its assessment. He may occupy a respectable position in the church, and in the society around it, if he contributes liberally, when called upon, to all the numerous demands which religious and charitable associations make upon him. It would be hard to conjecture how much of the money levied in this way would be got, if it were left to flow in solely by the spontaneous movements of the contributors. Certainly a very small portion. It is a regular system of business, this systematic benevolence; and if this feature be taken away, the whole must fall to the ground, unless some other life be breathed into it. A vast amount of good may be thus accomplished; many good Christians may mingle in these labours; yet this system is not Christianity, nor has it the purity or vitality of the Christian system.

We protest against Christianity being made responsible for this mode of operation, whatever of good or evil may be the result. It is rather an excrescence fastened upon Christianity by human frailty, and being so attached, it is regarded by too many beholders, who take not the trouble to examine, as a part of the Christian system. Let the probe be freely applied, and it will be found this excrescence is no part of the system which it overshadows, conceals, and deforms.

We mean not unqualified condemnation: every form or manifestation of Christianity must be more or less marred by human frailty. Let us be careful to separate that which is human from that which is divine: and, above all, let us be careful not to place that which is human above that which is divine. We merely point to a system professedly Christian, by which men commit their charity to the keeping of others, and permit their good works to grow upon other people's vines: by which we may do good to others, but get none for ourselves.

But let us not too much disparage this business-like philanthrophy: it is a tribute to the sublimer spirit of Christianity; yet not to be confounded with that system in which the gift of two mites may exceed in importance and in results the bestowal of millions. We would not condemn, we would not discourage this kind of effort; it may lead some to think they are fulfilling all their Christian duties, and thus lead them astray; but the general tendency must be to open the channels of good affections, to liberalize the mind, and to strengthen benevolent emotions.

Christianity designs the exercise of charity to be as useful to those who exercise it as to those in whose favour it is exercised—to him who gives alms as to him who receives them,

12

to those who visit the sick and suffering and
the imprisoned, who clothe the naked and
feed the hungry, to those who administer the
cup of cold water to the thirsty, as to those in
whose favour these kind offices are performed.
Christian charity is the overflowing of kindly
affections: it cannot commit to others that
which it can perform itself: it cannot wait for
direction nor arrangement, but promptly
stretches forth the hand of succour, wherever
it finds a claim for relief. Charity is poured
from the heart; that which springs up in the
soul, that loves its neighbour as it loves itself,
can never be satisfied by paying contributions
into the treasury of any association, however
praiseworthy its objects. The starving pauper
craves bread with no stronger sensations than
the charitable soul desires to minister to him
the succour and comfort he needs: the sons
and daughters of affliction crave sympathy
and consolation with no stronger emotions
than are felt by the charitable souls who fly
to commune with and comfort them. Charity

does not consist in any system which merely secures comfort to the poor and afflicted: it consists in the overflowing of those affections which prompt us to fly uncalled to the help of the miserable.

TOO MUCH RELIANCE ON LEARNING.—THE AFFECTIONS TO BE EXERCISED AS WELL AS THE MIND.

CHRISTIANITY has suffered from the labours of men in another aspect. While the spirit of business has invaded religion on one side, learning and theology have occupied too much ground on the other. It required but a few years of Christ's ministry to announce his great message. These simple but sublime truths are recorded by the four evangelists in very small space. They are so plain that he that runs may understand. Christ consummated his mission by suffering on the cross, and the work of redemption was accomplished.

His apostles went forth to proclaim the glad
tidings of salvation: they exhorted, explained,
argued, vindicated, and illustrated, according
to the circumstances in which they were
placed, and the persons to whom they addressed themselves, whether Jew or Gentile.
Both were opposed to the truth, and to both
were applied such motives and treatment as
their case required.

We mean not to urge any objections to
theology in itself, nor to deny that our spiritual teachers should be versed in such
knowledge. They may by such learning be
more thoroughly furnished to every good
work, and be enabled to prosecute their
labours with more success among all classes
of men. But all Christians cannot be versed
in theology: it cannot safely be asserted how
much knowledge is requisite to save a believer. This gauge is not placed in human
hands. It is true, the more knowledge of the
Christian system the better; but if this light
emit no heat, it is deceptive and injurious.

It is not the knowledge of God, but the love of God, which constitutes the Christian: it is not Christian doctrine as measured by human faculties which makes Christianity, but the perfect love of our neighbour. Men are not saved by their knowledge, but by their affections. Few can make high attainments in knowledge, but all may in the exercise of kindly feelings. Men are less answerable for the degree of their knowledge than they are for the use they make of it. If the temple is not warmed as well as lighted, it is not the abode of a Christian man.

We fear that too great prominence is given to doctrinal instruction. Too much effort is given to discipline men into parallel belief, to curb and restrain men's minds into one or a few channels of faith. All efforts thus applied have fallen far more short of success in reality than they have even in appearance. It is far from true that the individuals of any denominations of Christians agree in opinions; there are, probably, as many shades of belief

12*

as there are differences in minds. It is impossible to bring various mental capacities to one measure; to carry all to the same goal, or to stop all at the same place. Let not the attempt of equalizing men's belief be carried to extremes; Christian knowledge need not be carried beyond the bounds to which the heart can send the warmth and life of Christian affections. There is nothing now so much needed by Christianity from its professors as an earnest exemplification of Christ's teachings. This would preach louder than a thousand voices; this would be more eloquent than ten thousand volumes; this would carry conviction where no human instrumentality could ever penetrate.

THE ESTABLISHED CHURCH OF ENGLAND—ITS ABUSE
AT THE REFORMATION—ITS NEGLECT OF THE POOR
AND THE SUFFERING.

WE admit that other men, clothed with
powers similar to those wielded by the Romish ecclesiastics, would equally have abused
them. The very first steps of the Reformation afford striking examples. In no country
had the religious liberality of Catholic laity
been displayed on a larger scale than in England. This munificence, in the course of several centuries previous to the Reformation, had
placed in the hands of the clergy quite a large
proportion of the best estates in land of that
kingdom. The tendency to this kind of generosity, under priestly instigation, became so
great that legislative intervention became
necessary to restrain it. The immense estates
thus given to the church were, in a large degree, expressly bestowed for charitable pur-

poses, the fulfilment of which the givers supposed would assist to rescue their souls from the fires of purgatory. The bishops and priests, who knew what was necessary on that score, made what may be termed, all things considered, a very fair distribution of these spoils. They settled, as the law of apportionment, that the bishops should have one-fourth; the priests one-fourth; for repair of churches one-fourth; and the remaining one-fourth to the poor and the other general purposes for which the whole was expressly given. This distribution was, in some instances, or according to some authorities, one-third to the clergy, one-third for repair of churches, and one-third to purposes of charity. At the period of the Reformation, when Henry VIII. assumed the headship of the church of England, all these immense estates were confiscated and conferred upon the bishops and other clergy and leaders of the great reform. All that was given to the nobility and gentry has from that day to the present been held as

private property, without the slightest regard
.to the trusts upon which the grants were originally made. All that was given to the
English bishops and clergy has remained the
property of the establishment to this day. Its
yearly value is variously estimated, but is
safely put at fifty millions of dollars. Not the
slightest regard has been paid by these bishops
and clergy, any more than the lay grantees,
to the trusts under which these estates were
granted. The Catholic clergy applied a fourth,
or even a third, for the benefit of the poor;
the English clergy have retained the whole
as their exclusive perquisite. Thus arise the
enormous revenues of the English bishops,
which are a standing reproach to Christianity
in a country where millions upon millions are
groaning in poverty, with a clear right to all
the relief these riches could afford.

From its first establishment, the English
church not only appropriated the funds of the
poor, but cast the charge of the poor upon the
secular arm, where it remains to this day. It

would be difficult to point out in the history
of the papacy, any more daring and flagrant disregard of Christian principles than
this. The Romish church in all ages, and in
all countries, has admitted the claims of the
poor, and also the obligations which those
claims imposed. The Protestant church of
England commenced its career by seizing their
estates, and turning the poor over to the tender mercies of the government. The legislation for the poor was characterized, during the
reign of Henry VIII., by its fixing upon the
unemployed poor the epithet of " vagabonds,"
and by inflicting the penalties of whipping,
cropping, branding, and death for the offence
of being vagabonds. Many thousands were
hung in the reign of that first head of the
English church for being vagabonds; that is,
unemployed or idle poor. No doubt the dis-
solution of the monasteries and other religious
houses had sent forth a host of inmates
stripped of all means of support, and had deprived of their customary employments vast

troops of labourers, whose services were re-
placed by others more favoured by the new
occupants of the estates, and had driven away
in despair hosts of poor who had lived upon
the regular alms of the religious establishments. The mischiefs which arose from discharging such a multitude of destitute paupers
upon the community must have been grave
enough to require all the patience and all the
wisdom of the public authorities, and more
especially as the subject was new to them.
No wonder these persons, so suddenly and utterly stripped of their only comfort and hopes
for this life, became unruly, wandered like
vagabonds, and rendered stringent measures
necessary to keep them in awe. This is no
place to write the history of the English poor,
of the legislation applied to them, nor of the
administration of the poor-laws; whatever
may be said of the wisdom or the mercy or
the statesmanship displayed in the treatment
of English poor, the whole constitutes such a
disgrace to the established church, and to Pro-

testantism, as can never be adequately characterized. During three centuries, she has
shut her eyes from beholding, and shut her
ears from hearing, and withheld her hands
from removing the woes of ten generations of
increasing millions of suffering poor. She has
not fed them nor clothed them, nor visited
them in sickness nor in prison; she has left
them in charge of the national authorities.
And what have these done? In this long period, what have they devised for the poor?
They have long since reduced the treatment
of paupers to a system which has since been
adopted for criminals. They have invented
the poor-house, that stigma of Protestantism;
they have degraded the poor to the level of
the worst criminals; they have made charity
dependent on the parish boundaries; they
have enacted a scene of protracted and bitter
litigation to determine which parish may be
acquitted of the duty of relieving the poor;
they spend as much in efforts to cast off the
burden of a poor family as would relieve scores

of families; they let out the poor by contract
to the maintenance of a contractor; they look
upon the support of the poor as a grievous
burden, and regard it as a matter of business,
in which economy must rule, until the lowest
cost at which life can be sustained is found;
and accordingly the allowance of the poor has
gone far below that of the soldier or sailor, or
even the thief and murderer in prison. They
regard the pauper as a public evil, the cost of
which is to be kept at the lowest possible
point; and they deny the obligation of such
legislation as might have a tendency to amend
the condition of their hordes of poor.

Whether the English authorities have in all
this fulfilled their duties as legislators and
governors, is a question into which we cannot
enter. But the conduct of the established
church, which has for centuries looked upon
this scene of famine and nakedness and poor-
house imprisonment, without an effort as a
church to fulfil her Christian obligations to the
poor, is such as no language can with proper
13

severity stigmatize. The English poor have been increasing in comparative numbers and destitution from the Reformation to the present hour; and during this period, the confiscated revenues of the poor in the keeping of the church have been increasing. What possible affinity can that church, as such, have with the religion of Christ, which, whilst it absorbs the living of the poor, repudiates all care of them? Could such a church appear before Christ, without hearing the command, "Sell all that thou hast and give to the poor, and come follow me?" This is the lightest rebuke that is conceivable in the circumstances. But as this command was given to one whose heart was merely too much fixed on riches which were his own, the case of the church of England and the poor who are pining in want, and dying at her door, may be much more fitly illustrated by the parable of Lazarus and the rich man, who, for his hardness of heart, "in hell lifted up his eyes in torments." Even this does not reach the enormity of the case; for this rich man's goods were his own. The church of England turned the poor out of doors, and took possession of their houses and their goods; and whilst revelling in the enjoyment of these ill-gotten gains, myriads of paupers, lying at her gate, are suffering the extremities of sickness, nakedness, and want. If they ever reach Abraham's bosom, it will not be from any instruction or help given them by the establishment. But whether they do or not, who can doubt that it will be less tolerable for that church in the next world than for the rich man who neglected Lazarus?

When the truth first flashed on Zaccheus, the tax-gatherer of Judea, he broke out instantly, and said to Christ, "Behold, Lord, the half of my goods I give to the poor; and if I have taken any thing from any man by false accusation, I restore him fourfold." If this be the rule of restitution for a wrongful taking, it will not be hard to fix the sum which is due to the poor of England from the English church.

If our tone seems harsh towards the church of England, it is merely because the facts justify it. We believe no sect, as such, can vindicate all its acts. It is the more just to select that church for remark, in such an essay as this, because it imbodies what is regarded as the flower of Protestantism. The members of that church are distinguished throughout the world for wealth, liberality, learning, and many high qualities. It is fair to take them as a favourable sample of the fruits of the Reformation. We cannot say how far individuals or multitudes are responsible for the sins of the church with which they are connected; but we know that very many, in all ages of Christianity, have distinguished themselves far above the errors of their respective churches. No church has more to boast in this respect than that of England. It is well that the eternal welfare of the members does not depend on the character of the church to which they may belong. If so, what church or sect could save its members? Not one!—but least of all, perhaps, the church of England.

A natural result of this wicked neglect of the poor in England by the church, has been, that the poor in that country are regarded differently, and treated differently, from what they are in any other nation. What is not deemed the duty of the church has ceased to be regarded as the duty of individuals. The poor are restrained to the limits of their own parishes, under penalty of starvation or being carried back by the authorities to their own limits. They are not permitted to ask alms. They are turned off the land in England, and obliged to take refuge in the cities, working at wages which barely sustain life, to swell the products of the manufactories. They are, without judge or jury, convicted of poverty, sent to the poor-house, where husband and wife and children are separated and put to hard labour. The severity of this sentence is fully as great as that which awaits criminals under the present improved system of prison discipline. The poor are regarded as a burden upon society, to be diminished or got rid of by any course short of murder. They are not deemed to have any claims as fellow-men or fellow-christians, in a Christian land. England has a blessed constitution. She has long enjoyed the most wise and vigorous administration in the world, under all the advantages of a mild climate and productive soil, and yet paupers not only exist, but have greatly increased. It is plain they are an inevitable evil: nothing more can be done but by all proper means to prevent the increase of those who are only born to be burdens upon the community. This is the English feeling in regard to the poor.

It was reserved for a clergyman of the established church to work up this feeling and these views into a system of philosophy. The sum of the Rev. Mr. Malthus's work on population is thus given in his own words:—
" A man who is born into a world already

possessed, if he cannot get subsistence from
his parents, on whom he has a just demand,
and if the society does not want his labour,
has no claim of right to the smallest portion
of food, and, in fact, has no business to be
where he is. At nature's mighty feast there
is no cover for him. She tells him to be gone,
and will quickly execute her own orders, if he
do not work upon the compassion of some
of her guests. If these guests get up and
make room for him, other intruders immediately appear, demanding the same favour.
The report of a provision for all that come
fills the hall with numerous claimants.   The
order and harmony of the feast is disturbed :
the plenty that before reigned is changed into
scarcity : and the happiness of the guests is
destroyed by the spectacle of misery and dependence in every part of the hall, and by the
clamorous importunity of those who are justly
enraged at not finding the provision they had
been taught to expect.   The guests learn too
late their error in counteracting those strict

orders to all intruders issued by the great mistress of the feast, who, wishing that all her guests should have plenty, and knowing that she could not provide for unlimited numbers, humanely refused to admit fresh comers when her table was already full."*

Can inhumanity go a step farther? Can disobedience and contempt of the Divine command to love our neighbour as ourself imagine a farther step? It is a total denial of "the Fatherhood of God and the brotherhood of man," and consequently a total abjuration of Christianity. The remedial measure proposed by the Rev. Mr. Malthus is in strict accordance with his theory. He proposes that, notice being given, all children begotten afterwards should in every event be denied all official and private relief, or charity of any kind. If they perish, the responsibility will rest with the parents who brought them into the world after due warning of the consequences.

---

* Malthus on Population, first edition; and see sixth edition, vol. ii. p. 337.

By this means, the intruders into the hall of the great feast of life would be rapidly starved out of existence, the order and harmony of the feast restored, and the "happiness of the guests be no longer destroyed by the spectacle of misery" around them.

If this is not the doctrine of the church of England in regard to the poor, it is the philosophy which has grown out of her neglect to teach and exemplify the great duty of Christian charity : if it is not her doctrine, it is the very essence and theory of her practice.

THE SPIRIT OF PROTESTANTISM AT LARGE.—ENGLISH PROTESTANTISM.

THIS subject might justly be swelled into volumes. We might proceed to show that other Protestants besides those of England have fallen short of their duty to the poor; that they have not apprehended, taught, nor

practised the precepts of charity as inculcated
by Christ and his apostles : that, split into numerous sects, they have been far more zealous
in defining and defending their various shades
of belief than in fulfilling Christian duties :
that they have divided the vineyard which
has been given them to cultivate, into
innumerable subdivisions, and have spent
in contests about enclosures the time and
talents which they should have given to the
cultivation of the vines: that they have buried
themselves in theology, and neglected the
plainest teachings of Him whose name they
bear: that they have brought reproach upon
their Master by exhibiting all manner of uncharitableness in their mutual bearing towards each other: that while they utterly
scout the claim of the pope to infallibility,
they severally put forth pretensions in regard
to their own standards and creeds as exacting
as those of the pope; and whilst they thus
claim to be undoubtedly and severally right,
they have, almost without exception, exalted

their own creeds, catechisms, confessions, liturgies, and forms of service above the precepts
of their Master: that they have built temples
without number, and have preached the gospel, but not for nor to the poor: that whilst
all religious eloquence has been cultivated
with great assiduity, they have forgotten that
"though they speak with the tongues of angels, and have not charity, they are as sounding brass:" that whilst they have multiplied
religious books beyond all enumeration, and
pursued biblical lore with a zeal and success
truly wonderful, they have not remembered
that "though they had the gift of prophecy,
and understood all mysteries and all knowledge, and though they had all faith so that
they could remove mountains, and had not
charity, they are nothing:" that whilst their
liberality has frequently been large and greatly
diversified, and whilst they have suffered for
the truth's sake, they have forgotten that
"though they bestow all their goods to feed
the poor, and give their bodies to be burned,

and have not charity, it could profit them nothing."

There is, indeed, no church nor sect which can glory in its purity or perfection before God : there is none which would not be utterly condemned under the application of the same rules by which men must be finally judged. Let any of them give account of their stewardship in the administration of the great duty of Christian charity, and see how far, how very far they have fallen below the requirement. If this subject were pursued by some one fitted for the task, the picture drawn could not but lower that self-righteous spirit in which many Protestant churches so freely indulge. They would find that we may be very clear in perceiving error in others, without being right ourselves; and that so little room is there for any to indulge in self-righteousness before God, that, for the most part, those who are most positive and assuming are deepest in error. It may be well to think that whilst the great mass of Protestant theology may be in the main correct as far as it goes, yet it must be fatally deficient, because it has no soul. The statue may be faultless in its outlines, proportions, and faithfulness to the truth, but it is cold, hard, unyielding, and without sensation or affections.

The whole field of Protestantism being too wide for our purpose, we return to England, and confine our remarks to what is observable there, not in an invidious spirit, but because the facts are most easily ascertained and verified, and because, if English Protestants, with their world-wide reputation for liberality, have failed to fulfil the duties of Christian charity, there will be small ground for others to stand upon in the day of scrutiny.

If we have been successful in bringing to view the pressing obligations of our duties to our fellow-men in poverty, in sickness, and in confinement, few will deny the propriety of immediate obedience to every such call. But whilst we cheerfully give the cup of water to the thirsty, whilst we feed those who are actu-

14

ally starving, and clothe those who are actually naked or in rags, because these duties are specifically enjoined, does not the great law, "love thy neighbour as thyself," claim something more than these temporary acts of kindness and relief. We must not let these occasions of charity slip; we must not turn our back upon those who are suffering for what we can give them. But are we not equally bound to exert ourselves to afford permanent succour—to raise our suffering brethren to the same level in comfort with ourselves? We owe a duty not only in every particular case, but we owe a debt of love to every individual; and we are bound to pay that debt, not only in special acts of kindness, but in general efforts, not merely for the benefit of individuals, but of the whole human family. The obligations of Christian charity are as wide as the field of our action and of our influence; but we are not acquitted of these obligations by our individual efforts. We are bound as Christians to unite in the great work of bettering the condition of the human family. That which is the duty of every individual Christian in reference to his fellowmen, is the duty of the whole body; and the obligation upon the body is increased with the power and opportunity of doing good.

There can be no doubt that in any community where the individuals are full of the benign spirit of their great Exemplar, the whole mass will be enlivened and inspired by the same beneficence. If the community has not performed its duty, the responsibility lies upon the individuals.

We have thus imperfectly referred to the obligations of charity, because few will be disposed to question either their nature or extent. What has England, under such responsibilities, done for her millions of poor—poor so crushed and broken and pressed down, that the picture transcends the power of pencil, of pen, or of tongue? For those poor who have for three centuries been increasing in proportional numbers, and sinking to a deeper and deeper degradation, what has been done? We cannot reply, "nothing!" for though multitudes have sunk, from age to age, under the ills of poverty, yet masses have been kept alive to hand down their woes to increasing generations succeeding them. The church having repudiated the charge, the government has discharged the duty of saving, perhaps, the greater number of these outcasts from death by starvation or exposure. But what measures have been devised to lift these multitudes from their depths, and restore them to the level of living by their labour? Where shall we find the traces of any great movement among English Christians to redeem their poor from the chains of their hopeless bondage? They rouse themselves into energetic action to abolish the slave-trade—to emancipate the slaves of their West Indian colonies; they send Bibles by millions over the whole earth; they send missionaries to preach Christ to every people; yet how little will all this profit them, if they have neglected charity

at home. Christianity can only be successfully
propagated by those who practise it. English
Christians have done nothing worth naming
to redeem the poor from their abject condition. They have looked upon their myriads
of paupers in hopeless inaction : the problem
of relief seemed too difficult for solution, much
more of accomplishment.

The church of England has signally failed
in the fulfilment of her chief duty. Besides
having left unperformed every other duty to
the poor, she has, worst of all, not preached
the gospel to the poor. Whatever pre-eminence the Papist may claim over the Episcopa-
lian in this respect, even the Papal church
has in this fallen very far behind the line of
duty; and so, indeed, has every other church
or sect. The truth is, the work of the real
disciples of Christ must be performed by them
individually, and not by the church. The
good which flows from works of love and charity must benefit the giver as well as the re-
ceiver. No church has ever discharged, in its

14*

collective character, the duty of its members
in their individual capacities. Nor can that
love of men ever dwell in a corporation or
ecclesiastical organization which should glow
in the bosom of individual Christians. It was
not so intended, and is not so inculcated.
Every Christian association, however, of which
the members are fully warmed up to their
separate work, will be found partaking, in the
mass, of the life which pervades the individuals. The English church will never perform her duty to the poor, because she has
great possessions, and will continue to turn a
deaf ear to the command—"One thing thou
lackest: go thy way, sell whatsoever thou
hast, and give to the poor." How can that be
a church of Christ, which has great riches and
yet rejects the claims of the poor?

But whatever may be said of the guilt of
the church, if a church can be guilty, the responsibility lies upon its members. They are
the real stewards, to whom the various talents
are committed for which account will be ren-

dered at the coming of our Lord. The Christians of England are bound to relieve the poor to the extent of all their possessions, and to perform every other duty towards them required by the precepts of Christ, whatever may be the conduct of church dignitaries or political authorities. Nothing but performance can acquit them of this obligation. That performance would sweep from existence every vestige of the present unchristian system.

THE DUTY OF DEVISING AND CARRYING INTO EFFECT PLANS FOR THE GENERAL AMELIORATION AND PERMANENT RELIEF OF THE SUFFERING AND DEGRADED CLASSES.

BUT the duty of English Christians is not circumscribed, as we have insisted, to relieving the immediate and pressing wants of the poor, nor even to the present teaching them the way of life. Their numbers are so great, their degradation so low, their oppression so

heavy, that those whose duty it is to minister
to them, can only discharge their obligation
by adopting measures for permanent emancipation from evils so enormous. If we should
do unto others as we would have them do
unto us, if we should love our neighbours as
ourselves, we cannot escape the responsibility
of undertaking, in full earnest, the regeneration of the whole body of poor. This has
never occupied the minds of English Christians as it should : the feeling has been too
much that to which we have above referred :
' Our laws and institutions are the best in the
world; the result, visible in our hordes of
paupers, is inevitable : there is no remedy
but some check to this over-growing population.' No Christian who knows his Master's
will should hold such language, or entertain
such thoughts. In the eye of the Christian,
all men constitute one brotherhood, and there
is no avoiding the conclusion to which this
truth leads. The poor have as much right to
live as the rich; and the rich are equally

bound to help them, whether they give a good reason for coming into the world or not. The same Lord who has given freely to one, and denied to others, is over all, and has given the proper rules of action. How, then, can those who have wealth, or power, or influence, or wisdom, or knowledge, refuse to entertain as the great question of their lives,—What shall be done for the permanent amelioration of the condition of the poor? That in any possible state of society there must always be paupers, cannot be doubted; but in every society where Christian duties are discharged with even moderate faithfulness, the poor will be reduced to the smallest number possible. Is this so in England? Is it necessary—is it unavoidable, that there should be three millions of suffering poor in Great Britain? Is it inevitable that every tenth person should be a pauper? We say, no: that there should not be in Great Britain nor in Ireland more than one pauper to every hundred inhabitants. We say that this subject is seldom, if ever, approached, as it should be, in its Christian aspect.

All the world hears of the wealth of Great Britain. It is visible on every side to those who traverse the country. But all this wealth yields no income without labour: the industry of the people earns the enormous sum of two hundred and fifty millions of dollars, paid in annual revenue to the government, and five times the amount, which goes to swell the pockets of the rich. The income of the church is large, because it is drawn from the work of a large number of labourers. The large landholders are rich, because they receive the avails of the industry of a multitude of labourers. The manufacturers drive a large business, and make large profits at times, because they command the bones and sinews of as many labourers as they please to employ. It is labour which makes wealth available: without it, neither land, nor houses, nor machinery, nor mines, nor gold and silver, nor stocks of any description, could yield any per-

manent income. The labour of Great Britain
is absorbed by a comparatively few.   Their
income is large, and the streams of wealth and
liberal expenditure being large, the riches of
the country are rated accordingly.   But the
nation is none the richer for this unequal distribution of income.   England no longer appears so rich, if you divide her wealth by her
population : other countries will excel her in
wealth by that rule.   The industry of the
people is deeply mortgaged to produce this
result.   Masses of labourers are kept in
hopeless poverty and dependence; they are
allowed the scantiest subsistence which will
support life, that high taxes and high rents
may be paid, and that goods may be manufactured at prices so low as to secure them a
market throughout the world.   So long as
this system is maintained, there can indeed be
no amelioration of the bondage of the poor,
whose labour must go to make up this large
annual product; and it is because no suggestion of any change in this system is tolerated,

that the lot of the poor seems so hopeless in the eyes of Englishmen.

Such a policy, whether constructed upon the wisdom of this world or not, cannot be regarded in the light of Christian truth, without utter detestation. It is a duty from which Christians cannot escape, to search for the best mode of raising their brethren from this political degradation. The amelioration sought implies neither revolution, bloodshed, nor robbery : it demands adequate remuneration for labour : it implies that the bones and sinews of the people must not be sacrificed to that infatuation for foreign commerce which subjects them to the competition of the whole world. Great Britain presses her goods upon the markets of the world, and keeps prices everywhere at a rate ruinous to industry : she keeps the price of labour at home at such a point as leaves the labourer no choice but death or the offered wages : she keeps hosts of unemployed and starving labourers always pressing on the labour market, or working at a point between

life and death, to sustain that commercial
system which is absorbing the vitals of the
country.   Let Great Britain add five pounds
each to the annual wages of ten millions of her
poor operatives, and it will add fifty millions
sterling to her trade, because the whole sum
will be expended at home, in a way far more
beneficial to that country than any operation
of foreign trade.

If English Protestants have in three centuries weeded out the errors and superstitions of Romanism; if they have searched the
Scriptures and sifted from them the whole
truth, and formed a system of Christian theology by which they can abide, it is time they
should bear the fruits of Christian profession
so enlightened.   It is time they should exemplify the doctrines of their Master, and hold
up that exemplification in the display of England's greatness before the world.   This is
what is needed to send Christianity with rapid
pace round the world.   Let those deeds of
charity which are the legitimate fruit of a

15

truly Christian spirit, be exhibited in England
according to the urgency of that poverty
which calls for them, and according to the
beauty of that example which was set by Him
who went about continually ministering to
the wants of the poor, and the missionary
need only take the Bible in his hands and
point to this happy fulfilment of its precepts,
to insure among every people a ready obedience to its injunctions. How can English
Christians preach Christ successfully throughout the world, whilst myriads of her own
people are left to pine in ignorance, in want
and utter destitution? Can these be followers
of Christ, that permit this?—must be asked,
not only by the heathen abroad, but by the
skeptic or worldling at home. Every individual Christian of Great Britain is bound to
do all that he can, by his hand, his mind, his
voice and estate, to relieve and enlighten the
poor, presently and permanently; so, in like
manner, is the whole community of British
Christians bound to exert their united ener-

gies and means for the same end. Nothing less can acquit their obligations or fulfil their duties.

The Christians of Great Britain, if actuated by this spirit, could with ease guide the counsels of the nation: they would find many, very many, who now decline a profession of Christianity, prompt to engage with them in this great work, and ready to say, This, indeed, convinces us of the reality and truth of your religion. The solution of that problem which involves the social and religious elevation of the poor can never be reached by mere human wisdom; but British Christians, individually and in mass, are not the less bound to apply themselves to the task because it seems gigantic and above their knowledge; the effort is as necessary for their spiritual welfare as it is for the elevation of the poor. Every question of human well-being is solved directly or indirectly in the instructions left us by Christ. Every man is his steward; and if he has wealth, the principle upon which he is to hold it is plainly indicated. The rich man is not bound to divide his estate with his neighbour who may be in want, for the poor man may be utterly incapable of managing property. He is bound to relieve him, to the extent that love may dictate, necessity require, and prudence prescribe. The Christian who cannot hold riches upon this tenure, is in great danger if he hold them at all. It will be easier for a camel to pass through the eye of a needle than for him to enter the kingdom of God.

THE RESPONSIBILITIES OF CHRISTIANS IN THE UNITED STATES IN REGARD TO THE SUFFERING CLASSES.

WE have thus instanced the case of British Christians, and insisted upon their adopting the Christian solution of the great problem of pauperism. Their social difficulties are complicated by connection with the government, and hardened in texture by antiquity; but the duty is not less pressing and imperative. Lazarus is still lying at their gate: the wounded man in their streets is still bleeding—and the priest and Levite pass by on the other side, whilst the good Samaritan delays his coming. All this, however striking, removes no responsibility from the Christians of this country. Have we not among us those who are hungry, and require to be fed; those that are naked, and require to be clothed; those that are fainting with thirst, that require a cup of cold water; those that are sick and in prison that require to be visited? Alas! how many poor are already among us, and how fearfully the numbers are increasing! And what has been done for them by American Christians, upon whom their Master has heaped such bounteous favours? They have, as in England since the Reformation, been turned over to the public authorities. Christians, as such, have thus repudiated their

15*

highest obligations. They have not taken in Lazarus, to clothe and feed him: they have not taken up the wounded man: they have sent all to the poor-house; or rather, they have virtually assented to the doctrine that that is the proper place for them.

In some parts of the country, our poor-houses are fast growing populous, and we are, in this career, treading upon the heels of England. What have Christians done here to arrest this evil of pauperism? Their influence must be felt and exhibited in the action of our institutions, according to numbers, energy, and devotion to any good cause. If Christianity is not exemplified in the lives of its professors in this country, where lies the responsibility? If their united influence is not seen in the action of our various governments, what is the cause?

In point of fact, we find Christians forgetting their vocation in the exercise of their duty as citizens, and ranging themselves in the rank and file of political gamblers and demagogues. There are Christians enough, and light, and wisdom enough, if properly and zealously applied, to place every truly good cause in the ascendant, and to make our land as remarkable for its exemplification of Christian precepts as it has been for the favour of Providence. If the Christians of this country had only been as faithful to their religious obligations as they have been faithful to party discipline, they would now wield a moral and religious power which nothing within or without could long withstand.

Here is a field in which Christians, for more than half a century, have had full liberty and free scope to carry out their Master's injunctions. What have they done? What kind of Christianity is exhibited in this country, where the conscience is free; where religion is not complicated with the government; where abuses are not consecrated by antiquity; where superstitions are not fastened upon us by the habits and associations of ages; where the priesthood is without power, and where

the light of the Scriptures shines as freely as
the light of the sun? To what extent do we
behold the influence of Christians in our legislation, or in the working of our national or
state governments? Do we find that influence
in the fierce competition of trades, in the progress of which thousands upon thousands an-
nually fall into distress and poverty, while the
eager votaries of wealth sweep past, unheed-
ing the victims upon whom they trample?

But this is the mass which owns not Christ.
Look, then, at those who profess to be his followers, and bear his name. Scores of churches
surround us, mutually repelling and attack-
ing each other, and affording a scene of strife,
jealousy, animosity, and evil-speaking, with
scarce a parallel for virulence in the proceed-
ings of those who profess no fellowship with
Christ. Each of these various sects claim, in
terms the most unqualified, that they only
are right: no claim of infallibility is stronger
than that they arrogate. Some differ as wide
as terms can separate them: others agree so

nearly, that there is scarcely the shade of a phrase between them; yet the bitterness of division only increases with the less it has to fasten upon. But while this sectarianism is thus a spectacle to the world, it is eclipsed by the internal feuds to which these sects are themselves exposed. Many of them have been convulsed to their centres, or blown asunder by explosions of strife and evil passions which were a disgrace to civilization, let alone Christianity. Volumes might be filled with accounts of these fatal exhibitions; but, alas, they are too fresh in the memory of all, to need any reference even in the way of warning.

Apart from these flagrant departures from the spirit of Christianity, what does the current history of the various churches, in greater or less degree, disclose? Intense and often unscrupulous rivalry, incessant and unkind competition, a self-glorifying and haughty demeanour. Whatever a few individuals may do to correct or overcome the evil, churches seldom treat each other in a spirit of love or forbearance.

If, without, they are ever in a hostile attitude; within, they are far from being at peace with each other, or with the Master they profess to serve. If united, they are but too often frozen together: if at variance, it has all the acrimony of a family quarrel. They build sumptuous temples for the worship of God, and sell the seats to the highest bidder: they neither attend nor allow others to attend. The poor are virtually excluded from houses professedly devoted to the service of their best Friend; they are not invited to come to the services of these temples: much less are they compelled to come in: the streets and highways are never searched to find guests for the empty seats in these costly dwellings of sectarian worship.* The gospel is not preached to the poor, neither in them nor out of them. Christ is preached, but not obeyed; his various offices are magnified and proclaimed, but his precepts are neither ade-

---

* The few honourable exceptions to these statements do not save the necessity of making these and similar remarks.

quately explained nor exemplified. The
preaching is done in the churches to the rich,
or to the empty seats which belong to them.
The word of life is scattered abroad over the
world with a liberal hand, but it goes unac-
companied by any practical ratification of its
benign precepts, proving that it is confided
in and obeyed by those who send it. The
gospel is sent to the heathen of far distant
lands, but the heathen at home are neglected.
The world is the field committed to Christians for cultivation, and they employ themselves in dividing and subdividing the ground,
in building high walls, in planting hedges
of thorns, in digging deep ditches, and in
endless disputes about boundaries and lines
of demarcation, whilst the plants, the poor
plants, suffer for want of proper culture,
wither and die. The labourers in these artificial lines of circumvallation are not permitted to look over these walls, but are required to contract the range of vision and
thought to the lines prescribed. The culti-

vators of this great field, thus fearfully par-
titioned, employ themselves in studying and
discussing the philosophy of their work, down
to the minutest matter, and to the nicest possible distinctions; and while thus engaged,
plants perish by thousands at their feet, lack-
ing that attention which the simplest Christian could afford.   Thus that labour of Christians is expended in discussing, refining, and
distinguishing, which should be laid out in
exemplifying what they know.   Immense
efforts are made to induce and compel people
to believe the same things, and to think in
the same channels, which should be applied
to the practical illustration of what we believe
and know in common.   It is in vain that we
master chemistry, meteorology, and the whole
science of agriculture, if we do not likewise
perform the humble offices of ploughing,
manuring, planting and watering.   It is
equally in vain to pile up volumes of theology mountains high, if we are not thereby
stimulated to engage in those Christian

labours of love which it should be a main object of those works of theology, if they are of any value, to recommend and encourage.

The truth is, that theology has been exalted immeasurably above practical Christianity; although no theology can be wholly clear or convincing which is not accompanied by a practical illustration. Precept may go before example, but it must go unheeded unless the example quickly follows. The great work of Christianity being to love God and man, Christianity can only be successfully propagated by those whose lives illustrate these duties. The only solvent for the pride, asperity, hatred, jealousy, envy, and other evil passions of men, is charity. The only medium in which the truths of revelation can be clearly seen and appreciated in all their varied ramifications, is charity; it is the true test of all theology. The only atmosphere in which the rays of truth can reach the hearts of all the dwellers on earth with their full power, and in which the work

16

of bringing the whole race of men under the
dominion of Christ shall be successful, is
charity.

If this be so, a greater reformation is yet
to be accomplished than that of the sixteenth
century. How true that no flesh can glory
in its own doings before God! Let modern
Pharisees of every church, who imagine they
have attained unto the full measure of holiness, pause to inquire whether they are not
merely full of spiritual pride and uncharitableness: for sanctity cannot dwell but with
brotherly love.

Let a new reformation commence, which
shall exhibit in its consummation the " Fatherhood of God and the brotherhood of man."
Let it commence here, where there is no need
for such a protector as Frederic of Saxony,
nor any such champion as the detestable
Henry VIII. It demands the disruption of
no ties but those which bind us to evil. It
implies no revolution but that gradual one
which must take place as men change from

worse to better. Let every man examine himself, and see what talents are committed to
him for his master's service, and prepare himself by a proper fulfilment of his stewardship
to render his final account. There is no pleasure in this world so exalted and so pure as
this, in which our great duty consists in
honouring God and helping man. If all who
profess to be followers of Christ were to carry
out in their lives all his precepts in this respect, the spectacle would fill the world with
awe and admiration. Wickedness and cruelty
and oppression would shrink from that observation which now they do not fear.

But the world now looks on and beholds, in
Catholic countries, that great machine called
the church, contrived by crafty and ambitious
men to enrich themselves, to enslave and rule
the masses under cover of ignorance and superstition : where Protestantism prevails, a
free intellect, but a hard and unrelenting
selfishness, a devotion to mammon never before equalled, a grinding competition in all the

pursuits of life, a race for wealth and power,
in which the multitudes are distanced by a few,
who become masters, and wield their power
with unpitying severity; a scene of strife, of
endless divisions, of hot discussions about tri-
fles, of sectarian rivalry, in which every element of evil mingles, often without even a spice
of human kindness, much less religious charity.
Will the world adopt Christianity while this
picture is before it? No: the world has
already risen in judgment upon Christianity
as exemplified by those who are called Christians.   What are the characteristics of Christendom in the eye of the world? Civilization,
discord, war, priestcraft, sectarianism, greediness of gain, vigour of mind, heartless competition, domination of capital, pauperism, crime.
The world sees much to admire in Christendom, but fearful evidence that neither the
laws of brotherly kindness nor Christian charity control its institutions, social, political, or
religious.   Let not the Romanist flatter himself that the church can ultimately vindicate

Christianity, and set all right. His church has had her day of uncontrolled sway, and exhibited what men will invariably do when made the depositary of such powers: she abused her position shamefully, and sank Christianity into a long night of ignorance and superstition: his church is condemned already, and is clinging with unwise and depraved pertinacity to that power which the world will ere long tear from hands polluted with every crime. A few ill-balanced minds, darkened by drinking at the literary fountains of the middle ages, may betake themselves to the deep shadows of Romanism, and thus turn their eyes from the cheering light which the progress of humanity is shedding round them. Theirs is a mental vision which cannot endure human progress, nor undergo that change of light which must be encountered in the struggle for human brotherhood. They can perceive no beauty in the religion of Christ; they cannot be reconciled to any religion but that which involves all power in the hands

16*

of priests, and all submission on the part of the people. They may believe in Christ; they trust only in the church.

Let not the Protestant wrap himself in spiritual pride, and imagine that because he has escaped the errors of Romanism, he is safe from the judgment of the world. Let him not scorn that judgment because it often condemns what is right; but let him dread it, because it judges him for denying his Master and disgracing his cause. Let Protestants dread that rejection of Christianity which springs from their evil example. Let them fear their responsibility for retarding the cause they profess to befriend. Let them forbear proclaiming that Christianity is what their example makes it; the world may either refuse to accept such a religion, or condemn the pretensions of its professors.

Protestants are now zealously and successfully scattering the Scriptures in all languages to the ends of the earth, and all men are invited to read and judge for themselves. They will do so; they are doing so, and are disposed to interpret for themselves. They will not adopt all the sectarian dogmas; they will even question the piety of many of the straitest of the sects. They will decide that either these sects can find no warrant for many of their doings and doctrines in the New Testament, or that it can be no revelation from God. The independent readers of the evangelists will bow neither to Romish tradition nor to Protestant interpretation. They can read Christ for themselves, and the more they read, the more they will wonder how many who call themselves Christians can for a moment pretend to be followers of the meek and lowly Jesus, whose whole ministry was among the poor and the erring, and whose strongest rebukes were reserved for the proud, the rich, and the sanctimonious.

Christ went from village to village, healing the sick and personally solacing the cares of the poor : Protestants fulfil their charities, not personally, but by delegation, or by machinery;

they visit the sick, feed the hungry, and clothe
the naked by joint-stock associations, or by the
hands of public functionaries. The Romanists trust in the church; the Protestants trust
in theology. The former thinks to save himself by confessions, masses, and priestly abso-
lution; the other by preaching, by prayer-
meetings, and lectures. The one holds to the
accumulated errors of ages, and shuts out
Christ for the sake of the church; the other—
all right in theology—clings to a skeleton in
triumph, rejecting flesh and blood and spirit.
Both Romanist and Protestant hold up Christ
as a Saviour, and proclaim his personal sufferings, his cross, his crucifixion, his atonement,
his ascension, but they omit his life of toil
among the poor, and, above all, they neither
preach nor practise what he taught. The
person of Christ has long disappeared from
the earth, his earthly sufferings are long since
over, his personal mission has long since
ended, his atonement has long since been accomplished, but his precepts are handed down

to us unimpaired in sublimity, beauty, and
strength of obligation by the lapse of ages.
These constitute overpowering evidence that
He who delivered them "spake as never man
spake," and that his mission must have been
divine, which breathed so much love, so much
compassion, so much that is beyond and
above what any human teacher ever imagined or expressed. All this, we have now;
and this is what is not fairly incorporated
into the religious systems of either Protestant or Catholic. The former substitutes his
peculiar hobby of theology; his catechism,
prayer-book, creed, confession, articles, or other
frames of doctrine are carefully and assiduously taught to old and young, while the
teachings of Christ are comparatively neglected. The Romanist rejects the New Testament itself, as of no more authority than a
papal bull, and Christ as being no wiser than
the pope, both being infallible. But the
world is now reading this rejected book, and
the readers will compare Christians with

Christianity. This ordeal has begun: the motto of an advancing army of reformers is the "Fatherhood of God, the brotherhood of man." What arms can Christians oppose to such invaders? That policy may no longer suffice which has hitherto prevailed, of declaiming against the love of the world, and yet falling with savage severity upon him who offers to disturb a single brick in the grand structure of that society which constitutes this present world. There are no greater friends of political liberty than Protestants, but it is that liberty which lets every man take care of himself, and ruin seize the hindmost; it is that liberty which stimulates all to run, but permits the heat of competition to rise so high that none can stoop to pick up the multitudes who fall exhausted by the way.

GRADUAL DECLENSION OF CHRISTIANITY, UNTIL
IT LOSES THE IMAGE OF ITS ORIGIN.

HUMILIATING will be the effort of him who,
with a clear perception of the sublime and
simple instructions of Christ, betakes himself
to the task of searching the history of the
last eighteen centuries for any extended or
national exemplification of these pure lessons. He may experience all the admiration which the struggle of Christianity with
heathenism, during a few centuries of its infancy, is calculated to excite: he may be
struck with the vigour it infuses, the confidence it inspires, the unfailing courage and
fortitude it sustains; but he must suffer the
deep mortification of beholding that which
could triumph over a world of enemies suc-
cumbing to the treachery of professed friends.
Christianity was no sooner established than
its perversion commenced: crafty, covetous,

and ambitious men made it the instrument
of working out their designs, of absorbing
wealth, and wielding the power of nations.
Whatever of the truth was recognised by the
papal church, and whatever of piety may have
been displayed from age to age by individuals
in her communion, because they could not be
out of it, the church of Rome is a fabric as
purely human and as entirely opposed to the
true spirit of Christ's teachings as any system
of idolatry or false religion the world has
ever known.   The papacy has only honoured
and. used the truth as a means to sustain her
usurped power; and cannot therefore be defended on the ground of having merely disre-
garded the truth. Considered as a human invention, its great mistake was in the vastness
of the power committed to its priests; the
extent of this and its nature insured its abuse.
It was a power which could not be safely intrusted to human hands. The monstrous corruptions and the enormous wickedness displayed in the history of the papacy are such

as flowed from its constitution. Any other
men clothed with such powers would have
been as guilty. In all sects of Christians,
before and since the Reformation, human
nature displays its weaknesses and its depravity according to the power and opportunity afforded to weak or wicked men, who
are found in every community and congregation. What warrant has Christ left
for any complicated ecclesiastical organization, for high offices, for priestly power, for a
splendid ritual or pompous ceremonies! He
selected his assistants from the lowest orders
of the people : he gave them no power but to
declare the truth and to heal the sick : he
built no temples, and had not where to lay
his own head. His church, as he left it, was
the simplest possible form of organization.
In fact, in all its chief characteristics, it was
the opposite of the papacy. He used no ritual,
and left none for his followers. He enjoined
no ceremonies but those connected with

17

the simple and common acts of eating and washing.

It is plain that the institutions of this world, political, social, commercial, and industrial, we had almost said religious, partake little of the spirit of Christ; and yet his ministers and disciples are its most noted and uncompromising defenders. Is it because these ministers and disciples are so well treated by the world, that they are in such strict league with it, and are so prompt to take its part? All over Christendom, masses of men, long oppressed, are rising clamorous for relief, and a better condition. Light from Christianity has broken upon the night of their ignorance and helplessness, and they know that they are entitled to something better in the world's portion than has been allotted them. But the whole truth has not been told them, and their notions of remedy are wild and impracticable. This great movement should be met by Christians with rejoicing that light is at length penetrating such a dark mass of ignorance; and they should hasten to hold up to them the precepts of Christ, as meeting their entire case, and providing a complete remedy for all their grievances. But how is it that the outcries of these masses who have been hitherto strangers to the voice of Christian kindness, are now met by both Romanist and Protestant with a stern frown of rebuke and rejection? Christ is not preached to these poor, suffering millions, as all-sufficient for them; much less do they anywhere behold any Christian movement in their behalf, which might at once explain to them their errors and show them their remedy. They are not sought for in the lanes and highways, and invited, nay, compelled, to come into the feast of life; but they are rudely driven from the door as they present themselves, and are told that there is no room, no remedy, no alleviation; that the laws of property and the arrangements of society utterly forbid any amelioration of their sad condition. Thus it is

that religion purchases her peace with this
present world, by sustaining its institutions;
thus it is that Christ is denied, to purchase a
liberal provision for his ministers; thus it is
that, whilst these ministers assume the office
of denouncing this world, its maxims, its fol-
lies, its oppressions, its greediness of gain;
they deny that privilege to those who are
enduring the bitterest lot that can befall humanity.   Christ did not so : He went first
to the poor, and administered succour and
comfort to them; and that such is the chief
duty of his disciples now is as clear as the
words of inspiration can make it.   If Christ
were to appear again on a mission to earth,
he would go again to the multitudes; he
would be seen again in the abodes of the poor;
he would again claim no resting-place for his
head; he would again repeat his words of
solace to the lowly, and his works of mercy
to the suffering.   He would find little time
for Protestant observances, and little occasion
for their temples.   His ministry would con-

form to his precepts; and many who repeat
'Lord, Lord!' and claim to be his special and
favourite disciples, would find themselves objects of his sternest indignation and most
withering rebukes. The race of Pharisees
and priests and false teachers is not extinct;
they would again treat their Master with
contempt and scorn, or utter neglect, if his
associations were among the poor and lowly.

What, then, is to be done? No violent
revolution is required. No despot is to be
hunted from his place; no blood is to be shed;
no legislation is indispensable; no new sect
in religion or philosophy need be formed, nor,
in the first instance, need any one desert the
position in which Providence has placed him.
What is required is, that every one who is,
or who believes himself to be, a true disciple
of Christ, should at once resolve so far as in
his power, and so far as he might be favoured
with divine aid, to live in this world according
to the teachings of his Master. As soon as
the great law of doing to others as we would

17*

others should do to us begins to be exemplified, the reign of wrong, and injury, and extreme suffering will come rapidly to an end.   Instead of one Howard, one Mrs. Fry, and one Miss Dix in a century, we should have thousands upon thousands, in every department of charity.   When we look at what these three individuals have accomplished, what might we not expect from millions labouring with united strength and intellect in the great work of human welfare?

As soon as the law of charity is fulfilled on an extensive scale, in all its Christian beauty and loveliness, the world will pause to admire and believe and imitate.   The apostles as well as their great Master mingled their preaching with incessant care of the poor and the suffering; it should be so now. Christians may not fold their arms, and be inactive, because there is an almshouse, a poorhouse, or a benevolent society.   There should be no suffering within the reach of any Christian that he can relieve or alleviate, without making the attempt. It is not Christianity to attend weekly in the stately church and well-cushioned pew, to hear expositions of difficult passages of Scripture, while there is an utter failure to perform duties which are so plainly enjoined that the dullest intellect can comprehend. Nor does the most punctual attendance upon the Sunday-school, or upon lectures or weekly meetings for prayer, make up for neglect of the higher duties of charity. If the preacher and people in our rich and well-ordered congregations were, in the midst of the gravest sermon, suddenly visited from on high with a deep and adequate conception of their transgressions of the law of charity, and of the duties which they owe to those who are outside of the church; if they were made to realize the great contrast between their condition and that of those who were abroad and around them, their seats would in a moment become insupportable, and they would rush in a mass, preacher and people, from their splendid

edifice, to the courts and alleys and cellars,
to the abodes of destitution, ignorance, crime,
and suffering. They would carry succour for
present wants; and *all* would become teachers
of the way of life. In vain do we preach,
and in vain do we teach, unless we carry obedience to what we do understand, into our
lives; our progress in knowledge of divine
things must be limited by our actual progress
in the practical duties of Christianity.

No people can ever fully comprehend Christianity but those who comply with its requi-
sitions; and of course the world can never appreciate it until its laws of love are shown by
example. This distinguishing feature of Christianity is that which Christians have most
slighted. More attention has been given in
our churches and Sunday-schools to Jewish
manners, customs, ceremonies—to the ornaments of the tabernacle and temple—to breast-
plates and phylacteries, than to the obligations of brotherly kindness. There are fountains of tenderness in every human bosom;

they are not taught to gush forth and flow in
streams which no harshness of this world can
ever check : there are chords of love in every
breast; these are not taught to respond to
every appeal for sympathy and succour.

The purest joys of earth, the exercise of the
kindly affections, are nearly allied to the highest Christian duties of love to God and man.
Rare indeed is it to find a soul so dead as to
be insensible to kindness; and still more rare
is it to find one in the exercise of kindness,
who does not find the benefit of his good deeds
more than doubled in the happiness they reflect upon himself.   Rare is it to find a heart
so insensible as to be unmoved at even the
recital of noble deeds of charity, goodness, and
neighbourly kindness.   In this great channel
of charity the Deity has chosen, in his infinite
mercy, to fix the sphere of our chief duties
and our highest enjoyments.   Here is scope
for the employment of all our talents, and for
the exercise of all good affections.   Where all
these come into full use, under the law of

Christian charity, many things now deemed of vital importance will sink into comparative insignificance, or utterly disappear under the bright light of a purer Christianity.

THE CLERGY OF ALL CHURCHES—THEIR MISTAKES, DIFFICULTIES, AND DUTIES IN REFERENCE TO THIS SUBJECT.

WE cannot dismiss this topic without invoking to it the earnest attention of the clergy of all denominations, as well those who claim to be the successors of the apostles, as those who merely profess to be ministers of Christ. We are not of those who entertain any prejudices against them as a class. Like other classes, their history shows they have embraced in their ranks some of the best and some of the worst of men. It is plain they have their peculiarities as a class, and these are mainly what circumstances have created

and continued.   The frailties of human nature have been as apparent among them as
others : they have shown themselves as sus-
ceptible to temptation.   The developments of
their weaknesses have been more striking and
more painful from the sacredness of their calling.   The time has arrived when their influence for evil has sensibly diminished, and
when, we may trust, their labours for good
must be more successful.   The great error of
the ministers of Christ in the early ages of
Christianity, as already remarked, was in sup-
posing that the more power and influence
they had, the more useful they could be.   This
was a feeling very natural to human weakness, and the continuance and increase of it
built up the papacy, the spirit of which is, to
claim and exercise power, spiritual and temporal.   No doubt thousands upon thousands
of these early clergy honestly believed they
could better promote their Master's cause if
they were armed with a continual increase
of power.   They imagined in like manner that

if they could maintain a watch over the inner
man, while they had power to control his outward movements, they could efficiently serve
their Master, and promote the interests of his
kingdom in this world. They were daily en-
countering obstacles in the heathen world by
which they were surrounded, and in the per-
verseness or stubborn independence of nominal Christians, which tended to confirm in
them the conviction of the necessity of this
priestly power. They were regarding the subject as men; they forgot their Master's example, who had all power, both temporal and
spiritual, and yet worked only by love: who
did not even avail himself of power, or wealth,
or high office, or social position. He took the
lowest place in society, that he might reach
the multitudes who were more accessible to
the truth, and nearer to the kingdom of God,
because less wedded to this life than the rich
and great. They were not receiving the good
things of this world. He went among them
to carry them glad tidings of the world to

come. They were suffering in this world; he
appeared among them to carry succour, consolation, and hope. This should have been
to this day the conduct of his ministers; who,
by adopting the scheme of converting the
world to God by the power of the church over
mind and body, have committed an amount
of wickedness beyond any human estimate.

We thus notice this great mistake, as it prevails to this day, more or less, among those
denominations of Christians, or rather among
their clergy, who regard the church of Christ
as a great mysterious, spiritual corporation.
The temptation of magnifying their office over-
much assails the ministers of Christ continually, and they seek to magnify it, not by the
good they do, but by the power to do good.
But since the days of Christ, it has ever been
seen that power, temporal or spiritual, was a
dangerous possession to priests or ministers.
These have always been corrupt in proportion
to the power they wielded. All the power
they can employ successfully, is that of truth

18

and love. It is a mistake to suppose that this grasping after control has come to an end, or that it is confined to those who claim to have the only true priesthood. Many of the reformed churches are its victims. Those in the north of Europe have thus had all spiritual life extinguished : others have suffered more in this way than we can pause to tell. But this notion of the church, with power to do good, haunts the minds of many ministers all around us in a way that has produced, and still produces much mischief. Instead of bending all their energies to commend the truth to their hearers, and to back it by that kindness and love which is the seal of its genuineness, they struggle to build up the church, that is, their particular denomination; to bring their people to a strict adhesion to their peculiar tenets, to strict attendance upon their public worship, and to a general outward compliance with all its requirements. In this way, a hedge is carried round the people which is intended to secure submission to the discipline of the

church, and due attendance upon its prescribed routine. All this is very well within
proper bounds; but when the labours of the
clergy are chiefly devoted to congregational
management, the cause of Christ will suffer in
proportion as the minister is successful. He
may wield a dominion over his people as
strong as papal bondage, by establishing a
public opinion which few have courage to resist. He may secure an apparent unanimity
in matters of religion, which only proves the
tyranny which has been established. All such
attempts to promote the cause of Christ and
to extend his kingdom by church discipline,
by uniformity of opinion, by destroying freedom of expression, proceed upon false principles. The truth should be preached, but can-
dour should not be extinguished. Our profession of being Christ's disciples should bear
all the fruits of religion; but we should not
be constrained by artificial appliances to any
apparent obedience to Christ's commands.
The truth should make us free: free in

thought, in speech, and in action. How much
the mind is enslaved under papal rule is generally appreciated out of that church; but how
much bondage of opinion is endured under Protestant rule, is not so generally admitted or
considered. Others may point it out and display its special evils: we refer to it to show
how much time, attention, and mental effort
of ministers is employed in keeping up this
system, which should be employed upon the
more appropriate duties of the servants of
Christ. If half the time, labour, and mental
effort which have been expended in forging de-
nominational fetters, in fastening them on, and
in keeping them in their place, had been spent
by ministers in simply and honestly imitating
the ministry of Christ, how great an advance
would Christianity have made beyond what
is now seen!

This inclination to grasp power as a spiritual weapon, so congenial to human nature, has
been powerfully seconded in every age of
Christian history, as at this day, by a ten-

dency scarcely less strong on the part of the
people to flatter and pet their spiritual guides.
Multitudes act as if they must be safe for the
next world if they can secure the special
favour or smiles of their pastors in this world.
This has always been so obvious that even
the most humble and modest among the
clergy could not but see evidences of this
servility; and none but the most firm and
conscientious could help availing themselves
of it. By degrees, the temporal advantage
of being priest or minister reached such a
point, that it became an object of attraction
for many, very many who would never otherwise have been followers of Him who claimed
neither house nor home. The charge of a
pastor has grown to be an affair of business,
and no longer a mere mission of truth and
mercy to and among the poor. Salaries are
given, not to have the gospel preached to the
poor, not for a ministry like that of Christ,
but for hard study and much reading—for
the delivery on Sundays of elaborate treatises

on Scripture criticism, doctrinal points, or
practical duties. These discourses are not
addressed to the poor, and are not suited to
their comprehension; they are addressed to
the owners of the church in which they are
read, or to the empty seats belonging to these
proprietors. The poor enter these edifices in
very small numbers. Not half the poor in
any Protestant country ever find a seat in
the places of public worship. Not half their
numbers ever hear the gospel, even by accident, once in a year: a very small number
ever make the acquaintance of a minister of
Christ. They are born strangers to the truth,
and so remain during all their lives. They
live, perhaps, within sight of many churches
devoted to the service of God. But those
who swarm in the courts and alleys and
suburbs of our cities, the outskirts of our villages, and many a thronged locality of the
country, never enter a church, and seldom,
if ever, hear the accents of mercy and kindness which breathe in the teachings of our

Redeemer. As we cannot doubt that the poor and suffering of the present day are as much the objects of Divine compassion as during the personal ministry of Christ, so we cannot doubt what should be the mission of his disciples. If the clergy are prevented by circumstances beyond their control, by habits of the people not easily changed, by institutions and artificial duties not of their own arranging, but which time has fastened upon them, the example of Christ shines none the less brightly and its obligations lose none of their force, whether neglected or forgotten or found to be of difficult execution.

The clergy of the church of Rome and all denominations of Christians since the Reformation have failed, as we allege, to present Christianity to the world in the sublime and simple beauty in which it was clothed by its author in his ministrations. The papal clergy have overlaid it with the superstitious mummeries and traditions of ages of darkness : through which the faintest traces of the

divine and pure original can scarcely be perceived. The Protestant clergy have rescued
the Bible from the darkness of papal libraries
and have scattered it abroad over the whole
earth. They have exalted it in the highest
terms of human praise. They have studied,
commented, and explained, nay even tortured
every· word, phrase, and expression in the
original and translations, for every possible
interpretation : and this they continue to do
as one of the most meritorious works of Christian life. The result is, that Christianity is
smothered in theology and criticism : the
truths of revelation are wire-drawn and spun
and twisted into the most fantastical shapes
human fancy or human logic can devise. A
system of technical divinity has been constructed which rivals in complexity all the
machinery of the Romish church.

From this system, by a series of strainings,
condensations, and extractions, they have produced the catechisms, guides, and various
formularies of the different churches. These

resumés of theology are taught more than all Scripture, because they are regarded as authoritative abstracts of the truth. They constitute the landmarks of revelation, the skeleton of religion, the wires by which the Christian machinery is to be kept in successful operation. In all this system, man is mainly treated of and regarded as a lost sinner, as having fallen with his representative head, Adam, in his first transgression. Christ is mainly regarded as having become incarnate, as having endured the wrath of God, the scoffs of the Jews, the agony of the garden, the degrading death of the cross, and as having thus suffered and shed his blood as an expiatory sacrifice for the sins of men, thereby atoning for their offences and purchasing remission of their offences,—as having risen from the grave on the third day, and ascended to the right hand of the Father, there to be the head of the church founded by his incarnation, crucifixion, and resurrection.

But this hard and bony skeleton of truth can never be exalted into Christianity until it is clothed with desires, affections, kindness, charity, love to God, and love to men. The mission of Christ was not merely incarnation, death, resurrection, mediation, and redemption. It was also an humble and lowly ministration among the poor and suffering: this was his daily work. He went about doing good, ministering to the hungry, visiting the sick, and restoring the leprous, the blind and lame. He preached constantly the doctrines of his mission, which, wherever felt and apprehended, will secure a ministry engaged in the very same work. Now, whether we look upon the whole mass of those who are regarded as Christ's ministers, or at those of any particular denomination, we shall be equally at a loss to find any class of them who are imitating the ministry of their Lord and Master. Not only is there no such class of ministers, but it is rare to find one who walks in the footsteps of Him whom he professes to serve; it is rare to find one who even comprehends the scope of his teaching who spoke as never man spake. The mass of these nominal ministers of Christ aim constantly to maintain a position of authority and influence, which they have usurped, and not only strive to perpetuate, but to enlarge.

Vast numbers are engaged in teaching theology, in making weekly orations, in enforcing ecclesiastical discipline, and the performance of duties of routine required by church regulations, in reducing their hearers to the same level of faith and doctrine, in bringing them to the same line of conduct, and in performing a thousand church duties, which have no warrant in the teachings and no precedent in the example of Christ. Let them now be exhorted to review their course of ministration, comparing it honestly and intelligently with the instructions and the conduct of their Master: let their ministry become constantly more like His. This imports a great and vital change, and one which cannot be made at once. It will take time fully to comprehend the mighty scope of the mission which a thorough obedience to Christ dictates, and which following his example implies. There is room in this for all that human talents, or energy, or wisdom, or piety, or goodness can accomplish— room for the exercise of all the gifts the Deity has bestowed.

Passing over the main characteristics of a ministry after the example of Christ—merely remarking that the gospel is to be preached to the poor; the suffering are to be succoured; the sick, and those in prison, are to be visited; the hungry are to be fed, and water to be furnished for the thirsty—we proceed to designate other duties belonging to this service, not so obvious, but necessarily resulting from an enlarged view of the field of this ministry. The field is the world; and while the labours of the minister may be chiefly employed among the poor among whom his lot is cast, he is not to forget what he owes to all the race

of men. Whilst the servant of Christ finds
himself surrounded by many that require his
personal consolations, teachings, and aid, he
cannot but remember that the world is full of
sorrow and trouble, of want and degradation,
of oppression and cruelty. Far more than
half the human race is in a condition of poverty, ignorance, and abject wretchedness.
While the minister puts forth his hand for the
relief of those that are near him, his heart and
mind should embrace all that his voice and
hand cannot reach. Christianity offers amelioration to all cases of social evil—mitigation
to every human ill. No wisdom of man is
adequate to the rescue of humanity from the
social and physical evils which oppress it.
The wisdom of God has long since laid down
the rule which meets every possible exi-
gency:—" Love thy neighbour as thyself."

From this rule let all the practical duties
of life be developed. Christ himself furnished
many special deductions from this law; but,
as we have said, both his illustrations and

19

the law itself are almost unnoticed in Protestant literature : there has not been an approach to any adequate treatment of this subject by any Protestant hand. Let this reproach be speedily wiped away. Let ministers withdraw for a moment from the tread-mill work of church routine, and reflect upon the condition of all men, and the applicability of Christianity to social as well as religious renovation—to ameliorate the condition of men in this world as well as to save their souls in the next. Since the advent of Christ there have lived professed ministers enough, if they had performed a tithe of their duty, to have insured the blessings of Christianity to all the world in a much greater degree than they are now enjoyed by the most favoured portion. If one thousand ministers had only laboured in this cause as some have laboured—nay, if one hundred had so laboured in every generation since the Christian era, we might now look abroad upon a Christian world. A hundred ministers as devoted to their Master's cause in general as Howard was to one department of that cause, would, in less than a century, bring all the world to the knowledge of God in Christ. No mere proclamation of the truth, whether by voice or by types, could effect such a desirable renovation : the seal of charity must go with the book, and the liberal hand must accompany the voice.   Men will never be made to know what Christianity is, until they are made to see and feel it in the conduct of Christians.

It is time that ministers were waking up to some better conception of their mission; for the world is already awake, and masses of men, sensible that their condition in this world is, without fault of theirs, below their true position, are groping for amendment, seeking for light, and demanding aid in the name of a common humanity. They are struggling in the mists of ignorance for better things; they are devising plans for social improvement, and attempting to carry them out in revolutions and bloodshed.   Their efforts are convulsing civilization to its centre. They have been oppressed, trodden down, kept in ignorance, buried in superstition. What has been done for them by ministers of state, or ministers of Christ? They have felt no kind hand from the state extended for their relief; they have seen no effort of Christianity in their behalf, nor any adequate example of its success in ameliorating the ills of humanity. When these men arise in mass to seek justice, to hunt for that charity which has not found them, the ears of slumbering ministers of Christ should tingle with mortification and shame for having so long neglected to preach the gospel to these poor, and for having so long withheld from them the blessings of Christianity.

Let not stern Christian conservatives now deride their erroneous schemes of social improvement, and denounce as bad men and citizens all who make such attempts; rather let the voice of Christian ministers be heard addressing them in tones of kindness and encouragement, giving assurance that in Christianity they can find the only hope of a better system of society, and the only solution of social problems: that if it has not performed any mighty achievement in social regeneratiőn, it was not the fault of its principles or its maxims, but of those who professed but did not practise them. The highest aspiration of the most earnest reformer never reached a point so lofty as, "Thou shalt love thy neighbour as thyself." Let those who are sighing for reform be invited to unite in a system enjoining on its members, and on all men, more kindness, more charity, and more brotherly love than all the social schemes they ever listened to could imagine. Let them be told that its invitations, promises, assurances, and rewards are specially addressed to the poor, the suffering and oppressed; that it requires for its success no political revolution, permits no bloodshed, but a simple surrender of human wisdom, and an acceptance of that of the Deity; that they should not only ask

Christ to come to them, but arise at once and
go to Him. But topics need not be suggested;
they abound, and every minister will be fruitful in them when he has once opened his mind
and heart to regard all the human family as
within the scope of Christian sympathies, and,
in so far as opportunities offered, within the
scope of clerical labours. Let the world clearly
perceive that Christians are labouring with
untiring zeal, not merely for the purpose of
making proselytes to a sect, or slaves to a
church—not merely to swell the numbers and
glory of a sect, or to increase the taxables of
a church, but to promote the temporal comfort and eternal welfare of all to whom they
have access, and the world will soon be found
sending its hosts heavenward. But the world
must first be fed and cured of its ailments and
sorrows before it will hear; it must be convinced over a banquet of "loaves and fishes."
The poor must be sure of the disinterested-
ness of the teacher before they will receive his
teachings.   Personal kindness will win more

friends among them than the highest eloquence or the most orthodox theology. They will believe you are truly desirous of their eternal welfare when you show yourself truly desirous of promoting their temporal well-being.

This is no harsh judgment. The great point to be gained, in the progress of truth, is to make people willing to hear, and willing to be convinced. As soon as they are satisfied, by your personal kindness or steady zeal for their good, that you are a fast friend, they become ready to hear from you the truths of the gospel. If Christ himself commenced and carried on his ministry by continual displays of regard for the poor, how much more necessary for his ministers to make their ministry one of continual kindness and compassion! No amount of preaching or of prayer can compensate for the neglect of this essential part of clerical duty. But in this, as in many other Christian duties, the minister or priest can only lead in kind offices;

it will be nearly in vain, if those who profess to be Christians do not follow. In this career of charity, the clergy must not only embark, but their people must be induced to embark with them.

It is strange, indeed, that with the example and instructions of the Saviour before them, ministers should have so forgotten their duties to their fellow-men as not to perceive that the hand of charity must accompany the tongue of truth; the latter must enter into the heart, but the former must open the door. In what Protestant country are the clergy regarded by the mass of the poor as their special friends? or rather, in which do the poor look to or receive from ministers or bishops, as such, any evidences of special regard, temporal or spiritual, beyond what may be dictated by and subserve the interests of such ministers and bishops themselves? Where has the impression been adequately made upon the poor that Christ is as much the friend of the poor now as in the days of his sojourning upon earth, only that now his disciples are appointed to do his will and execute his works of mercy? Until this impression is made, and that by a veritable fulfilment of the law of love, the gospel cannot be preached to the poor, as prescribed and intended in the New Testament.

It may be said, the clergy are already burdened beyond their strength, and that they cannot assume such duties as are here designated. True, they are so burdened, and they are constantly sacrificing health and life to a mistaken system. Two-thirds of their present current duties should be dispensed with, to make room for the ministry of kindness, which would promote health instead of destroying it, and prolong life instead of shortening it. The personal effort required by a ministry of consolation and succour among the poor, the afflicted, the sick, and the imprisoned, would give vigour to the body and nerve to the mind; it would deepen the affections and enlarge the views; it would confer a knowledge of human nature and an insight into the ways of Providence which no other clerical training can accomplish. It would show that he who makes such acquisitions may carry to the study of the Scriptures a commentary shedding a holier and purer light than all the volumes which human intellect without such experience has yet devoted to that purpose. A servant of Christ engaged in the very work in which his Master laboured must acquire the very knowledge and experience which will enable him fully to understand and appreciate the lessons delivered by Christ whilst so engaged. The whole of that sublime and exquisite system of divinity and charity which is taught in the evangelists will be gradually unfolded to his admiring view. He will soon glory in his Master, in his instructions, and in his work. With this clear comprehension of the Scriptures which lie before him, of the wants of his fellow-men around him, he can soon extend his vision to the whole field of labour, the inha-

bited world. By this torch, he will begin to
see the compromise now subsisting between
the spirit of this world and the professed disciples of Christ, of which the ministers of Christ
are, of every name, the most determined supporters. His mind will gradually open to
the consideration of topics and questions now
utterly eschewed by nearly all the clergy
of every church. Looking with indignation
beyond that political economy which regards
men as machines to create and distribute
wealth; which upholds a competition which
grinds the labourer into a condition far below
that of the slave; which looks upon the poor
as having come "unbidden to the banquet
of life," he will inquire anxiously and boldly
what can be done to ameliorate the condition
of the millions upon millions of his brethren
of the same family and children of the same
Heavenly Father. Whilst he will bow to
every ordinance of man for conscience' sake,
and will neither meditate nor counsel violence, nor any uncharitable or evil proceed-

ing, to attain a good end, he will permit no
false principles of honour, or trade, or property,
however consecrated by time, or upheld by
rank, wealth, or legislation, to restrain him
from looking at the naked truth, and from
pursuing what he shall deem the path that
leads to human well-being in that way which
may be consonant with the teachings of Christ.

FURTHER MISTAKES OF THE CLERGY.

THE clergy fell into another grievous error
in the first ages of the church of Christ,
which clings in greater or less degree to
all churches down to the present time.
This error is equally due to human weakness, and is therefore as likely to prevail in
time to come as in time past.   It is the
more necessary, then, to be fully aware of
the mischief, that some effort be exerted
towards counteraction.   We refer to the con-

stant disposition to enlarge or restrict the
bounds of revelation.   It was early displayed in the exertions of the Jewish converts to impose on the disciples of Christ
the yoke of Judaism : this was followed by
a system of tradition, and this, by the erec-
tion of a hierarchy, at the head of which
was the bishop of Rome as pope claiming
equal authority in matters of truth with
Christ himself.   This tendency is displayed in
later times, in the adoption of creeds, articles
and confessions of faith, prayer-books, catechisms, and such formularies.   Whatever the
advantage a proper use of such helps may be,
the constant abuse of them has been their
substitution for the plain and simple teachings of Christ and his apostles.   There seems
to be a constant apprehension that the latter
are insufficient, and that men must inevitably
go astray if left to interpret the word of God
for themselves.   It must, therefore, be taken
away from them, and an entire system of man's
devising substituted in its stead, as is done by

20·

the Romanists; or strict forms of faith and
practice must be submitted for the adoption
of believers, who are required to believe, not
in the New Testament, but that the system
submitted is drawn from it, or is in accordance
with it.   None of these are so easily understood as Christ's own words, but are yet
put forward as standards of faith, as summa-
ries of knowledge, as compends of instruction
for the old and the young.   We do not venture to depreciate these productions nor to
estimate their true value.   It is their abuse
of which we complain; it is the constant tendency to rest upon the paraphrase instead
of the text, to rely upon long-drawn conclusions instead of direct revelation; it is the disposition, not merely to insist upon our taking
the Scriptures as our guide, but to prescribe
how we must take them; it is the limiting
the right of individual judgment, and nar-
rowing the ground of private opinion, until
nothing is left for the exercise of the believer's
mind.   He is required to believe, not to think;

to receive the conclusions of others, and not to draw any for himself. It may appear best to the trained mind of the theologian to bring the minds of believers at one step to the conclusions of that science, but they forget that the assent which is thus given is of no advantage to him who gives it—his mind has not derived it from the word of God. It may appear safest and most expedient and a saving of labour thus to tax men's credence, but it clearly involves the danger of a desertion of the Scriptures, which contain the very truths upon which the minds of believers are to be employed, and stated in the way which the same inspiration dictated. Who can teach higher things than Christ himself taught, and illustrated by his life,—and who can make them plainer to common minds than they now are? Even Protestant clergy have failed to hold up the Scriptures as the only word of life, upon the revelations of which every man must pass his own judgment, enlightened as much as may be by clerical exposition. Christ said, "Suffer little children to come unto me;" now that Christ is no more on the earth, this exhortation means, "Suffer little children to come to me" through the study of my life and precepts; but the clergy now lead little children to the catechism—to a compend of theology. Even where the study of the Scriptures is zealously pursued and inculcated, the formula of faith is put forward as of equal importance and authority. Scores of thousands of volumes are written for the purpose of enforcing, explaining, and defending these formularies, which should be given to the plainer duties of the shepherds of a flock, many of which are sick, deserted, in trouble, or straying from the fold.

This is no special or singular dereliction of the clergy of the present day: it is a phase of the present state of Christianity. The ministers of Christ being what the abuses and errors of the age have made them, the cause of Christ must suffer grievously in their hands, for they are not so much the servants of Christ as of their congregations or clerical superiors. They are no longer ministers of peace, meekness, and charity, but of study, of learned polemical war, of worldly, imperious, and unyielding habits. What hosts of candidates for the pastorship of rich churches, and yet how few able and popular ministers are found labouring among the degraded and the poor! In fine, however much many may perceive the inconsistency of their course of life with the profession they make, they feel their inability to stem the current which sweeps them onward in the beaten track of sectarian forms. How few clergymen of any church could be strict imitators of their Master without losing caste, or suffering excommunication! Those who can and do come nearest to their Master's example are the missionaries, who give up the comforts of home and the enjoyments of social life, to brave the opposition, the blindness, or the besotted idolatry of remote and frequently barbarous people.

Many of these devoted men have, in such positions, at once perceived the true nature of their mission. They felt that the truths they had to announce could only find access to darkened minds by channels opened through the affections. They went among the poor, and carried relief and succour wherever they were able. They visited the sick, administering medical aid without charge. The lame and the blind and the suffering, in many cases, resorted to them in multitudes. When the missionary is a physician, or is accompanied by one, the resemblance of his mission approximates more closely to that of his Master. How profound the impression which has at various times been made by such missionaries! The pagan is made to feel that nothing in his religion approaches in sublimity the beautiful kindness of the disinterested messenger of Christ: his great difficulty is to realize that such kindness is real; that there is not some lurking selfishness, some covert design concealed from sight.

Every doubt, however, falls before a continued ministry of kindness to the poor, to the afflicted, and to children : the missionary might rejoice in conquests for his Master greater than his most sanguine dreams ever anticipated, but for the practical repudiation which Christendom affords of Christian principles · and practice.

What can the missionary in India say to objections raised upon the conduct of officers, agents, soldiers, and servants of the East India Company, who are all reputed to be Christians by the natives ? What can the missionary in China say in defence of that Christianity which forces opium upon the Chinese at the cannon's mouth ? What can the missionary to the Sandwich Islands say for the conduct of the people of Christian nations who touch there; and of those who force brandy upon them under the guns of men-of-war; and what can the missionaries to the poor Indians of this country say to the policy which has driven them from their homes, de-

prived them of their lands, and exterminated
tribe after tribe?

Mere Protestantism makes no claim upon
the sympathies or affections of any people;
and when the law of kindness is held up as
the law of Christian life, the idolater points
to the conduct of Christian nations and the
lives of the people. Some among them are
always ready to avail themselves of this means
of discrediting the new worship, and show
themselves well-informed as to the delin-
quencies of Christian life. The barrier to the
success of the missionary is not merely the
inconsistency between Christian precepts and
practice—it is the practical denial of the great
law of charity which the missionary preaches,
and in his own life exemplifies. This law or
rule of life, which would soon bear Christianity
into all the world, not being respected by
Christians, cannot secure the confidence of the
heathen, multitudes of whom regard it as a
pretence and a covering for more designing
selfishness and deeper iniquity. We think it

right thus to distinguish between the missionaries and other clergy, because the former
present to our minds the only true exemplars
of a Christian ministry. When once engaged
in their work of love, they look back upon
the narrowness of sectarian views with horror
and surprise. They regard the squabbles of
ecclesiastical assemblies with pain and mortification. They begin to understand their mission as ministers of Christ, and to see how little that mission is comprehended by theologians and divines, the well-paid ministers of
rich congregations, many of whom plume
themselves chiefly upon being the successors
of the apostles, whilst they are certainly not
even earning the title of the humblest of
Christ's servants.

TOPICS FOR THE CONSIDERATION OF CHRISTIAN TEACHERS.

THE sins of society are the sins of the individuals of which it is composed, however willing the individuals are to shift or cast off the responsibility. Christians are thus accountable for much iniquity which they might prevent. They become hardened, by custom, to that which is occurring all around them; but their duty is not less binding, to overcome the ills of society, and to point out the errors which are consecrated by habit. When they become able to lay aside the pride of position, the conservative stubbornness of an easy life, and to regard the present constitution of society under the full light of Christ's life and precepts, they will find abundant cause of lamentation. They will find that almost all the maxims and requirements of business are opposed in spirit and results to these precepts.

That stern punctuality which is the essence
of business morality, and which exacts a fulfilment of engagements with so little forbearance that thousands are ruined whom a very
little forbearance would save, may be indispensable to the progress of commerce, but is
irreconcilable with those precepts which en-
join upon us to love our neighbour as ourselves, and with that prayer which asks " for-
giveness of sins, for we also forgive every one
that is indebted to us."

That fierce and unfaltering competition in
the race of business so much exalted by political economists as the best regulator of industry, may be very useful in extinguishing
all those sympathies which weaken human
efforts when directed against each other, and
in sharpening all those energies which are applied to the purpose of amassing wealth, grasping power, and ministering to all other ends
of human selfishness; but little accords with
the demands of human brotherhood.   That
ravenous and untiring pursuit of wealth so cha-

racteristic of Protestant activity—that adding of field to field and barn to barn, or heaping up treasures of this world, or that lavish expenditure which squanders with as much zeal as it accumulates—may be a necessary accompaniment of the doctrine which teaches the propriety of encouraging whatever gives vigour to the mind and body, and confirms the sacred rights of property, that is, of doing what we please with our own; but all this little comports with the stewardship of Christ's disciples, or with the command, " Go sell that thou hast and give to the poor."

This buying at the cheapest possible rate, not regarding the hardship to him who sells, and selling at the dearest rate possible, not regarding the interest of him who buys—this position in trade or in society which makes it not only the interest, but the natural course, of every one to prey upon his fellow-men to the full extent of his power and cunning, is well fitted to carry selfishness to its highest limits, and to extinguish every spark of mutual kindness, but is very inconsistent with the duty or the policy of keeping out of the way of temptation.   This idea of considering men as mere machines for the purpose of creating and distributing wealth, may do very well to round off the periods, the syllogisms, and statements of political economists; but the whole notion is totally and irreconcileably at variance with Christianity, which teaches that all the world is of less value than one soul; and that, in ascertaining the true interests of men, we should first direct our attention to those measures which may best secure physical comfort, peace, and happiness in this world, and the best preparation for the world to come; and afterwards to those which may create the largest amount of wealth, not merely for the benefit of free trade,—that unrestrained action of merchants, which makes them arbiters of the condition of millions who toil to produce what they buy and sell, and fetch and carry, at charges fixed by themselves.

21

The doctrine that property, real and personal, must, under all circumstances, remain inviolate, always under the ever watchful vigilance of the law, and its invaders subject to the severest penalties of dungeon or damages, may be very essential to the maintenance of our present social system, but totally disregards the consideration that labour, the poor man's capital, his only property, should, as his only means of securing a comfortable subsistence, be also under the special care and safeguard of the law. The doctrine that trade should be entirely free—that is, that merchants should be perfectly at liberty, throughout the world, to manage their business in that way which best promotes their interests, may suit very well for merchants, making them masters of the industry of the world; but it will be giving a small body of men a power over the bones and sinews of their fellow-men, which it would be contrary to all our knowledge of human nature if they do not fatally abuse; because they are interested to reduce the avails of labour to the lowest attainable point, as the best means of enlarging their business and increasing their gains.

That philosophy which teaches that men should always be left to the care of themselves; that labour is a merely marketable article, which should be left, like others, to find its own market value, without reference to the welfare of the man, may appear plausible to those who forget the Fatherhood of God and the brotherhood of man; but is utterly at variance with His precepts who taught that those who were sent to work at the eleventh hour should receive the same as those who had borne the burden and heat of the day.

We might thus go on, indicating topic after topic, in endless variety, linked by their relations with the welfare of men in this world and their hope of the world to come, all of which deserve the serious examination of those who are shepherds of Christ's flock. These and many more such subjects are not

merely political, or politico-economical; they
concern men's temporal well-being, and,
through that, have a vital bearing on their
eternal prospects. They demand, therefore,
the most earnest attention of Christians and
Christian ministers, as of far greater importance to the progress of religion than innumerable topics of theology which have heretofore and do yet engross so large a portion
of their time and talents. If the scrutiny and
time and talents which have thus been misapplied, had, with equal industry and zeal,
been turned to the science of human well-being, we should not now lament the little progress which has been made in that great and
much-abused department of knowledge.

What has been so long neglected remains
to be done; the social economy which will resolve the most difficult questions yet proposed,
must be developed by Christians from the
teachings of Christ and his apostles. And so
developed that the exemplification may accompany the truth; that precept and practice

may travel together, and reflect a mutual light on their progress. In this lies the problem, the solution of which will determine the advance of real Christianity and all the blessings it bestows.

PRINCIPLES UPON WHICH REFORMS, SOCIAL AND RELIGIOUS, SHOULD BE CONDUCTED.

IN reference to the advance of human well-being, there is, perhaps, no subject which more requires the close attention of Christian men and ministers of the gospel than the manner of effecting reforms in religion and politics and social economy. It is so much more easy to see and tell what is best in these respects than to advise how it is to be accomplished, that whilst the world has never been without attractive schemes and theories of human welfare, very few have been found who could successfully accomplish any beneficial change.

21*

It would be impossible to estimate or conjecture the amount of evil inflicted on the human family by ill-conducted efforts at reform. How many laudable plans have wholly failed for want of wisdom and moderation in their supporters! How much has real progress been retarded by unseasonable, unwise, and ill-directed labours! It is not enough that Christians should desire to promote the highest interests of humanity; that, under the light of Christian truth, they should enter into all the subjects which pertain to human welfare, social and religious; but it is equally their duty to step into the arena of active reform, and carry thither all the light, all the wisdom, self-control, and influence they can command. They should be ready to take the lead in every movement which promises to ameliorate the condition of men. They should not permit the direction of such movements to fall into the hands of those who are prompt to seize it from motives of interest or ambition.

Men emancipated from the clouds of superstition, and the grasp of power, whose minds are free to act, will not be idle in thought or in deed. Who shall direct the masses that are now, and soon are to become, thus free? Who should be the best friends of the poor, the ignorant, and the inquiring? If these multitudes should be promptly acted upon and led into error by designing and mistaken men, who should be the first to extend a hand to guide them into the true path? Who so properly, as those who have in their hands, and should have in their hearts and minds, that true philosophy which alone affords elements for the solution of all questions of human well-being?

It is difficult to detect all the errors, fallacies, and temptations to wrong which have lain in the path of reformers, and on which some of the most beautiful and richly-laden vessels ever freighted with human interests have suffered wreck and destruction. These rocks cannot all be pointed out and laid down; but some of the more dangerous may be selected for special remark.

God speaks to us none the less plainly and authoritatively in the volumes of Nature and Providence because he speaks to us also in a special revelation. We may not fully understand this teaching of Nature or Providence but with the aid of revelation; yet with this aid, we must not neglect to study and try to comprehend. God is the Creator and Governor of the world, as well as the Author of the Scriptures. His precepts and his administration must be consistent: we must therefore construe these volumes of Nature, and Providence, and Holy Writ, by the light they mutually reflect upon each other. He that is blind to Providence and deaf to the voice of Nature, can never adequately understand the instructions of revelation. It is a common sin of men to exalt themselves above God, and to pretend to a wisdom above his wisdom. Many reformers would stem the whole current of the Divine administration, and stop the course of Providence. They would instantaneously banish all evil from the world, and extirpate all that is hurtful, dangerous, and offensive in the kingdom of nature and in the province of humanity.   Upon their showing, these things should never have existed, and should now, without a moment's delay, be brought to an unconditional termination.   They take no account of the origin of evil, nor of its permitted continuance by a Being who could bring the movements of the universe to an end, if he chose; but they would, without hesitation, under guidance of their own wisdom, change the whole order of Providence, and reverse the course of the Divine government.

Even the Scriptures, taken alone, furnish the same blended picture of good and evil, all occurring under the same wise Ruler.   Those, then, who would put an end to evil in any other way than that which is contemplated in the Divine teachings, are making themselves wiser than the Governor of the universe.   The Deity has ever permitted the existence and the use of evil in his administration of the affairs of men: to how many is the way to heaven through the furnace of afflictions! Who can recount the sufferings and the sorrows of the people of God? or who describe a tithe of the agony which men have endured in this world? By far the largest number of human beings who have had a place on the earth since the dawn of history, have been slaves—slaves in the usual acceptation of the word; slaves to despotic sway; slaves to military rule; slaves to priestly domination; slaves to the feudal system; slaves to capital, to competition, to the fear of starvation. The worst passions of men have long rioted in mutual injuries and in endless wars about the most unimportant things. Thrice as many men have fallen by the hands of their fellow-men as are now living on earth.

Against evils of such enormous magnitude, no other weapon has been provided by Christianity than those of charity—brotherly kindness. The Christian scheme is to renew and regenerate the man; to inspire him with new tastes, new feelings, new aims, higher aspira-

tions, and, by making better men, to put an
end to the crimes, excesses, bloodshed, and oppression which have so long reigned in the
world. When the disciples of Christ would
have invoked the fire of heaven upon his enemies, he rebuked them, and told them they
little knew the spirit they were of; that is,
they little knew they were instigated in this
by the spirit of the prince of this world. We
must, therefore, under his teaching, give up
the spirit of revenge for wrong suffered, the
spirit of violence, and the spirit of reproach, in
accomplishing all reforms, and expect the Divine approval only when we proceed in the
way of Divine appointment. We may not, if
we have the power, destroy the oppressor, nor
even overwhelm him with indignant reproach.
We may not seize the combatants at the moment they are about to engage in deadly
strife, and hold them in iron grasp while their
veins swell with increasing rage; but we must
change the oppressor into a benefactor, and
the deadly combatants into brethren and

peacemakers. If this be a long process, the delay is unavoidable; for God permits no other mode. If generations pass away before this reform is effected, it is our fault, who hold the truth, but do not exemplify it. But the delay is unavoidable; for no other mode is in accordance with the Divine government.

It cannot be denied, that the cause of reform in religion, politics, and social economy has suffered, and not undeservedly, from the faults and vagaries of those who have, in all ages of the world, offered themselves as reformers. It has too often happened that the prosecution of the best reforms has fallen into the hands of the worst men. All reform requires industry, energy, and indomitable perseverance. These qualities are frequently found among those who are destitute of all good principles, and who embark in the cause of reformation from interested motives, or for the mere sake of the excitement and distinction which a new career affords. Such men, not having the main object in view, turn the whole progress of events to serve their own purposes, or commit such excesses and are guilty of such outrages as bring reproach and contempt upon the cause they advocate, and finally beget a resistance to further progress which cannot be overcome. Reforms are thus often wholly ruined by the unfitness or wickedness of those who usurp their management, or smothered by the imprudent zeal of those who need better guidance. Seeing how thorny and difficult this path has always been, and how many a good cause has suffered shipwreck for want of good pilots, it is not to be wondered that good men stand aloof, fearing to enter a career in which so many not only fail to achieve the good they aim at, but commit a world of mischief, which, perhaps, they did not contemplate. It is so common for those who leave the beaten track on the great subjects of religion and the temporal interests of humanity, to wander far beyond the sphere of truth—once swung from their accustomed moorings, to push far out into a trackless and

uncertain ocean, without compass or chart—
that many of the most prudent, dreading the
loss of present advantages, refuse to step from
the trodden road of routine, or to cast their
eyes into regions beyond the ordinary range
of their vision; and regard such wanderings
as sinful and dangerous. As soon as they ob-
serve a man adventuring upon new ground
or unused investigations, they look upon him
as in the path of danger, if not in the road to
destruction. Thus is born a stern and im-
movable conservatism, which reverences prudence more than truth—which fears error
more than it loves wisdom. Into this mistaken disposition the best may fall, because
the best are most apt to mistrust their own
powers and doubt their own fitness. Where
this prevails in any community, the spirit of
inquiry is repressed, if not extinguished, and
none but erratic, ill-balanced, and ill-disci-
plined minds venture, against the weight of
public opinion, to depart from the usual routes
of thought and action. The prudence of the

wise, carried too far, but heightens the absurdity of the foolish, and thus, unhappily, throws additional discredit upon the path of research and reformation.

But although all these snares, temptations, and obstacles beset the path of reform, it is none the less our duty to struggle onward. It is in the order of God's providence thus to try our courage and fortitude at every step, and thus to strengthen the intellect, the good affections, and the watchfulness of his servants, by giving full exercise to every faculty of progressive energy and passive endurance. It is His will, that whilst His people are doing good to their fellow-men, they shall be building themselves up in spiritual vigour and mental power, thus enlarging their capacities for higher enjoyment in the world of spirits. Christians must not stand still while by far the largest portion of men are estranged from their Master, and while strife, oppression, bloodshed, and evil rule throughout all the world. They must not only fulfil the vocation to brotherly kindness to the individuals around them, but they must study every problem of humanity which is displayed before them, and do what they can for multitudes both near and at a distance. It should be true, and be known to be true, that they are incessantly occupied in studying the temporal and eternal interests of men; that they are ready to go forward upon every occasion and every moment when relief can be afforded, sorrow soothed, suffering alleviated—when any reform can be effected, with advantage in the mode of accomplishing it and permanent results for the end.

It should be known and felt by the masses of degraded and suffering men, that Christians seize every occasion of labouring for their good—as it should be known to the rulers of all countries, that reforms conducted by Christians involve neither bloodshed, nor rebellion, nor disorganization, but the best interests of all concerned, social, intellectual, and religious. But Christians can only create this

impression by engaging efficiently in this
work, by wise solutions of the various questions involved, and by perseveringly pursuing
the instructions and footsteps of their divine
Master. His precepts contain elements for the
solution of all the problems of social well-being, and the mode of accomplishing all desirable reforms. When the object is to abolish
slavery, the Christian process will be to incite
masters to love and cherish their slaves as
immortal beings under their charge, and to
teach the slaves to love and obey their masters, under whom, in the order of Providence,
they are placed. Under this teaching, a pa-
triarchal relation will arise between the master and his slave; the fetters will drop off;
the one will become a father, and the others
children; and, finally, when the master is
brought to the point of emancipation, the servants are brought to that preparation for
liberty which enables them to accept the boon
with advantage, and to begin the career of
freedom under the more than friendly eye

of their former master, and now employer; or to enter upon any other enterprise for which their habits or education might fit them.

So in political reform. The precepts and example of Christ should be brought to bear, by love and acts of kindness, upon kings and rulers, and upon subjects and citizens, at the same time. This wisdom, which came from on high, if properly applied by such as exemplify what they teach, will, in due time, leaven the whole mass. The grasp of authority will be relaxed, the complaints of the oppressed will gradually cease, as the process of that reform goes on, which lightens the cares and labours of authority while it removes the burdens of obedience.

But all these are labours of love, as well as words of truth. These lessons must be imparted to the master as well as the slave, to the despot as well as the subject, by those who never forget the example nor the precepts of their Divine Teacher. There can be no doubt that those, whether many or few, who conform to His rules, may go everywhere and deliver the words of warning and of truth to everybody, rich and poor, bond and free, high and low.

INFIDELITY, AND SOME OF ITS EXCITING CAUSES.

MANY Christian writers have attempted the task of exposing the causes and progress of infidelity. If we have been in any degree successful in bringing our train of thought and inquiry before the reader, we think he will be satisfied that the grand cause of unbelief is to be found in the abuses of Christianity. The prevalent unbelief has for its object not the truths of revelation, but the opinions and conduct of those who profess to be Christians. We all know how this operates on a small scale among the individuals around us; and we may well infer that it operates still more potently upon multitudes

than upon individuals. In Catholic countries,
the most of those who escape the fetters of
ignorance and superstition regard Christianity
as a system of fraud and oppression, designed
to cheat and govern men. They become infidels, because they confound Christianity with
its professors. In Protestant countries, the
wrangling disputes and uncharitable bearing
of the various churches carry disgust and
dislike wherever they are witnessed. Men
cannot believe that is a pure fountain from
which such uncleanness flows. They are
repelled and not attracted by the exhibition,
and easily draw the conclusion that whether
there is anything real in Christianity or not,
they must be as safe for eternity as those
whose profession accords so ill with their
lives. It would be difficult to over-estimate
the prevalence of such feelings, or their influence in turning men from the path of obedience and piety. Many say in their hearts,
if they do not pronounce aloud, that if certain
persons or classes of men are really bound

heavenward, they do not wish to go—they will take an opposite direction. Are they excusable for thus rejecting Christianity, through the fault of its professed friends? Certainly not: but how is that to be reconciled with the Christian duty of winning souls to Christ, when their conduct repels more than it attracts? It may be said that the aversion of the natural man to Christianity is such that it need not be wondered if he turns away from holiness. Something is due to this consideration, but it has less foundation than many good people imagine. It is true that in the days of Christ's sojourn on earth, the priests, the rich, and noble, for the most part, rejected his mission with scorn; but it is equally true that multitudes, attracted by his kindness, and by his preaching, flocked after him: these multitudes were so great, that the priests feared the people, although they had all the authorities and the Roman soldiers at their command. How many were deterred by the threats and management of the priests from following Christ, we know not. The fact was that the ministrations of Christ were in a high degree attractive, and nine-tenths of the whole nation would probably have followed after him, but for the measures taken to repress the movement. So the persecutions encountered by the early Christians in pagan lands came from emperors, governors, priests, and prophets, who feared that the new doctrine would undermine their authority: the people everywhere welcomed the advent of Christianity. This is not that they naturally inclined to love its doctrines or obey its precepts, but that they always, unless in positions of advantage supposed to be endangered by innovation, revered and loved every personal exemplification of the gentle spirit of Christianity. They loved the Christian, even when they did not at once cordially embrace his faith and partake of his hope.

The aversion to the pure requirements of Christian truth may still be influential and

visible in the natural man, but he has no
such aversion to the Christians who obey
these requirements and display them in their
lives. It is even true that the very men who
read the Bible are forcibly struck with the
beauty of its precepts, and feel themselves
strongly attracted to the Author of our present
dispensation; and this is the strong inducement
to the present extensive distribution of the
Holy Scriptures. But where one man would be
thus favourably influenced by the mere reading of the word, a thousand would behold
with admiration and sincere regard any fair
exemplification of the precepts of the Saviour.
It is a matter worthy of special remark that
the exercise of charity, of brotherly love, of
humanity, embracing those duties which Christians most overlook and neglect, are the very
duties in which the men of the world are most
willing to engage and carry on independently
or in company with Christians. It is further
to be noted that very many of the benevolent
and Christian enterprises of the day are in

fact more indebted to the liberality of men not professing to be Christians, than to those who are. It is upon this very ground, in which Christians are most deficient, that men of the world are most efficient—most inclined to act. This is the field in which the least repulsion is to be expected, and in which the most complete success would immediately crown any rightly-directed Christian effort.

It is because this effort is not made, because this field, which, even in the estimation of the men of the world, belongs to the domain of Christianity, is not fully and strongly occupied by Christians, that many, very many disbelieve in its power over the human heart and mind, whilst they admit its abstract purity. They regard that, as a neglected philosophy—as the Utopia of an amiable philanthropist, which assumes to be an active religious principle—a divine power. It is only when Christianity is in action, when the example of its Author is followed even at the distance from divinity to humanity, that its beauties and graces reveal all their attractions. So, in like manner, when a semblance of Christianity is set up in which the chief beauties and graces are omitted, the men of the world turn away from the counterfeit, with contempt and hatred added to natural aversion.

It is this failure on the part of Christians to commend their Master's pure and benign cause by lives of meekness and charity that turns away so many of the strict moralists of this world, who, feeling that their own conduct, even in what they deem a Christian aspect, is so much superior to that of professed Christians, that they cannot reverence a religion which bears no better fruits than those they behold. Ah, how should such considerations arrest the attention of all followers of Christ! Here is an aspect of duty which fixes heavy responsibilities upon every individual of them; not upon the clergy alone, but upon the whole body of Christians. This is a field of labour in which the efforts of the laity may be more potent than all the labours of the clergy.

23

Here lies the path to an effectual refutation
of by far the largest portion of infidel objections.   When these responsibilities are fairly
met, the clergy will no longer fulfil the heavy
task of preaching that gospel which none
obey—of enforcing those precepts which find
no verification.

It is a fact worthy of note and careful reflection, though we cannot enter into any full
analysis of it at present, that many of the
most zealous friends of humanity, in some
cases only professed friends, have either been
infidels or have shown a strong bias in that
direction.   So far as this zeal for the interests
of humanity can have been real, or can be
supposed to have been real, it presents a case
of moral and intellectual obliquity of the
most extraordinary kind.   The reasons may
be worked out at length by those who have
leisure and ability for the task.   We only
point to the fact.   We refer not to those who
are merely seeking political reforms, but to
those who apparently desire to go deeper and

effect more radical changes for the better
in human condition. To go no farther
back than Paine, a long list of men might
be formed whose zeal for humanity made
them infidels, or whose infidelity begot their
zeal for human welfare. In general, these
men were not ignorant of, and could not be
blind to, the claims of Christianity, upon a
survey of all history since its advent, to being
considered the greatest benefactor of mankind
the world has ever known. But they were
not men who busied themselves with past
claims or merits : they were looking to
something to be accomplished which was before them. They find Christians arrayed
against their plans, and they immediately
array themselves against Christianity. The
Christians may be right, and the reformers
may be wrong, or there may be right and
wrong on both sides, but what is chiefly to be
lamented is that Christians suffer these controversies to assume a shape and aspect which
have the appearance of infidelity being on the

side of human well-being, while Christianity
stands up in defence of ancient abuses, oppres-
sive legislation, and social enormities. Whose
fault is it that the good of Christianity is thus
brought into a position to be " evil spoken
of?"   Is it that Christianity has so complicated her interests with those of governments,
with the course of legislation, with the existing social evils, that Christians fear to have
any of these touched lest the fabric of their
respective churches may suffer?   Is it so, that
those who set themselves to examine existing
institutions and the evils which afflict humanity are brought to the conclusion that Christianity is one of the chief barriers to progress
in the path of charity and social well-being?
Can Christianity be so far put in the wrong
as to appear even in the slightest degree
adverse to any policy which promises the least
addition to the comforts, the happiness or best
interests of the great masses of men?

Let no one wince if the probe has to be
applied in finding a reply to these queries,

and if it wounds the complacency of those Christians who are so perfectly satisfied with things and institutions as they are that they tremble at any suggestions of change. It is very easy for those who are sitting in abundance, in the enjoyment of competent salaries, a good inheritance, a well-established business, or enjoying the sure patronage of powerful or rich friends, or in possession of other adventitious or well-earned advantages, to be very much opposed to all propositions of reform which do not meet their views or comport with their interests. And as it is not probable that any plan can be devised to secure the assent of all, common sympathy unites the respectable classes in opposition to every scheme which implies much change. They feel easy and comfortable, and, having the power in their hands, they cannot perceive why they should jeopardize their position by assenting to reforms which, after all, may not fulfil their design. These sentiments and

23*

this state of feeling, is in perfect accordance with the natural dictates of the human heart.

But they are certainly wide as the poles from the genuine spirit of Christianity, which should not be used as a cloak for such selfishness. It seems to be the order of Providence that, in the path of life, at least two-thirds of the human race fall behind, and become more or less dependent on the other third, upon whom greater industry or strength, or bodily vigour, or special talents, or accidental advantages have conferred power, or wealth, or influence, which enables them not merely to live upon the labour of their less fortunate brethren, but at will to prey upon them, and reduce them to absolute or virtual servitude. Now, it so happens, in Christendom, that this happy third, in Catholic countries, consists of the priesthood, and the nobles, public officers, gentry, and men of wealth, who find many reasons for sustaining their exclusive position; in Protestant countries, the deposit of power and influence is in equivalent hands.

Thus Christianity sits enthroned on high places, while poverty is struggling below. Christians find matters very well arranged for them; they are reaping the fruits of sobriety, economy, industry, and honesty, while the multitudes below are suffering the consequences of idleness, ignorance, vagrancy, intemperance, dishonesty, and crime. The complacency of the upper class is complete, but dangerous. Between these vast classes of the higher and lower range is a multitude that skirt the boundaries of both, and are no indifferent spectators of what passes above and below them. A portion of them may, with all the energies of selfishness, be working their way upwards; but many, of medium capacities, are constitutionally content with a quiet life and frugal living; and these become special observers of the effects of disease, hunger, nakedness, ignorance, crime, and the indescribable suffering and anguish which are below, and of the cool indifference, the hardness of heart, the exclusiveness which dictates relief to a few of some particular church, or some who have fallen from higher fortunes, but which repudiates the kindredship of the human family: they become indignant observers of the barriers and obstacles, legal, political, religious, and moral, which are carefully and industriously raised, not only against any actual measures of relief for these suffering millions, but even against any fair and candid, much less Christian discussion of the questions involved in any attempt to elevate and permanently improve their condition. Does all this beget in them no abhorrence of power, no infidelity, no tendency to democracy and other levelling doctrines? Let the literature of the past century speak in reply. Let the progress of republicanism in Europe and America answer—let chartism, and above all socialism, respond. In chartism, in democracy, in socialism, there is not necessarily any ingredient of infidelity; and yet in fact, we find them to a large extent blended and travelling together, because

Christians, as such, and those who pretend to be such, have, without just discrimination, opposed every movement of reform, as dangerous to society. There is then no avoiding the conclusion which should be uppermost in the minds of all,—that Christians should promote every reform which has human welfare for its object, provided it can furnish good assurance of its claims, and that it is to be carried out in the true spirit of Christianity. They should not only be prompt to perform all that it is wise to do, but ready to devise all that their minds can compass for that end, and be ready to hear all that can be suggested. No discussion should be more welcome to a Christian's ear, than that which concerns the true interests of men, even for this world; because, when Christians find the means of promoting the temporal interests of men, they have found a door open to secure their interests for eternity. Christians should, therefore, be the known patrons of every measure involving the progress of humanity:

that their patronage may be effectual, they must keep their minds and their duties balanced, not allowing any one measure to swallow up all others and all other considerations. There is but one rule for doing this, and but one Being who can aid us in applying it: we must love the emperor and serf alike, the master and slave, the captor and his prisoner, the man in the palace and the man in the hovel, the man that is a friend and the man that is a foe: the rule is to love all these as we love ourselves; and if we have not strength to keep this precept, we must look for aid to Him who. gave this "new commandment."

But we find many besides those in this middle range of life who become deeply grieved at the apparent indifference of Christians to the cause of humanity : these exceptions exist both in the higher and lower ranks : they exist among the poor, mingled with bitterness, if not hatred; and among the rich, mingled with scorn and contempt.*

It is no sign of wisdom, or of meekness, or of charity, that Christians despise and disregard these opinions and sentiments, how-

---

* Take the case of Stephen Girard. We hear there is a feeling of resentment among many of the clergy of Pennsylvania, coupled with branding him always as an infidel, for his exclusion of their order from his college of orphans. We know nothing of Mr. Girard's reasons beyond what he says, nor of his religious sentiments, but on the face of the transaction there is every reason why the clergy should bow in anguish before an event which speaks so loud a reproach to their order. That a man who could conceive so vast a project of charity towards children, the most favoured class under the dispensation of mercy ; that one, who could so approximate the spirit of the apostle's declaration,—"Pure religion and undefiled before God and the Father is this, to visit the fatherless and the widows in their affliction," (James i. 27 ;) that one who knew the world so well, and had lived in it so long, and desired that the orphans taken in charge should be taught "*the purest principles of morality*, so that, on their entrance into active life, they may, from inclination and habit, evince *benevolence towards their fellow-creatures*, and *a love of truth, sobriety, and industry*,"— should not be willing to commit this teaching to the clergy, or to their supervision, or even to their occasional inspection, should rather justify strong self-distrust and apprehension than a tone of reproach or condemnation.

It may serve to extenuate this much mooted offence of Mr. Girard against religion, to state that the management of the British and Foreign Bible Society, the London Sunday-school Union, and our own Sunday-school Union is committed exclusively to laymen.

ever mistaken, and attempt to wrap themselves complacently in robes of orthodoxy
and self-righteousness, wondering at such
ignorance and presumption. This is an error
even more fatal than that at which it is directed. It is cause of profound mortification
and humility in Christians, that such sentiments prevail in certain quarters. There is
no escaping this conclusion by contempt or
disregard, any more than the ostrich escapes
its pursuers by thrusting its head in the sand;
nor will it meet the case to say "that the
heart of man is deceitful above all things and
desperately wicked,"—that "enmity against
God" is the explanation of this enmity to his
servants. When the day of judgment comes,
and all hearts are laid open, it will be determined how far it is safe or proper for one set
of men to assume that their righteousness
was the cause of offence in other men.

Religion and its institutions, whether from
compactness or strength of organization or
from a command of public opinion, constitute

a very effective power, which is wielded by
human hands under all the influences to
which human nature is subject. It is inevitable, therefore, that it must be abused, and
the more especially because no human possession is more apt to be abused than power,
however derived. This power is abused both
positively and negatively,—by what it does,
and what it prohibits being done :—it is efficient of evil and repressive of good. Those
enjoying such control have always been inclined, not only to stifle inquiry into abuses
which might expose themselves, but also all
free expression of opinion which might, in
any way, bring the validity of their dogmas
in question. It was easier for them to sit
tranquil in their places and hold men to one
track of thought, than to be kept constantly
on the alert, to examine, understand, and try
the soundness of positions as fast as they
might be advanced. They deemed that, by
having grasped this power, they had earned a
right to the quiet enjoyment of its exercise,

24

although that exercise affected ten times
their number of people, vitally interested
to question the validity of the rights claimed,
and more especially interested to inquire if
neither religion, nor humanity, nor politics,
nor political economy had any thing better
in store for them.   It is therefore in perfect
accordance with human nature that we find
this power for repression of truth and all
disturbing investigations freely exercised, not
only in cases where the truth or the subject
of inquiry plainly points to defects of existing systems, or suggests remedies, but even
from tyranny or caprice, in cases where no
possible danger to the powers that be is involved.   Thus the Catholic opposition to the
astronomical discoveries of the middle ages;
thus the modern opposition to the conclusions
of geology, and thus the almost universal
opposition among rigid churchmen and the
severely orthodox to all free inquiries into
human condition, the rights and wrongs of
the poor, and into the great problem of proper

security for human labour.   This is proclaimed, by some from whom better things
might be expected, to be ground which free
inquiry should not touch; as within the domain of religion, and therefore not to be
touched by profane hands.   And yet these
same persons do not so much as touch these
subjects with their little fingers.   They do
not enter in themselves, and they would
fain prevent others also from entering.   The
odium of this tyranny falls not merely upon
the guilty, but upon that Christianity they
unworthily represent.

When will it be understood and fairly admitted, that however men may have cause
to fear the truth, and however they may be
interested to sustain abusive doctrines and
institutions, Christianity has nothing to fear
from the truth, and much less cause to fear
open enemies than pretended or mistaken
friends? When will it be felt and understood,
that whatever virtue there may be in conservatism, whatever caution should be ob-

served in reforms, whatever barriers may be
raised against the progress of truth or science,
Christianity cannot be enlisted against humanity, nor against any cause that promotes
social well-being : that whilst millions upon
millions of human beings in Christendom,
under the very shadow of Christianity, are
suffering the extremities of want, of ignorance, degradation, crime, and oppression,
Christians cannot, in the slightest accordance with their profession, oppose all searching inquiries into these miseries and all active
and effectual methods of relief? It is unchristian to say that nothing can be done for
these millions : it is wicked to deny that very
much can be done : it is treason to the cause
of Christ if infidelity is permitted to take
precedence in the career of social and moral
reformation.   Let Christian kindness be so
prompt and conspicuous in whatever concerns human amelioration, that whilst every
mind is encouraged to put forth all its powers
in that direction, every scheme of improve-

ment shall be tinged, if not imbued, with heavenly wisdom, and every plan shall instinctively seek the approval of Christian Charity and the co-operation of Christian enterprise. Let the science of social well-being—the art of doing good—be exalted to its true elevation, of making all other sciences and arts subordinate, and contributory to its perfection and efficiency, and then it shall be found that every good cause will stand in its true place and the harmony of the whole will constitute a soil on which Christianity shall reap her greatest triumphs in this world.

NOTES.

WE have not in the English language any elaborate work on Christian Charity. A great many beautiful things have been said and written on this subject, which it would be at once profitable and pleasant to collect and compare. How many charity sermons have been preached in English since the Reformation! How many essays, how many touching passages, poetical and prosaic, might be brought together by a diligent search! How far all these might go to vindicate Protestantism in Great Britain and America from the reproach of having produced no great work on Charity we cannot conjecture. Whether these choice extracts would be found most abundant in sacred or profane literature we cannot tell. We trust the work will be done by some thoroughly industrious explorer, whom nothing worthy of notice shall escape. If the collection shall prove too extensive for publication, let us at least have a descriptive catalogue, indicating the localities and the nature of these hidden treasures. When this task is to be performed, we trust that our religious literature will be especially examined; that every system of theology, every guide to piety, every book of daily meditations, every work descriptive of the divine life, every volume that professes to set forth Christianity in general, and every one that professes to point out the paths of a Christian life in particular, shall be diligently searched, to discover what any and all may yield on the great subject of Christian Charity. Enough may be found perhaps to encourage some competent person to wipe away our reproach, and furnish in our language a great and adequate work on Christian Charity—on the leading instructions of Christ, on the more prominent acts of Christ's life, on the duties that Christian ministers owe to the ignorant poor, and on the obligations of Christian people to all that require their aid, sympathy, and protection.

Our inquiries have furnished us in English religious literature with only one work on the subject of Christian Charity, which, though far from being comprehensive or thorough, is nevertheless a very good book. The author is one who was capable of doing better justice to this vital topic, but unfortunately, it did not come within the scope of his undertaking to embrace its whole range. He gives frequent proofs in its pages of having felt the importance and pressure of the subject. We trust he may yet return to it and furnish a systematic treatise, covering the whole ground of love to God and love to man. We refer to "CHRISTIAN CHARITY EXPLAINED, &c., in an Exposition of the Thirteenth Chapter of the First Epistle to the Corinthians," by John Angell James.

The mode of treatment suggested by the weekly duty of furnishing a lecture was unfavourable to system and shut out elementary and comprehensive views, whilst perhaps it gave earnestness and pungency to his exhortations. We offer a few extracts, which, whilst they confirm many of our author's positions, show that the writer fell short of a full conception of the subject.

"Our Lord has resolved all piety and all morality into LOVE. This shows us at once that religion has its seat in the heart, and is of a free, and noble, and generous nature. From a persuasion that this view of it is too rarely taken, too little understood, and too imperfectly felt, I was induced to enter upon the exposition of Paul's most interesting description of Christian Charity."

"It is impossible to read this chapter without being convinced that the religion of Jesus Christ has excellences and beauties in its nature, which, in consequence of the depravity of our hearts, have been yet but very imperfectly developed to the world. Unfortunately for the reputation of Christianity, it has been generally looked at, not as it appears, in mild but unclouded effulgence, in its own hemisphere, the Bible, but as it is feebly and dimly reflected from the dull surface of what is called the Christian world."

"Were this rule of conduct accurately and universally conformed to by all who bear the name of Christ, what a scene would the church of God present! how striking would it appear, when thus exhibited as the dwelling-place of love, amidst a region of selfishness and cruelty,—a verdant oasis in this desert world."

"Religion, in the *present* day especially, is too exclusively a *public* business—a thing of times and places—an observance of forms, and an enjoyment of public means: its efforts are confined to the hearing of sermons, and a voluptuous enjoyment of devotional seasons."

"The religion of the age is all bustle, and hurry, and flutter; the consequence is, that many really know not what manner of spirit they are of."

"The *mode* of doing business, also, in the present day, is often shockingly at variance with the "whatsoever things are true, and just, and honest." It has been said by some, that trade is a lie from beginning to end. This is an extravagant expression, but it is *partially* true; so that what with the bad practices which custom too easily reconciles to the conscience of even pious people, and what with the time which is usually employed, even where there is no departure from the strictest integrity,—personal religion is in imminent peril."

"Miracles were but the credentials of Christianity, but CHARITY is its essence; miracles but its witnesses, which, having ushered it into the world, and borne their testimony, retired for ever;—but CHARITY is its very soul, which, when disencumbered of all that is earthly, shall ascend to its native seat—the paradise and the presence of the eternal God."

"This is love, blended with all our living habits, diffused through all our conduct, forming our character, breathing in our desires, speaking in our words, beaming in our eyes; in short, a living part of our living selves. And *this*, be it remembered, is religion—practical religion."

After quoting a number of the leading passages in the New Testament on the subject of Charity, the author bursts forth as follows :—

"What encomiums are these! what striking proofs of the supreme importance of the disposition now under consideration! Who has not been guilty of some neglect of it? Who has not had his attention drawn too much from it? Who can read these passages of Holy Writ, and not feel convinced that not only mankind in general, but the professors of spiritual religion also, have too much mistaken the nature of true piety? What are clear and orthodox views—what are strong feelings—what is our faith—what our enjoyment—what our freedom from gross immorality,—without this spirit of pure and universal benevolence?"

"Some conclude, that because *they are regular in their attendance upon the services of religion* they are true Christians; they go punctually to church or to meeting—they receive the Lord's supper—they frequent the meetings for social prayer—they, perhaps, repeat prayers in secret, and read the Scriptures. All this is well, if it be done with right views, and in connection with right dispositions: but it is the whole of their religion; a mere abstraction of devotional exercise; a thing separate and apart from the heart, and temper, and conduct; a business of the closet, and of the sanctuary; a sort of composition paid to the Almighty, to be released from all the other demands of Scripture, and obligations of piety; an expression of their willingness to be devout in the church, and on the Sabbath, provided they may be as earthly-minded, as selfish, as malicious, and as unkind as they please, in all places and all times besides. *This* is not religion."

"Doctrine is every thing; clear views of the gospel are the great desideratum: and in their zeal for these things, they suppose they can never say things extravagant enough, nor absurd enough, nor angry enough, against good works, practical religion, or Christian temper. Puffed up with pride, selfish, unkind, irritable, censorious, malicious,—they manifest a total want of that humility and kindness which are the prominent features of true Christianity. Let it be known however, that clear views, even where they have no resemblance to the monstrous caricatures and frightful deformities of modern Antinomianism, are of themselves no evidence of religion, any more than right theoretical notions of the constitution are the proofs of loyalty; and as a man with these notions in his mind may be a traitor in his heart, so may a professor of religion be an enemy to God in his soul, with an evangelical creed upon his tongue. Many profess to be very fond of the lamp of truth, grasp it firmly in their hands, admire its flame, pity or blame those who are following the delusive and me-teoric fires of error; but after all, make no other use of it than to illuminate the path that leads them to perdition; their religion begins and ends in adopt-ing a form of sound words for their creed, approving an evangelical ministry, admiring the popular champions of the truth, and joining in the reproba-tion of fundamental error. As to any spirituality of mind, any heavenliness of affection, any Christian love,—in short, as to any of the natural tendency, the appropriate energy, the vital, elevating influence, of those very doctrines to which they profess to be attached—they are as destitute as the veriest world-ling; and like him, are perhaps selfish, revengeful, implacable, and unkind. This is a religion but too common in the present day, when evangelical senti-ments are becoming increasingly popular; a religion but too common in our churches: a religion, cold, heartless, and uninfluential; a sort of lunar light, which reflects the beams of the sun, but not his warmth."

"It is to be feared that many, in the present day, satisfy themselves that they are Christians, *because of their zeal in the cause of religion.* Happily for the church of God, happily for the world at large, there is now a great and general eagerness for the diffusion of knowledge and piety. Throwing off the torpor of ages, the friends of Christ are labouring to extend his kingdom in every di-rection. Almost every possible object of Christian philanthropy is seized upon; societies are organized; means adapted to every kind of instruments are em-ployed; the whole levy *en masse* of the religious world is called out; and Christendom presents an interesting scene of benevolent energy. Such a state of things, however, has its dangers in reference to personal religion, and may become an occasion of delusion to many. It does not require genuine piety to associate us with these movements: from a natural liberality of disposition, or regard to reputation, or a desire of influence, or by the compulsion of example, we may give our property; for all these motives are, no doubt, in partial ope-ration, when giving is in fashion. And as to personal exertions, how many inducements may lead to this, besides a sincere and an ardent love to Christ! An inherent fondness for activity, a love of display, the spirit of party, the per-suasion of friends, may all operate, and unquestionably do operate in many cases, to produce astonishing effects in the cause of religious benevolence, where there is a total absence of genuine piety. The mind of man, prone to self-deception, and anxious to find some reasons to satisfy itself in reference to its eternal state, short of the true evidence of a renewed heart, is too apt to derive a false peace from the contemplation of its zeal. In proportion as the cause of the delusion approximates to the nature of true religion, is its power to blind and to mislead the judgment. If the mind can perceive any thing in itself, or in its operations, which bears the semblance of godliness, it will con-vert it into a means of lulling the conscience and removing anxiety. To many persons the fatal opiate, the soul-destroying imposture—is their activity in the cause of Christian zeal: none are more diligent in their devotedness to the duties of committees, none are more constant in their attendance upon public meetings; others, again, weary themselves in their weekly rounds to collect the contributions of the rich or the offerings of the poor. These things, if they do not lead them coolly to reason and to conclude that they are believers, take off their attention from the real condition of their souls, leave them no leisure for reflection, repress the rising fear, and either stifle the voice of conscience, or enable them to drown its remonstrances in the eloquence of the platform or in the discussion of the committee-room. We doubt not that some unworthy professors of religion, in the present age, resort to public meetings for the same reason as many a guilty votary of pleasure does to public amusements,—to forget his own condition, and to turn away his ear, for a short season, from the voice that speaks to him from within. Individuals are known to us all, who, amidst the greatest zeal for various public institutions, are living in malice and all uncharitableness, in the indulgence of a predominant selfishness and uncontrolled wrath. But it will not do. This is not piety. Could we support the whole expenditure of the Missionary Society by our affluence, and direct its counsels by our wisdom, and keep alive its energy by our ardour, and yet at the same time were destitute of love,—we should perish eternally, amidst the munificence of our liberality."

"Mammon, or Covetousness, the Sin of the Christian Church, by the Rev. John Harris, author of The Great Teacher."

This was a vigorous effort of an English divine to bring the sins of the English churches against charity to their notice. It was a prize essay, and made a strong impression on the public mind. It partakes, however, of the same defects as the work of Mr. James—it does not cover the whole ground; because, doubtless, the author did not contemplate so large a task. A few extracts will give its tone:—

"It is clear, then, that the entire economy of salvation is constructed on the principle of restoring to the world the lost spirit of love. Its advent was an era in the universe." . . . "It was confronting selfishness in its own native region with a system of benevolence prepared, as its avowed antagonist, by the hand of God itself."—P. 27. "But has its object been realized? more than 1800 years have elapsed since it was brought into operation—has its design succeeded. Succeeded! Alas! the question seems a taunt, a mockery. . . But why is it thus? why has the gospel been hitherto threatened with the failure of a mere business experiment?"—P. 28. Speaking of the success of the earliest preachers of Christianity: "The world was taken by surprise—never before had it beheld such men—every thing gave way before them—city after city, and province after province capitulated—yet the whole secret of their power was *love*." . . . . "A fire had been kindled in the earth which consumed the selfishness of men wherever it came."—P. 30. . . . "But who does not feel that the era of effective benevolence has yet to commence? Let him sketch the most simple scheme of benevolence which the gospel can approve, and he will perceive

at every step that he is writing the condemnation of the church."—238 . . .
"The great lesson taught by our Lord's voluntary selection of a state of poverty
is yet to be fully understood, the evident application of many plain passages of
Scripture to be made, doctrines startling to selfishness to become familiar and
welcome, the word benevolence itself to be differently understood, the demon
of covetousness to be cast out of the church, and the whole economy of benevolence to be revised."—239.

"Every nation has its idol. In some countries that idol is pleasure; in
others, glory; in others, liberty: but the name of our idol (in Great Britain) is
mammon." If it be true that each succeeding age has its representative; that
it beholds itself reflected in some leading school, and impresses its image on the
philosophy of the day, where shall we look for the image of the existing age,
but in our systems of political economy."—80 . . . . "Mammon is marching
through the land in triumph."—81. . . . . "To the same unhallowed spirit of
gain is to be traced that fierce 'competition,' of which the labourer, the arti-
san, the dealer, the manufacturer, and even the members of all the liberal professions alike complain." . . . . . "But when it rises to a struggle in which
neither time nor strength is left for higher pursuits, in which every new com-
petitor is looked upon in the light of an enemy, in which every personal exertion and practicable retrenchment do but barely leave a subsistence, there
must be something essentially wrong in our ruling spirit or social constitution."—83. . . . "And on all hands it is admitted that the way in which business is now conducted, involves all the risk, uncertainty, and unnatural excitement of a game of chance."—84. Edit. Am. Tract Soc. 7.

Three prize tracts on Benevolence or Christianity, have been recently published by the American Tract Society, entitled as follows :

The Divine Law of Beneficence, by Rev. Parsons Cook, Lynn.
Zaccheus, or the Scriptural Plan of Benevolence, by Rev. Samuel Harris,
Conway, Massachusetts.
The Mission of the Church, or Systematic Beneficence, by Rev. Edward A.
Lawrence, Marblehead.

These tracts have great merit, but are confined to urging liberality in support of the various Christian enterprises of the day,
and to the propriety of systematic appropriations of a regular portion
of our incomes to charitable purposes. They are really good as far as
they go, but fall short of developing the great principle of love to God
and man as the motive of all giving to religious objects. Their
tendency is more to make giving a business, to foster habits of
giving, than to plant that deep spirit of Christian sympathy which
promptly, spontaneously offers the needful aid, the sustaining hand,
the cup of cold water, without staying to consult the state of *the charitable fund,* or acting from the impulse of a regular habit.

ON THE ENGLISH POOR-LAWS, AND THE LITERATURE TO WHICH THEY
HAVE GIVEN ORIGIN.

If the English Church has abjured all charge of the poor, neither
feeding them, nor lodging them, nor clothing them, nor visiting them
in prison, nor administering the cup of cold water to the thirsty; if
English libraries furnish, neither by churchman, nor statesman, nor philanthropist, any complete treatise upon Christian Charity, the language
is by no means deficient in literature of the poor; we mean, not poor
literature, nor literature for the poor, but literature of the "Poor-
laws." When the English civil authorities assumed the charge of the
poor, whom the Church rejected, they undertook a most dangerous
and difficult task, as the whole history of their poor-administration
proves. We do not say it would have been done better by any other
authorities, for we admit it was the most difficult undertaking ever
assumed by civil authorities. The management of the poor in England has given birth to volumes of legislative enactments, volumes of
judicial decisions on questions as to whether a pauper belonged to
one parish or another, as to what sort of residence constituted a claim
to relief, as to which parish the burden of the pauper belonged to, and
which should be exempted from affording any aid; volumes upon the
most economical mode of feeding and keeping these burdens of the
parishes; volumes on the history of the poor-laws and their administration; on the management of the poor; on their employment,
on workhouses, on the history of the poor, and on the poor-rates.
This literature is unique—there is no parallel to it in any country. It
exhibits a constant series of writers struggling against the whole
system, disgusted with it, or approving it only as an inevitable evil
without remedy; but all unable to rise to the Christian solution of the
subject. The Protestants of England had absolutely lost sight of the
relations between Christianity and poverty, and numberless humane
writers were racking their brains during centuries to find some plan
or theory in regard to the poor which might meet the object and quiet
disturbed consciences. But no solution appeared, and the evil continually increased. We may characterize the actual state of the poor
and the legislation for the poor during nearly the whole of this period
by the following extract from a work of the highest authority, "The
History of the Poor Laws," by Richard Burn, L.L. D. 1 vol. 8vo.
London, 1764.

"THE OFFICE OF AN OVERSEER OF THE POOR seems to be understood to be this:
To keep an extraordinary lookout to prevent persons coming to inhabit [his
parish] without certificates, and to fly to the justices to remove them; and if a
man brings a certificate, then to caution all the inhabitants not to let him a
farm of £10 a year, [which would give him a settlement in the parish,] and to
take care to keep him out of all parish offices; to warn them, if they will hire
servants, to hire them half-yearly, or by the month, or by the week, or by the
day, rather than by any way that shall give them a settlement [which entitles
them to relief in case of their becoming poor;] or, if they do hire them for a year,
then to try and pick a quarrel with them before the year's end, and so to get rid
of them. To maintain their poor as cheaply as possibly they can, at all events;
not to lay out twopence in prospect of any future good, but only to serve the
present necessity. To bargain with some sturdy person to take them by the
lump, who yet is not intended to take them, but to hang over them *in terrorem*,
if they shall complain to the justices for want of maintenance. To send them
out into the country abegging; for why not they, as well as others? To bind
out poor children apprentices, no matter to whom or to what trade, so that the
master live in another parish. To move heaven and earth, if any dispute happens about a settlement, and, in that particular, to invert the general rule, and
stick at no expense. To pull down cottages. To drive out as many inhabitants
and admit as few as possibly they can; that is, to depopulate the parish in
order to lessen the poor-rate.   To be generous indeed, in sometimes giving a
portion with the mother of a bastard child to the reputed father, on condition
that he will marry her [and support her;] or with a poor widow, for why should
she be without the comforts of matrimony?—always provided that the husband
is settled in another parish. Or, if a poor man with a large family appears to
be industrious, they will charitably assist him in taking a farm in another
parish at £10 a year, and give him the money to pay his first year's rent; and
if any of the poor have a mercantile genius, they will purchase him a box of
pins, needles, laces, buckles, and such-like wares, and send him abroad in the
quality of a petty chapman: with the profits thereof, and a moderate knack at
stealing, he can decently support himself, and educate his children in the same
industrious way."—Page 211.

A CATALOGUE OF SOME ENGLISH WORKS ON THE POOR-LAWS AND
THEIR ADMINISTRATION, AND ON THE POOR.

Proposals for Employing the Poor, by T. Firmin,	London,	1678
Provision for the Poor, by Sir M. Hale,	"	1683
Proposals for a College of Industry, by John Bellers,	"	1696
Giving Alms no Charity, by Daniel Defoe,	"	1704
Effectual Provision for the Poor, by H. Fielding,	"	1753
Defects of the Poor-laws, by Th. Alcock, 8vo.	"	1752
Considerations on Better Management of the Poor, 4to.	"	1752
Of the Care of the Poor in most Civilized Nations, by Richard Onely, 4to.	"	1758

Causes of the Increase of the Poor, by Josiah Tucker, 4to.······London, 1760
Letters on the Rising Generation of the Labouring Part of our
    Fellow-subjects, by Jonas Hanway, 2 vols. 8vo. ·········· " 1767
A Dissertation on the Poor-laws, by Rev. Joseph Townsend, 8vo. " 1786
Causes of Increase of Poor and Poor-rates, by Rev. John
    Howlett, 8vo.··· " 1788
History of the Poor, by Thomas Ruggles, 2 vols. 8vo.·········· " 1793

This writer first clearly announced the wrong which the Established Church had done to the poor, by taking possession of and holding the church property given for the relief of the poor. It is said he was compelled by clerical influence to expurgate his work and publish without these objectionable allegations upon the purity of the Church.

Means of Providing Employment for the People, a Prize Essay,
    by Samuel Crumpe, 8vo.······························London, 1795
The Case of Labourers in Husbandry stated, by Rev. D. Davis, 4to. " 1795
The State of the Poor; or, a History of the Labouring Classes in
    England from the Conquest to the Present Period; their
    Domestic Economy, with respect to diet, dress, fuel, habi-
    tation, and plans adopted for their relief, by Sir F. M.
    Eden, 3 vols. 4to. ····································· " 1797

This is the most elaborate work to which this fruitful topic has given rise. It is highly valuable in the sense in which this subject was viewed. It descends to the merest minutiæ of food and clothing, and sifts numberless reports, documents, and accounts, to exhibit the true cost of maintaining the poor during the period to which it relates. The treatment of the poor is discussed solely in the light of economy. It is the best history of prices for the last three centuries extant, and is, otherwise, an important collection of facts. Can any thing more strongly exhibit the blindness of English people to the true relations of this subject, than that a work of 3 vols. 4to. could be written upon the State of the Poor, from the Conquest to the year 1797, on which so little should be said upon the true nature of the claims of the poor and the obligations of the rich? The author has, however, said enough to show that he was not ignorant of the truth, but he evidently considers that view of the subject as one of small importance.

Inquiry into the Policy and Humanity of the poor laws, by J.
    Weyland, 8vo.···London.
A Treatise on Indigence, by P. Colquhoun, 8vo. [This is not ele-
    mentary, as its title imports.]························· " 1808
Systematic Relief of Poor in different Countries, by J. Duncan, · Bath, 1815

Report and Evidence on Mendicity in the Metropolis, to House
of Commons, folio·······································London, 1815
Condition of Labouring Classes of Society, by John Barton, 8vo. " 1817
Report to House of Commons on Poor-laws, ················ 1817
Remarks on the Report on the Poor-laws, by J. H. Moggridge, 8vo. Bristol, 1818
Causes of Depreciation of Agricultural Labour, by J. Barton,···London, 1820
Administration of the Poor-laws, by Rev. C. D. Brereton, 8vo.··Norwich, 1823
Workhouse System,···························same···· " ·· " 1826
Causes and Remedies of Modern Pauperism, ···same····· " ·· " 1827
Poor-laws, as a Scheme of Benevolence and as to their Political
Economy, by J. E. Bicheno, 8vo.·······················London, 1824
Principle of English Poor-laws Defended, by F. Page, 8vo. Bath, 1822 " 1830
Reports to House of Commons, 1824 and 1825, on Condition of
Manufacturing Population, folio,·····················
Nature, Extent, and Effects of Pauperism, by Thos. Walker,··· " 1826
Administration of Poor-laws, by T. Calvert, ················ " 1831
Christian and Civic Economy of Large Towns, by Thomas Chal-
mers, D. D., 3 vols. 8vo.····························· 1821-26
Causes and Remedies of Pauperism in Great Britain, by R. Wil-
mot Horton, 8vo.·······································London, 1830
Moral and Physical Condition of Working Classes, by J. H.
Kay, M. D., 8vo.·· " 1832
The Poor and the Labouring Classes in America and Europe, by
N. W. Senior, 8vo.····································· " 1835
Manufacturing Population of England, Moral, Social, and Physi-
cal, by P. Gaskell, 8vo.································· " 1833
The History of the Middle and Working Classes,—the Economi-
cal and Political Principles which have influenced the
Past and Present Condition of the Industrious Orders, by
John Wade,·· " 1833

Several editions of this valuable work have appeared since.

The Agricultural Classes of Great Britain and Ireland, with
Extracts from Parliamentary Reports from 1833 to 1840,
Remarks of the French Editor, published at Vienna, with
a Preface, by Henry Drummond, Esq., 2 vols. 8vo.······· " 1842

This mystified title, doubtless, is but a thin covering to the fact that
H. Drummond is responsible for the work.

National Distress, its Causes and Remedies, by Samuel Laing,
Esq. Jun., 8vo. ·····································London, 1844
The Working Classes, their Moral, Social, and Intellectual con-
dition, with Suggestions for their Improvement, by G.
Simmons, 12mo.·· " 1849
The Social Condition and Education of the People in England
and Europe, by Joseph Kay, 2 vols. 8vo. ················ " 1850

THE POPULATION QUESTION AND ITS DISCUSSIONS.

The discussions carried on in the books on the subject of the poor and poor-laws were much enlivened by the publication of the Rev. T. R. Malthus, in 1798, of "An Essay on the Principle of Population, as it Affects the Future Improvement of Society," London, 8vo., already referred to by our author, who has quoted some of its positions, (*ante,* page 150.)

Malthus produced nothing very original; he merely reduced English feeling and usages in regard to the poor into a philosophy. Previous to this publication, the questions discussed had been chiefly as to points of economy in keeping the poor, and the very point of feeding had been assiduously ascertained, discussed, and tried: it had also been a matter of much inquiry how far and in what way the labour of paupers might be made to pay for their maintenance. In these inquiries, nothing, however small or unimportant, escaped remark: in a question of economy, a very small saving, even that of a few pence in a year, made a large sum when multiplied by the poor of England. The keeper of one of the workhouses once made the important discovery that the constant use of the same scales in weighing out paupers' rations had worn upon one side of the scales so as sensibly to affect the adjustment. This was brought forward at the meeting of the superintendents as indicating the means of a considerable economy. But no one, who has not looked into the details which occupied the attention of writers and administrators of the poor-laws, can conceive to what a nicety of management this economy was carried. A question of moment was debated by many, while the attention of others was directed to the point of economy,—that of the propriety of any compulsory provision for the poor; some alleging that the poor ought to be left to the charity of individuals—any public provision made for them only encouraging idleness and consequent pauperism. Others averred that there must be paupers, and that they could be more economically kept upon some general plan, applicable to all, and that allowing hordes of beggars to stroll through the kingdom was an annoyance not to be endured. It was much discussed whether paupers should be confined, families being separated, in poorhouses, or let out to the farmers, upon the best terms obtainable. In the midst of these and many like debates, Mr. Malthus appeared, and announced that he had discovered the philosophy of the

whole matter. He took the discussion by the horns, and rejected all
the previous plans and opinions, compulsory provision, economy, and
all. He told the people of England, they were fast approaching a period when the population would exceed the supply of food, and that it
was unjust and unphilosophical to nurture and keep alive men who
would soon take the bread out of the mouths of those who were now so
generously feeding them. Let them alone, they will only die by privation—they came unbidden to the banquet of life—there is no place
for them; do not let them usurp your places at the feast; do not give
them a morsel; if let alone, nature will execute her decrees, and send
them out of the way. This philosophy of Mr. Malthus made a great
sensation: to some it appeared as clear a truth as ever was announced:
others regarded it with unmingled horror and detestation. The political economists, who are supposed to look upon men as machines for the
production and distribution of wealth, took sides with Mr. Malthus.
The humane classes took the other side. After the appearance of Mr.
Malthus's work, one branch of the discussion turned upon his views,
while the others followed the old tracks. It is worthy of remark that
the cry of horror which was uttered at the first appearance of Mr.
Malthus's work, induced him to omit in subsequent editions the most
objectionable passages, and, among others, that quoted above, page 150.
But these omissions leave his theory unimpaired in its full scope.
And that is, that no one has any business to remain in this world who
cannot of himself make himself comfortable; and that great care
should be taken to avoid the increase of such people, by withdrawing
all countenance and aid from them. This theory was not suffered to
go untouched. It was attacked with great vigour and eloquence, both
in England and on the continent, and defended by Mr. Malthus and
others, with talent and learning. We give a list of a few of the works
which followed Mr. Malthus on the subject of "population."

The State of the Poor. The Principle of Mr. Malthus's Essay on Population and the Manufacturing System. Robert Southey. 80 pp.
12mo. 1812
The State of the Poor and the Means pursued by the Society for Bettering their Condition. Robert Southey. 87 pp. 12mo. 1816
A Treatise on the Records of Creation, &c., showing the Consistency of
the Principle of Population, with the Wisdom and Goodness of the
Deity, by J. B. Sumner, Bishop of Chester, 2 vols. 8vo. .... London, 1815
The Principles of Population and Production, as they are Affected by the

Progress of Society, with a view to moral and political conse-
quences. John Weyland, Jun., F. R. S. 8vo. .... London, 1816
An Inquiry into the Population of Nations, containing a Refutation of
Malthus's Essay on Population. George Ensor, 8 vo. ....London, 1818
Of Population. An Inquiry concerning the Power of Increase in the
Numbers of Mankind, being an Answer to Mr. Malthus, &c. Wm.
Godwin, 8vo.···· ....London, 1820
Illustrations and Proofs of the Principle of Population, by Francis
Place, 8vo. ....London, 1822
New Ideas of Population, with Remarks on Malthus and Godwin, by Alex.
H. Everett, Minister of the U. S. at the Netherlands, 8vo. London, 1823
Lectures on Population, with a Correspondence between the Author and
Mr. Malthus, by N. W. Senior, 8vo.......................London, 1829
The Law of Population, a Treatise in Disproof of the Super-fecundity of
Human Beings and developing the real principle of their Increase,
by M. T. Saddler, M. P., 2 vols. 8vo.......................London, 1830
An Inquiry into the Principles of Population, exhibiting a System of
Regulations for the Poor, designed to lessen and finally remove the
evils pressing upon the Labouring Classes of Society, 8vo. London, 1832
The Principles of Population and their Connection with Human Happi-
ness, by Archd. Allison, 2 vols. 8vo.....................Edinburgh, 1840
The True Law of Population shown to be connected with the Food of the
People, by Thomas Doubleday, 8vo. ....London, 1842

Besides these, very many other separate publications were made in
this controversy, which gave birth also to a large issue of pamphlets;
and the subject was largely introduced into most of the works on political economy which have appeared since the beginning of this century. It is far beyond our present purpose to offer any appreciation
of these works separately.

We regard this whole discussion as among the most remarkable of
modern times. It exhibits a virtual disregard of Christianity scarcely
to be equalled. This is evidently no special fault of the respective
writers; for they and their readers were alike involved in this utter
neglect or utter misconception of Christianity. These writers were,
many of them, far from being infidels: their reference to religion is
frequent and respectful. The marvel is that, for the solution of the
great points in dispute, they neither take nor seek any aid from Christianity. The whole subject is man, and yet humanity, in its full
meaning, is excluded from consideration. The topics are, the law of
increase; the laws of limitation; the supply of food; economy of
feeding; restraints of marriage, moral and political; police; compulsory provision; poorhouse regulations; labour, manufacturing and

agricultural. The statistics of the world were ransacked to supply materials for these and very many similar subjects. Learning and ability worthy of a better cause were most profusely expended in the wide range of these treatises. These authors and their readers grapple with a great difficulty, and, for more than a generation after the work of Malthus appeared, they struggled to produce some grand solution. But they never advanced a step. They never can, in that path. So long as those who, for the time, are rich or comfortable in life, confine themselves to the inquiry how they can perpetuate such a desirable state of things; how they can manage to hold a heavy mortgage on the labour of the masses, and make them work it out; how they can keep down the numbers of the poor to the point at which they can by their labour make up the incomes of the rich and comfortable, without risk of becoming a burden; how food and labour can be kept plenty and cheap; how one-tenth of the population can manage to live in elegance, and ease, and English comfort, whilst the nine-tenths are suffering all the degradation of mind and body, all the nakedness, and hunger, and other privations of utter poverty; and, in fine, how the poor can be best managed, to get a large living out of them, without danger of having that living absorbed in keeping them alive,—so long the Christian and only true solution of the great problem of human well-being will never be reached. In England, the rich man cannot endure to have Lazarus at his gate; he cannot endure a beggar in the highway or in his private path. The Englishman of wealth is eminently respectable. He sends the beggar to some secluded spot, where his shabby looks can offend no gentle eyes, nor spoil a landscape in which all that is permitted to be seen is beautiful and rich; he gives him work, when he has any, and food to keep him alive. But labour may be always kept plenty and cheap when nine-tenths of the people labour for one-tenth, and a very large profit may be realized on the operation; for though only half-work is required from these people, yet they are only half-fed and half-clothed. If the poor were full-fed, full-clothed, and full-worked, they would rapidly save enough to become sufficiently independent to make their own terms for their labour, and thus gradually bring about a more equal and just distribution of the avails of labour.

In all this prolonged discussion, none of those engaged ever fairly rose to the conception that every Christian man is a guardian of the poor, under religious obligations to succour all the suffering within his reach, and, not only to assist individuals, but, according to the example of his Divine Master, to feed and help the multitudes. The sacrifice necessary to accomplish any great change in the position of the poor in England appeared greater than any government dared require of the governed, or was able to effect without some flagrant and unjustifiable violations of the right of property. It did not occur to these authors that this sacrifice could come from the spontaneous action of the people under the pressure of religious motives. Less effort, and, perhaps, less money than was expended upon the attempt to abolish the slave-trade, and the emancipation of the slaves in the West Indies, would have been sufficient to accomplish a thorough change of policy in regard to the poor, by which, if they were not immediately lifted above the state of poverty, they would be lifted into a state of hope, and the energies of men, long paralyzed with despair, would be roused to successful action.

We believe that no ingenuity, no talent, no effort of any human intellect can solve the questions involved in those discussions, so long as such data are assumed as a basis of discussion. That door is irrevocably shut against human eyes and human strength. It is not for men to adjust the food of the world to the population of the world, and much less is it for them, as assumed by Malthus and those of his school, to adjust the population of the world to the food of the world. This partakes rather too much of an intervention in the Divine government—of assuming the reins of Providence. There were questions to be solved, doubtless, growing out of the position of the poor in England, but the true solution could never be reached by speculations upon the possible increase of food or the possible increase of population, compulsory provision, parish charge, out-door, in-door, or workhouse relief. All these questions assumed that all was right in British institutions except what was referred to, and of course the disputants did not even touch the elements of the subject. The real questions are,—How can the labour of man be best applied to subserve the necessities and comforts of man ? As it is plain, from the order of Providence, from the inequalities in the mental and physical energies and faculties of men, that some must act under the direction of others, or, perhaps, fall under their dominion, what should be the limit of the power thus attainable? To what extent may the labour of a few or of many be mortgaged for the benefit of those who, by superior industry, or talents, or energy, may be able to subject them to their power?

And, if Christianity be heard on a subject so vitally interwoven with its precepts, what light is shed upon this topic by the life and instructions of its Great Author?

If it be objected that this abstract consideration of the subject could not lead to any practical result, because all such questions arise under actual governments and established institutions, which must, more or less, modify every decision, the reply is, that the abstract truth must be discovered and fully understood before it can be ascertained how far existing laws and institutions stand in the way of reform. When the truth shall be known, the obstacles will be known, and plans of reform can be devised, including such political changes as may be needful for complete success. Shall this whole discussion be excluded from the pale of Christianity? In all matters of politics, and in all of humanity, shall Christians always walk through the world with their lights deeply shaded, that they may appear to be as much in the dark as those who are groping round them?

In all this controversy about "population," no event is more striking than the advent upon the arena of Dr. Thomas Chalmers, the great Scottish divine. He entered upon the subject with all the zeal which belonged to his character, and, though he shed a flood of light upon it, and has left a mine of materials for future labourers in that career, he has added another to the many instances, that clear and powerful thinkers do not always, nor even soonest, reach the truth. He failed to assume the proper elements in his outset, to lay the right foundation for his structure, and therefore failed in erecting a well-proportioned superstructure. He saw, at a glance, that the English system of providing for the poor was both impolitic and unchristian. He dashed into the contest and made his efforts felt on every side. He was the first who fairly carried Christianity into the field, and demonstrated that to Christians and Christian ministers belonged the care of the poor. Himself a minister of the Established Church of Scotland, he unfortunately took his whole survey of the subject from that point of view. He set out with the proposition in his mind, that to the parishes, as such, of an Established Church, belonged the charge of the poor. Having once assumed this wrong ground, he went into the discussion with extraordinary power and ardour, carrying with him, in far greater degree than any who had preceded him, a truly Christian desire to redress the wrongs of the poor. It can scarcely be doubted that the absorbing interest of this subject, and his ardour in maintaining a position which he deemed to be the only one consonant with Christianity, accounts for that almost bigoted devotion to an established church, which Dr. Chalmers displayed for many years of his life. Looking upon the parish churches and their officers as the proper guardians of the poor, he could not but regard with impatience any voluntary system or dissenting churches, as so many disorganizers, who complicated his plans for the poor and weakened the only churches upon whom he supposed any reliance could be placed for performing the great office of relieving suffering humanity. It is pleasant to discover what thus accounts so favourably for what appeared to be the greatest defect in Dr. Chalmers's character. His zeal for the poor made him, for a time, an uncompromising opponent of Christian freedom. The severe lesson he received before his death, in the disruption of the Scotch Establishment, and the noble sacrifice of sentiment he made by uniting in the secession, showed how far he was above preserving consistency at the expense of truth. He suffered in this more mental agony, probably, than any other individual who left the Establishment. How his opinions were modified, in regard to the poor, we are not informed, but we feel confident, that if the occasion had offered to produce another work on the subject, it would have been what is yet a *desideratum* in Christian literature. Dr. Chalmers's error, in the first place, was assuming the parish churches to be the proper guardians of the poor, instead of taking the higher ground that every Christian is a guardian of the poor, and insisting upon the great law which requires us to love our neighbour as ourselves. His system of action should have been developed from that law, and not from the duty of parish churches. He could then, without difficulty, have reached and brought in the agency of congregations under all systems of religion, both established and voluntary. When the duties of individual Christians towards the suffering are all discharged, there will not be much left for parish churches or separate congregations to perform.

But though Dr. Chalmers committed this error, and though he failed in his "Christian and Civic Economy of Large Towns," to produce the work which was needed, and though political economists, so called, have not assigned a high rank to that production, it contains more truth, more profound Christian philosophy, more pure Christian sympathy for the poor than any one to which the controversy has given rise.

The following extracts from Chalmers's "Christian and Civic Economy" will help to illustrate the subject of the foregoing pages, and afford a specimen of the manner and tone of his work:

" There are many towns in our empire, where the Establishment has not provided room in churches for one-tenth of the inhabitants." . . . . " It is clear, in these circumstances, that the vast majority must be left to wander without the pale of Christian ministrations, and Christian ordinances, altogether— where they have settled down into a mass of heathenism, which, to the eye of common experience, looks completely irrecoverable. There is a very general feeling of helplessness and despair upon this subject, as if the profligacy and ungodliness of cities were elements in every way as unconquerable as is physical necessity itself." . . . .

" All serving to confirm the general hopelessness that there is upon the subject, and to afford a plausible warrant for the contempt wherewith schemes of philanthropy are so apt to be regarded by the more secular and sober-minded of our citizens, who feel satisfied with things as they are, nor want their quiescence to be at all disturbed by any suggestion or demonstration, whatever, of things as they should be."

" It has transformed the whole character of charity, by turning a matter of love into a matter of litigation: and so, has seared and shut many a heart, out of which the spontaneous emanations of good-will would have gone plentifully forth among the abodes of the destitute. We know not how a more freezing arrest can be laid on the current of benevolence, than when it is met in the tone of a rightful, and perhaps, indignant demand for that, wherewith it was ready, on its own proper impulse, to pour refreshment and relief over the whole field of ascertained wretchedness. There is a mighty difference of effect between an imperative and an imploring application. The one calls out the jealousy of our nature, and puts us upon the attitude of surly and determined resistance. The other calls out the compassion of our nature, and inclines us to the free and willing movements of generosity. It is in the former attitude, that, under a system of overgrown pauperism, we now, generally speaking, behold the wealthy in reference to the working classes of England. They stand to each other in a grim array of hostility— the one thankless and dissatisfied, and stoutly challenging as its due, what the other reluctantly yields, and that as sparingly as possible. Had such been a right state of things, then pity would have been more a superfluous feeling in our constitution; as its functions would have been nearly superseded by the operation of law and justice. And the truth is, that this sweetener of the ills of life has been greatly stifled by legislation; while the amount of actual and unrelieved wretchedness among the peasantry of England too plainly demonstrates, that the economy of pauperism has failed to provide an adequate substitute in its room. Were this economy simply broken up, and the fountain of human sympathy again left free to be operated upon by its wonted excitements, and to send out its wonted streams throughout those manifold subordinations by which the various classes of society are bound and amalgamated together—we doubt not that from this alone a more abundant, or, at least, a far more efficient and better spread tide of charity would be diffused throughout the habitations of indigence." . . . .

" And we fear not, on the other hand, the dislike of the theologian to our announcement, that the pauperism itself is a moral nuisance, which must be swept away from these realms, ere we can rationally hope for a very powerful or prevalent spirit of Christianity in the land. That which letteth must be taken out of the way. It is, indeed, a heavy incumbrance on the work of a clergyman, whose office it is to substitute among his people the graces of a new character, for the hardness, and selfishness, and the depraved tendencies of nature, that, in addition to the primary and essential evils of the human constitution, he has to struggle, in his holy warfare, against a system so replete as pauperism is, with all that can minister to the worst, or that can wither up the best affections of our species." . . . .

" We hold pauperism to be a still more deadly antagonist to the morality of our nation." . . . . " Like the Malaire in Italy, it has now attained a progress and a virulency, which begin to be contemplated with the awe of some great approaching desolation ; and a sense of helplessness mingles with the terror which is inspired by the forebodings of a mighty disaster, that has been gathering along the lapse of time, into a more distinct shape and more appalling magnitude. It is indeed, a frightful spectacle ; and the heart of the Christian, as well as of the civil philanthropist, ought to be solemnized by it. He, of all men, should not look on with indifference, while the vapour of this teeming exhalation so thickens and spreads itself throughout the whole moral atmosphere of our land : And, when he witnesses the fell malignity of its operation, both on the graver and more amiable virtues of our nature,—when he sees how diligence in the callings, and economy in the habits of individuals, are alike extinguished by it, and both the tendernesses of relationship and the wider charities of life, are chilled and overborne—we should expect of this friend to the higher interests of our species, that he, among all his fellows, would be most intent on the destruction of a system that so nips the best promises of spiritual cultivation, and, under the balefulness of whose shadow, are now withering into rapid decay, and sure annihilation, the very fairest of the fruits of righteousness."

If companionship in crime or in adversity make strange bedfellows, so companionship in error affords not less curious specimens of incongruous fellowship. Parties, having taken their sides with little or no reference to Christianity, lug it in to serve the purposes of the discussion, to turn a period or to point a sneer, according to the disposition of the writer. It was not the object of even Chalmers to solve the question by means of Christian truth, but to establish his position that compulsory provisions for the poor were of evil tendency, and that the proper charge of the poor belonged to the parish officials of an

established church. This view did not afford him a fair opportunity
to explain the nature of Christian charity; it was not his topic,—he
did not attempt a full exposition, and Christianity only plays a subordinate part in the system of Dr. Chalmers. Wayland, in his work on
" Population," refers to revelation throughout, as offering the only true
solution, but, though his book is in many respects well written, his exhibition of the bearing of Christianity on this subject is very feeble,
and shows how slightly he felt its power, and how little he knew its
scope. It is worth observing, in these various authors, their various
modes of referring to the truths of Holy Writ as furnishing a curious
and instructive exhibition of the human mind and human nature.
But no one can fully understand the relations of Christianity to this
subject, as fixed by the various writers, who has not fully mastered
the spirit and details of the leading author, Malthus, whose " Essay
on Population" has, ever since it appeared, ruled the faith of a large
number of disciples. It would be difficult to point out a publication
as thoroughly infidel in its spirit and tendencies. When taken up, out
of the controversy about population, and regarded from the side of
Christianity, the book cannot be read without an accumulating sense
of contempt, horror, and indignation. Yet this is the standard book
in English literature on this subject; its positions are regarded as impregnable by a very large body of the educated people of Great Britain; and its contents are the received doctrine of all the political
economists, strictly so called, of Europe and America.

Yet Dr. Chalmers is found battling by the side of Malthus, both
agreeing in the opposition to a compulsory legal provision for the poor ;
and we find him writing to his friend Morton—

" Mr. Malthus's theory upon this subject would have carried me without examples. But it seldom happens that a speculation so apparently paradoxical,
is so well supported by the most triumphant exemplifications."*

It is scarcely to be wondered that, when such a man can receive such
theories and speculations so kindly, the world around him should do so
likewise. But, whatever the number of Malthus's innocent disciples,
there were not wanting many who detected the cloven foot. On the
Continent, especially, many, who did not belong to the stricter school of
political economists, denounced the work as atrocious and unchristian.
It required an infidel to detect an infidel, according to the spirit of the
old proverb: and thus was effected a complete exposure of the fallacies,

---

* Life of Chalmers, vol. ii. 386.

the inhumanity, and the infidelity of a work professedly friendly to Christianity, the production of one of its ministers. It was Wm. Godwin, who, writing "Of Population," gave the first effectual check to the spread of Malthusian doctrines. Without any reference to the argument and the facts of Godwin, in which unusual ability is evinced, as opposed to those of Malthus, we cannot but advert to the effectiveness of the excoriation which he applied to Malthus and his opinions: not content with ·this, he crushes him indignantly as a venomous reptile. The morbid exposure is frightful ; such a literary smashing was rarely or never seen, and never more richly merited. If a butchery like this, were unbecoming a Christian, it is the only pretence upon which the shame of leaving its execution to an infidel can be justified.

Of course, such a punishment will neither bear transfer nor abridgment, but we must not let the occasion pass without giving a specimen of Mr. Godwin. The portentous evil which Mr. Malthus held up to frighten the world was, the fact asserted by him, that population tended to increase in a geometrical ratio, and subsistence in an arithmetical ratio :

Thus, Food,   1 2 3 4 5 6 7   8   9
Population, 1 2 4 8 16 32 64 128 256.

"This, then, is the precise outline of Mr. Malthus's system. The evils against which he would guard are hunger and famine ; the remedies for these evils are vice and misery."* Unimpeded increase would, "in less than two thousand years, people the whole visible universe, at the rate of four men to every yard square."† It must, of course, have required a vast deal of vice and misery to counteract such a ratio of increase as that imports. Mr. Malthus, to remove some of the harshness of his conclusions in the earlier editions of his work, introduces another check to population, which he calls "moral restraint," but he constantly insinuates a caution against any reliance upon it. He finds that "in past ages it has operated with very inconsiderable force," and he is not visionary enough to entertain "any opinion respecting the future improvement of society, in which he is not borne out by the experience of the past." His main dependence, therefore, against the enormous calamity of an over-peopled world, is vice and misery. Mr. Malthus "sits remote, like a malignant providence dispensing from his magazine all the various iniquities and miseries of life, which, sooner or later," in

---

* Godwin on Population, chap. i. book vi. 516.   † Malthus, vol. ii. p. 344, note.

various degrees, contribute to shorten the natural duration of human
life. "That is the desideratum."*

He examines the population of all the countries of the world, and
finds confirmation of his doctrine everywhere—vice and misery in
abundance ; he does not discriminate, and cares not for kind or degree,
so it be inherent and effective. If inherent in the constitution of all
societies, it must operate in every condition of the human family. He
finds, therefore, that " human institutions, however they may appear to
be the causes of much mischief to society, are in reality light and
superficial,—mere feathers that float on the surface, in comparison with
those deeper causes of evil which result from the laws of nature and
the passions of men." It is visionary to think that any improved form
of government could overcome the vice and misery which prevail as
checks to population, and if they could, they would become the cause
of still greater evils. Mr. Malthus can descant pleasantly upon the
benefits and beauties of Christianity, but these benefits and beauties are reserved for those only in the higher walks of life, and if it
were otherwise, Christianity must of itself become a nuisance. A large
portion of the pages of the " Essay on Population" are devoted to
speculations on the diminution of mortality. This would seem, at first
sight, against the spirit of the whole treatise. A closer examination
reveals the harmony of his opinions.

It will be found, that all the plans of reducing mortality involve
the previous processes of thinning the ranks from which death can
pluck his victims. If vice and misery can be made to reduce the
numbers of the present generation below the average, then there must
be fewer deaths hereafter, because fewer men to die. As the world will
go on to double its population every twenty-five years, unless something is done to prevent it, and as Mr. Malthus feels it to be rather
awkward to rely entirely for remedy upon vice and misery, without,
at least, mentioning other remedies, he discusses divers modes of reducing the numbers of mankind. As men are coming into the world
faster than they can be provided for, it becomes a question what is to
be done with the new-comers. Mr. Malthus discovers the law which
must, of necessity, govern the case. They come into a world already
possessed and fully occupied. There is not room for all,—who must
give way, the possessors or the interlopers ? It is perfectly clear that
those who have the ground and the property, " have a right to do what

---

* Godwin on Population, chap. i. book vi. 520.

they please with their own." It follows, that "we are bound in justice and honour, formally, to disclaim the *right* of the poor to support." This includes all the poor, the maimed, the blind, the sick, and suffering of every description. The poor-laws of England are, in his estimation, "an evil, in comparison of which, the national debt, with all its magnitude of terror, is of little moment."* The law of Mr. Malthus, then, is, that men who came into the world must support themselves, or those who bring them in must support them: if they fail or die in the attempt, they but execute the laws of nature upon themselves; they have no right to obtrude themselves upon the notice of those who are comfortably enjoying the banquet of life, much less any right to claim any portion from a feast to which they were not invited.

Mr. Godwin quotes freely from the New Testament the law of love as set forth in the precepts of Christ—the command to the young man who alleged he had kept all the commandments from his youth up, "Go sell that thou hast and give to the poor." On this, Godwin remarks :—

"There is a kind of oriental boldness in this, at least, considered as a general exposition of the moral law; for it would be reasonable to answer, If it is my duty to render the greatest benefit to my fellow-creatures, and if my mind is well prepared to discharge this duty, it will, probably, be better done by my devoting my income to this purpose, than by at once divesting myself of the principal."

"But nothing can be more clear than the general tenor of revelation on this question. By it we are instructed that we are stewards, not proprietors of the good things of this life, we are forbidden to pamper our appetites or our vanity, we are commanded to be fellow-workers with and impartial ministers of the bountiful principle of nature, and we are told that, when we have done all, we have done nothing of which we have any right to boast."

"Such are the dictates of Christian revelation, and such is the answer to Mr. Malthus's position that 'every man has a right to do what he will with his own.'"—Godwin, Of Population, chap. iii. book vi. p. 544.

"Thus stood the principles of morality," remarks Mr. Godwin, after making these quotations from the teaching of Christ, "before Mr. Malthus wrote his Essay on Population." The rich man believed in them, though he constantly violated them by wantonly expending on his appetites and vanity, sums for which his conscience as con-

---

* Malthus, Vol. II. 307. The public debt was then £850,000,000, and the interest £47,000,000. The poor-rates were £3,000,000.

stantly reproached him. This was some check. The poor man
believed in them, though he saw how little they prevailed in the
world. He believed that the unfortunate, the disabled, and deserving
poor had a right to support, "a belief in which he was borne out by
the light of nature and by the gospel. Neither the evangelists, nor
apostles, nor the Holy Spirit that inspired them, were aware that all
these maxims were subverted by the principle of population." Mr.
Malthus has changed the situation of the rich and poor. To the poor
he has taught that, if they receive any relief, they owe it not to any
right, but to what he calls the spontaneous charity and pure benevolence of the rich; his opinion being that "private charity almost
invariably leads to pernicious consequences," and public charity he
condemns without any reservation.

"To the rich he has read an important lesson. A great portion of this class
of society are sufficiently indisposed to acts of charity, and eminently disposed
to the indulgence of their appetites and their vanity. But hitherto they had
secretly reproached themselves with this as an offence against God and man.
Mr. Malthus has been the first man to perform the grateful task of reconciling
their conduct and their consciences, and to show them that when they thought
they were indulging themselves in vice, they were in reality conferring a most
eminent and praiseworthy benefit upon the community."—Godwin, p. 548.

THE PUSEYITES.—ANOTHER PHASE OF THE CONTROVERSY ABOUT
POPULATION AND PAUPERISM.

We have seen that Chalmers and Malthus were found side by side
in their opposition to a compulsory provision for the poor, but, with
what different ultimate objects! Chalmers, to secure a kinder administration, and a more effectual maintenance; Malthus, to let their own
improvidence and misery bring them to a rapid end, that, by thinning
the ranks of men now, the mortality hereafter might be diminished.
We now bring forward another collaborator, from a different school,
having his point of agreement, also, with these anti-champions of the
poor-laws. A class of religionists has become conspicuous in Great
Britain since Malthus and Chalmers wrote, who, as is generally the
case with new sects, are divisible into two camps. The Puseyites may
be divided into the sincere, but deluded and mistaken; and the designing and unprincipled, who are always ready to lead any squadrons
of the ignorant or superstitious. No drifting mob of humanity can go
long without a leader. It may be well feared that, as we find many
good and sincere people among the Puseyites, they were made so by

contemplating Protestantism as it is displayed in the Church of England. The purer and more conscientious they were, the greater their detestation of her character and doings. If too religious to become infidels, and too refined to become mere disciples of Christ, they naturally turned their faces towards Rome. Among this class of the sincere and deluded, many writers have appeared whose pages breathe a spirit of pure piety, which is destined to meet very little sympathy in the Romish Church, to which it is tending. The leaders who are steadily guiding this deluded cohort to Rome, no doubt suffer the expression of such opinions among those in their train, knowing that, once safe in Popedom, such absurd goodness will soon be rubbed off or laughed out of countenance. The writer to whom we are now to refer is the Rev. Wm. Sewell, B. D., Author of CHRISTIAN POLITICS, and late Professor of Moral Philosophy in the University of Oxford. He plainly sees the incompatibility of the English poor-laws with Christianity; he freely admits that the poor are the charge of Christians, and, with Chalmers, he sees no way of discharging that duty but through the officials of an established church—not such as Chalmers had in his eye, nor such as exists in England, but a real priesthood after the order of the papacy of the Middle Ages. But, however antiquated the plan of Mr. Sewell for the care of the poor, what he says about them is deserving the attention of all; and evinces clearly that his heart is in the right place, however wrong his head or perverted his judgment.

"Poverty, in some shape or other, is an essential condition of political society, and it will increase in proportion with the accumulation of money; because capital has always a tendency to drain and absorb into itself all the lesser springs of wealth by its command over labour, and competition will drive wages down to the lowest possible prices. But these questions, and the whole theory of national wealth, require to be examined at length; and a Christian political economy would form a necessary appendage to Christian politics, and must be reserved for such a place.

"But, as a fact, the mass of poverty has now swelled in this country to a pitch which threatens to overflow and devastate society itself. With a free trade and a manufacturing system, it could not be otherwise. The interference of the legislature is demanded. All eyes are turned to its omnipotent arm; and it proceeds to act. It gathers under its protection the starving, houseless, miserable beings, whom the avarice of their employers has called into existence by the demand for labour, and then left them to perish in the fluctuations of employment, or has reduced them to the minimum of subsistence, and therefore to demoralization and despair. But it is compelled to gather them in masses, by broad, palpable lines of distinction; because the state has no delicate discriminating eyes, none of the finer organs of prehension and selection, which are required to separate between the bad and the good; the industrious and the idle; the poverty which is a fault, from that which is misfortune; that which demands consolation, from that which requires chastisement; the improving from the reprobate and lost. Its seat of action is too far removed to penetrate into the cottage and the hovel, to hear the tale of distress, and to balance degrees of indiscretion, or suffering, or crime. And no instruments can it create to execute such a task, because it can retain them by pay only, and hired servants can have neither the feeling nor the zeal to attempt it well. There is, indeed, in every parish, one or more persons, of whose sacred and appointed functions it is an especial part to care for the poor—the servants of a Divine Master who was born in a stable and laid in a manger; who, as far as personal enjoyment is concerned, are themselves pledged to poverty; whose office it is to watch over the souls of those around them, and therefore to discriminate characters; who can give alms without degrading the receivers; who can add to them a double grace and double comfort by words of blessing and advice; who are solemnly devoted to this work, whether the state employ their services or not; and who, by the ministrations of religion, can render even destitution tolerable, and raise even idleness and profligacy to an honest and respectable industry. The clergy are the clergy for the poor." . . . .

"The clergy must be set aside; and the poor must be fed and clothed by a Board of Poor-law Commissioners, who have no religious preference whatever. What follows? Destitute of the means of discriminating character, and justly afraid of encouraging every kind of vice and evil by an indiscriminating charity, they are compelled, I will not say to regard poverty as a crime, but to deal with it as if it were such; to reduce their alms down to the lowest possible point at which life can be maintained—life without hope, without dignity, without enjoyment, without possibility of improvement—one stern, cheerless, dreary, dismal protraction of imprisonment and privation, that all may be discouraged from approaching it. Whether it be from prudence towards the poor, or from selfish economy for itself, the civil power cannot hold out any alms, which are not wrung and counted out like drops of blood, and given with a curse, the curse of niggardliness and reproach, rather than with a blessing.

"But the necessity of economy and privation renders another step equally necessary. The home cannot be permitted to remain; expenses cannot be curtailed, nor enjoyments restricted, where the poor are allowed to expend what they receive in the bosom of their families; and therefore they must be gathered together under one roof. Oh, how thwarted nature and despised truth will avenge themselves at last; and, if we refuse to receive and honour them in their genuine forms, will compel us to fall down and worship some deformed idol, which we erect, without knowing it, after their mutilated image! It is necessary that some men be poor. It may be good for us all to abandon wealth, even if we are not abandoned by it. And social life is a blessing: and for those who have no firesides, it is charity to provide a home, after the model of a family, where they may live under a wise and merciful restraint, and have their affections developed and their energies exercised, and even accomplish

many a grand and noble work, by united labour, which cannot be attempted
by individuals." . . . .

"And in the nineteenth century, when we boast of having receded so far
from such ignorance and superstition, that we cannot possibly relapse to it,
suddenly, at the call of the most vague latitudinarianism, there rise up on
every side vast houses and refuges of the poor, maintained not by religious
alms, but by extorted taxes; and, containing in their system, almost every cir-
cumstance which has been either wrongly ridiculed by the bad, or justly condemned by the good, in the system of monasticism; omitting only that which
commanded the reverence of all—religion.

"There is poverty, but forced, not voluntary; privation and fasting, but
reluctant sufferings, not self-denying and repentant discipline. There is seclu-
sion from the world without contemplation, or any of the benefits of retirement.
There is endless, hopeless fixedness of lot, but riveted by the denial of all
means of improving the condition, not by vows, which, however erroneously
taken, were at least dignified by their sacredness. There is labour, wasted and
unproductive; society, without any bond of union but common degradation
and restraint; and dependence upon others, but on their grudging penurious-
ness, not on their benevolence and love. There is celibacy, or a compulsory
disruption of the marriage-ties, but with no holy thoughts or high aspirations
to purify and guard it from crime. There is a breaking up of the family and
the home, but without creating any community of love to supply its place.
There is a badge stamped upon all inmates, separating them from the rest of
their fellows, but neither holding up before the world the memorial of higher
duties and purer feelings than the world at large permits, no giving dignity
and elevation to them who bear it, but branding them with a mark of infamy,
as the paupers of a poorhouse. And there are no duties to animate or dignify.
Shame, but not for sin—fear, but not of God—inactivity without repose—labour without hope—ignominy without self-reproach—and punishment without
crime; such are the essential and inseparable characteristics of a system which
gathers together the good and the bad into one abode of poverty, and feeds, and
clothes, and shelters, and employs them by the hands, not of the church, but
of the state.

" For religion is excluded; or, if admitted, it can come before them only in
the rare and grudged ministrations of a single chaplain; set side by side with
the authorized teaching of others, who denounce his doctrines as false, and
his commission as invalid. Heresy and schism, and, following on them, unbelief, must pursue the civil power, even into the poorhouse. And the last
refuge for its miserable inhabitants, the belief in a God, and the hopes of
heaven, must be shut against them by the distractions of doubt and controversy, which the state, instead of excluding, forces on them; which it brings
into their very home—gathering the war of words and the strife of tongues, as
before round the bewildered child, so now in the ear of the ignorant, the aged,
the sinful, the miserable, the hard of heart, the bereaved and the friendless,
the dull and dead of hearing and understanding, even round the decay of
sickness, and the agonies of the death-bed. The state will acknowledge no

exclusive truth in religion, and listen to no controversies, because truth is full of doubt, and controversies the destruction of peace; and therefore the miserable pauper is compelled by it to listen to them himself, and to end where the state begins, in disbelieving all that he hears." . . . .

"And then turn to another relation of domestic life—that of master and servant. Christianity set the slave free. It struck off his chains, not by any violent infraction of an established system—not by encouraging that restless and dangerous spirit of independence which refuses to own any master—not by indulging in vain and fanatical clamours against an institution which had not been excluded even from the divinely appointed polity of the Jews—which nature herself had in some degree adopted—and the very name of which had been assumed into the most ennobling relations of the gospel. She knew that where the spirit of Christian love is infused, there the outward form of slavery not only loses its terrors, but becomes capable of generating great virtues. And, however capable of abuse may be the power of one human being over another, she knew that far greater abuses prevail in the unrestricted rule of each man over himself. The highest virtues of our nature—patience, fortitude, humility, faith, may be cherished and exercised in the slave, even under the harshest bondage; and mercy, and pity, and love, and self-denial may be practised by the master even when armed with absolute power. But no virtue whatever can be generated in the license of self-will, except it be the self-command taught to us by bitter suffering, and resolute to abandon its freedom and to confine itself under an external rule. If a Christian was born a slave, by the advice of the apostle he was not to seek to become free." . . . .

"Labour—the labour of human beings—is now an article for the market. It is a subject of competition. It is open to the same rivalry, and its value is fixed by the same irregular struggle between two contending selfishnesses, as the price of a bale of cotton or a loaf of bread. The hirer and hired have each but a single object: the one to purchase as cheap, the other to sell his toil as dear, as possible. But in such a conflict the master must ultimately be the vanquisher. The servant who outstands his market must starve. And thus, we have seen the price of the labour of the poor throughout the kingdom, in almost every department, reduced to so low a rate, that life can scarcely be supported. And the wretched workman is left to starve, throughout the vigour of his life, in a miserable hovel, and to die in a poorhouse, while the master is apparently exempt from all responsibility, as he is untouched by any compassion, because the relation between himself and his servant has been stripped of all moral obligation and religious character, and has been reduced to a mere act of barter. Faith and fear have perished from it. And so it must be, when the dependence of man upon man ceases to be regarded in a religious light—as a positive dispensation of Providence; when, instead of submitting to, and acquiescing in, the position in which we are placed at our birth, until some other call from heaven summon us from it, we are taught from our childhood, that there is no law or rule for our temporal conduct, but to secure, each of us, what we deem to be our own advancement in the world; when, in this way, a perpetual fretting fever of restless ambition is diffused through every class;

when the master, to increase his gains, reduces his servants to starvation, and the servant serves, not as an act of duty, and in the Lord, but simply to earn his bread." . . . .

"We sigh over the imprisonment of the canary-bird, exclaim against the cruelty of its oppressor, unbar the doors of its cage without a moment's delay, and the poor bird claps its wings with joy, flutters into the open air, regains its liberty, its blessed liberty,—and the next day is found dead of cold and hunger. It is not for a Christian to argue in favour of slavery; still less to speak of it, except with abhorrence, when the master abuses his power, and the slave, instead of being raised by him, by degrees, to the capability and enjoyment of his freedom, is rivetted in his chains for ever. But a Christian may indeed ask, whether the total exclusion of all constraint, of all fear, of all positive external obligation from the relation of master and servant, has not ended in reducing the servant in this country to a condition far worse—far more abject and degraded—far more hopeless—far more vitiated—than that of any slave in any period or country of the world. Our mines, our factories, our common workshops—even our farms and agricultural cottages—full of crippled children and deformed women, of famine and fever, of drunkenness and vice, of depraved, miserable, hopeless beings, doomed by their own free act—the free act of a being in the agony of starvation—to the severest toil in darkness, at midnight; deprived of rest, stinted in food, selling their children to the same misery with their own for a few shillings, or sickening over hours of toil to earn their pence—all the horrible scenes revealed by late inquiries into the state of our lower classes,—what is there in the records of slavery to be found more heart-breaking, or more appalling, to those who believe that nations, like individuals, are visited by curses from the Almighty, and that the first curse denounced in His commandments is uttered against those who depart, even in the slightest degree, from His positive, external, revealed truth, and shape out ideas of the Divine nature after their own fancy."—pp. 313—328.

THE SUBJECT OF HUMANITY APPROACHED WITH TIMIDITY IN ENGLAND, THROUGH DREAD OF UNSETTLING THE FOUNDATIONS OF THEIR SYSTEM.

The writers of England have come slowly and reluctantly to the persuasion that something must be done for the working classes. All the searching and thorough expositions of parliamentary reports, in which the condition of the poor was set forth with a fidelity of detail and power of truth have failed to conquer public apathy, for the mass of evidence proved too heavy for the public digestion. No doubt it had some weight even in England, by furnishing sources of information to the few who were inquiring. Some reforms followed in the hours of labour, in the employment of children in factories, and females in mines. These documents never touched the great social problems involved. A large class of writers discoursed abundantly of wealth, labour, production, distribution, and other topics of political economy, without a kind thought or expression for the men whose industry furnished the subject of their thoughts; they treated of commerce, and of the productive powers of nations, without shedding a ray of light on the questions of human welfare and happiness involved in these discussions. Wealth and industry are treated as abstractly and as separately from human well-being, as if the whole productive power was nothing but steam-engines or water-wheels. Perhaps no department of literary labour has suffered more from not being placed on a right basis, than this of political economy. Being a science, if one at all, pertaining exclusively to human well-being—to the progress of social economy, it was early divorced from this basis and assumed the shape of speculations upon commerce, the productive power of labour, consumption, rent, capital, value, money, exchange, interest, banking, circulation, credit, and similar topics; all which were discussed theoretically and developed largely, as if imbodying an abstract science, apart from the men whom they concerned. That there is no agreement among these writers, and that their productions command the assent, or even the comprehension of very few, cannot be surprising, when it is considered they are brain-spun theories, and not actual deductions from history or experience. The reason why political economy took this shape was, doubtless, chiefly, because despotic rule and priestly domination forbade any attempt on the continent of Europe at erecting a system of political economy with a strict view to the best interests of men. The Church of Rome has always assumed to be infallible in matters of this world, as well as of those in the world to come; it was not possible, therefore, for authors to shed light on any subject of which "the Church" chose to take jurisdiction. Whatever ground "the Church" left was covered by the various claims of despotic governments. In England, where these obstacles did not intervene, the incubus of the poor-laws effectually prevented any inquiry into the science of human welfare which would tend to disturb the existing order of things. Under these manifold disadvantages the science of political economy has received its expansion; and, as might be expected, it is neither consistent with itself nor adapted to its object. According to its literal expression, however, it has no legitimate end; it contemplates the production, distribution, and consumption of wealth; but does not inform us in what way this can be done with a view to the best interests, temporal and eternal, of the producer.

"It considers the lord of the creation merely as a sensitive machine, with eyes, arms, hands, and fingers formed to manufacture some commodity saleable in the marts of commerce; merely an animated engine, to be worked at the will of opulence and power for pecuniary gain; merely as a breathing mill or animal automaton, which cannot stand still a moment for the purposes of moral and religious discipline, without irreparable loss of time and unpardonable waste of wealth."*

But the pressure of new ideas and the advancing tide of reform is invading the "godless wisdom" of political economy. Its votaries begin to perceive they cannot much longer overlook man in their speculations. The last and best work of its class, "The Principles of Political Economy, by John Stuart Mill," thus steps out of its way to speak of man :—

"In the details of political economy, general views of society and politics are out of place; but, in the more comprehensive, it is impossible to exclude them." .... "Considered in its moral and social aspect, the state of the labouring people has lately been a subject of much more speculation and discussion than formerly; and the opinion, that it is not now what it ought to be, has become very general." .... "The working classes have taken their interests into their own hands, and are perpetually showing that they think the interests of their employers are not identical with their own, but opposite to them." .... "The principles of the Reformation have reached as low down in society as reading and writing, and the poor will no longer accept morals and religion of other people's prescribing." .... "The poor have come out of leading-strings and cannot any longer be governed or treated like children." .... "But whatever advice, exhortation, or guidance is held out to the labouring classes, must henceforth be tendered to them as equals." .... "The problem is, to obtain the efficiency and economy of production on a large scale, without dividing the producers into two parties with hostile interests, employers and employed, the many who do the work being mere servants under the command of the one who supplies the funds, and having no interest of their own in the enterprise, except to fulfil their contract and earn their wages."†

These are certainly remarkable concessions to the spirit of the age, appearing in the pages of an elaborate work on political economy. No doubt, the writer felt it to be impossible for even one of his school to be deaf to the cries of humanity; and therefore, some twenty pages, in over eleven hundred and fifty, are devoted to the connection between humanity and industry.

The progress of opinion shows that the time cannot be distant when the science or system of political economy will receive its just appre-

---

* V. Knox's Works, vol. vi. p. 428. † Book iv. chap. vii.

ciation—when the absurdity of constructing a system of industry or trade without any reference to the men for whom it is intended will be seen in its naked deformity. It must be known soon that any system of social economy which leaves out of view both divinity and humanity must at first encounter resistance and reproach, and at last utter failure.

"The system which produces the happiest moral effects will be found, also, most beneficial to the interest of the individual and to the general weal. Upon this basis the science of political economy will rest at last, when the ponderous volumes with which it has been overlaid shall have sunk by their own weight into the dead sea of oblivion."*

For half a century, the philanthropy of Great Britain has been conspicuous in many remarkable manifestations. The abolition of the slave-trade, the emancipation of the slaves in the West Indies, the immense sums paid for the distribution of the Bible, and for the support of missionaries, the searching inquiry made by committees of parliament into the condition of all the suffering classes, all show that the public mind was deeply moved with compassion. There has, however, been visible there a great reluctance to enter into the real questions pertaining to their domestic population. The few could afford to be liberal, while the many were oppressed. No inquiry could be stirred in relation to the permanent relief of the masses, which did not point to some sacrifices on the part of the few. The constitution was sacred, ancient usages were sacred, property was sacred, personal rights were sacred: all these and many like barriers rose in the way of any organic changes, by which labour might be increased and its rewards enlarged. The difficulty of overcoming these barriers was greater, and so still remains, than even at first sight strikes the inquirer. Three-fourths of the labouring population of Great Britain have been long sunk into a state of utter poverty and dependence: they live from day to day, and the least misfortune precipitates them into pauperism. They have no voice in fixing their wages, but are compelled, by sheer necessity, to labour for what they can get. This is a dreadful alternative for the multitudes, and shows how hopeless their condition. But it is the real foundation upon which the apparent strength, wealth, and grandeur of Great Britain now rest. Her manufactures increased by

---

* Essay on the State of the Poor and the Means Pursued by the Society for Bettering their Condition, 1816, by Robert Southey.

the aid of steam and machinery, and this cheap labour can enter all the markets of the world at a price low enough to encounter any competition; her nobles and men of capital can sport the largest individual incomes in the world, because the labour that earns that income is inadequately compensated; the government can with certainty raise the largest revenue in the world, because it is the proceeds of the labour of her millions of poor, who must toil incessantly, and give the whole avails of their incessant toil to the men of capital who employ them, receiving for their share a pittance which imperfectly sustains life. The men of capital, having this command of the bones and sinews of the poor, can afford to pay high taxes to sustain the government which sustains this system. The strength of this system is the extreme subordination of the labourers, which is only maintained by their inability to make any provision ahead to resist a system which reduces them to worse than African bondage. Now it is clear that the questions which arise in any attempt to bring this whole subject to the light of day are delicate and complicated in the extreme. It is no wonder that few have courage to approach it, and that those most interested in maintaining the present order of things can scarcely endure to have it touched. It is very evident that any sudden reform, however directed, must be fatal in the extreme to the present social system of Great Britain. One great error has prevailed, which must soon be dispelled by the light which is rapidly gathering over the true interests of humanity;—we cannot much longer shut our eyes to the truth: we must receive it with full credit: if its bearings are adverse to some cherished notions or interests, it will become a matter of conscience, of prudence, and consideration, when and how the reforms which this truth dictates shall be accomplished. We should no longer fear light, though we may well pause and ponder in the path of reform. We believe that if the truth in regard to the social system of Great Britain was brought home to the minds and consciences of the intelligent people of that empire, a quarter of a century would not elapse, without exhibiting an entire renovation and political reformation, effected without violent revolution or bloodshed, and mainly by concessions made by those now holding positions of power and the possession of capital. Let it be understood, then, that while no consideration should extinguish or repress the truth, the methods of reform, however effectual, should be fraught with neither violence, nor injustice, nor even dangerous haste.

It is quite curious to trace the cautious and slow approaches which have been made in Great Britain, in the last half-century, towards a thorough consideration of the condition of their labouring population. We may readily imagine many grounds for this caution, all of which were magnified in the minds of those whom they influenced. The whole contributed to form a public sentiment so intensely conservative as to be at times ridiculous, tremblingly sensitive, and often odious, if not positively anti-christian. All who belonged directly or indirectly to the established church, all who were connected with the government, executive, legislative, or judicial, or expected or aimed to be so—all who supposed their interests to be deeply concerned in the great questions touching the rights of property, were alive to every topic that might remotely or directly affect any of these great interests. The influence of the church and the government, and the wealth of the country were arrayed on the side of the severest conservatism, and formed, together, a public sentiment which it was not only hard to stem, but which those who were educated in it found it almost impossible to think against. It formed a shell which the mind could not break through. It would be easy to illustrate it by extracts, but for the space it would require. Those who desire, may find its tone and polished surface well exemplified in the pages of John Foster, whose conception of human depravity and the hopelessness of all amendment, was of the strongest kind. According to him, if the wickedness of the world was concentrated in any one country, it would furnish a land of infernal spirits, except that they would be incarnate, "which last, they would soon, through mutual destruction, cease to be," and thus become naked spirits infernal. He brands all reform with ridicule and contempt, and says "that revolutions, great discoveries, augmented science, and new forms of policy shall become, in effect, what may be denominated the sublime mechanics of depravity."*

This essayist had a profound respect for religion, and expressly excepted its ministers from the odium he attached to the profession and idea of reform; but he expressly cautions them not to hope for any great things from that; and the utmost stretch of expectation which he allows for the time to come, is measured by what has been accomplished in times past. Happily for the world, even the profound essayist was obliged, in subsequent editions of his popular essays, to make some acknowledgment of advance, in the face of his "ominous conjectures" and profound immovableness.

---

* Letter IV. on the Application of the Epithet *Romantic*. John Foster.

We have already seen that those who most frequently attacked this discouraging philosophy were known as avowed infidels. The truth is, the tone assumed by many of this conservative school was such, that very few could venture to attack it without risk of being called infidels. Note the extreme care which runs throughout the work entitled, "*Hampden in the XIX. Century,*" in which the author, evidently strongly imbued with enlarged feelings of humanity, and anxious to enter upon the career of investigation and reform, is but too apprehensive that Christianity and humanity cannot be reconciled. Southey, in his "*Progress of Society,*" availing himself of the conversational form in which it is written, takes both sides, the hopeful and hopeless, and gives no decided opinion, although his writings generally show his sympathies were strongly on the side of humanity. Dr. Chalmers was bold enough to break this barrier of truth, and, in spite of all the influences bearing on the path of reform and free expression, he not only said what he thought, but did what he could. Hear him, in 1819, addressing an assemblage in Glasgow, met on the subject of the schools for the poor, got up and endowed by his exertions:

"Here will I prophesy, if the world is to stand, there will be a great amelioration in the life of general humanity. The labouring classes are destined to attain a far more secure place of comfort and independence in the commonwealth than they have ever yet occupied; and this will come about, not as the fruit of any victory gained on the arena of angry and discordant politics, but far more surely, as the result of growing virtue and intelligence and worth among the labourers themselves. I trust, the day is coming, when humble life will be dignified both by leisure and literature . . . . . when many a lettered sage, as well as many an enlightened Christian, will be met with, even in the very lowest walks of society; when the elements of science and philanthropy and high scholarship, will so ripen throughout the general mind of the country, as to exalt it prodigiously above the level of its present character and acquirements."*

Many works have appeared within the last ten years, which show that the question of human well-being is falling by degrees within the public domain. Apprehension is wearing off, the friends of humanity are growing bolder, Christians are extending their vision over a wider field, and beginning to be ashamed of leaving the championship of humanity so much to infidels. To this result the efforts of Robert Hall and Thomas Arnold contributed their full share: the latter was, however, far ahead of the former in his appreciation of questions

---

* Life of Chalmers, by the Rev. Wm. Hanna, 2d vol. p. 250, Am. Ed.

involving the interests of the human race.   In answer to the question,
" What is the progress spoken of?" Arnold replied, " It is in the application of Christianity to human things,—the progress in this is as
endless as the progress from our imperfection to perfection can be."*

  Besides the later works enumerated in our catalogue above, some of
which go freely into the question of the improvement of the labouring
classes, is one which deserves a special mention,—*"The Philosophy of
Necessity, or the Law of Consequences as applicable to Mental, Moral, and
Social Science, by Charles Bray."*† This work, though far from being
elaborate, when the extent of its scope is considered, is yet highly deserving, as a direct attempt to open up the subject of the "science of
man," and spread its topics before the world in logical order.   We are not
prepared to furnish an appreciation of a work of so much thought, but
deem it worth while to give some indication of its contents.

  " The object of the work is to inquire into the nature and constitution of man :
to ascertain his place in creation, the object and aim of his existence, and the
boundaries of his mind :—'to vindicate the ways of God to man,' by tracing
the law of consequences, and pointing to the *good of evil* : to inquire what sanction nature affords to morality, or what obligation she lays us under to regard
the happiness of others : to analyze the present constitution of society : to trace
the cause of its numerous evils : to suggest a remedy, and to show how we may
best avail ourselves of our present knowledge and power, to live together in
the most happy manner possible."‡

  In the body of his work the author classes his subject under the
three main divisions,—MENTAL SCIENCE, MORAL SCIENCE, and SOCIAL
SCIENCE.   Under the head of MENTAL SCIENCE, he treats of the *mental faculties, animal feelings, social feelings, moral sentiments, external
senses, perceptive faculties,* and *reasoning faculties ; the origin of our
knowledge,* and the *adaptation of the intellectual faculties to the external world ; belief ; truth ; the connection of the mind with organization ;*
and the subjects of *materialism, consciousness, ideality,* and *association.*   Under the head of MORAL SCIENCE, we have *philosophical
necessity,* the doctrine of which he derived from Edwards's "Inquiry
into Freedom of Will," *and its application to responsibility, praise
and blame, reward and punishment, virtue and vice ; the origin, objects, and advantages of evil ; pain considered as the most effective*

* Miscellaneous Works, Am. Ed. p. 441.
† In two volumes, 8vo., London, 1841.   ‡ Preface.

guardian of that system of organization upon which happiness depends ; pain necessary as a stimulus to action ; evils consequent upon the varieties of condition among mankind ; death. Morality, pain and pleasure, man in relation to external objects ; man in relation to his fellow-man. Under the head of SOCIAL SCIENCE, he treats of the *present condition of society, division of society, annual income of the kingdom and its distribution, income of the working classes and its expenditure, condition of the working classes. Measures proposed for the amelioration of the condition of the people,—governmental reform, free-trade, emigration, education, religion. Causes of the poverty of the working classes, social reform, summary, &c.*

We mention this work as a bold and well-sustained attempt to take up the subject of human welfare on its own merits. It is readily seen that the prevalent theories of political economy have had little room in the mind of the author. We can easily perceive that, labouring under the prevailing error of estimating the value and importance of Christianity through the medium of the conduct of Christians, he did not comprehend the true relations of religion with his subject. This error, so common and so fatal to the progress of correct notions, is equivalent to ascertaining the constitution and laws of a nation by the conduct of the people, instead of comparing the conduct of a people with their written constitution and laws.

Mr. Bray is the author of a very useful book as a help in these studies,—"*An Outline of the Various Social Systems and Communities which have been founded on the Principle of Co-operation: London,* 1846." In this he briefly indicates, under more than sixty heads, some of the more prominent schemes of reform and co-operation, from early to modern times ; such as *Crete, Sparta, Peru, Egypt, the Essenes, Early Christians, Moravians, Shakers, Rappites, Godwin's, St. Simon's, and Owen's Systems, Poor Colonies of Holland, Socialism, Fourierism, Hofwyl, Port Royal: the various Utopists,—Plato, More, Bacon, Harrington.* This indication of these various plans is confined to exposition and dwells not upon merits or demerits, but is preceded by an introduction on the general subjects, which contains a variety of information on the condition of the working classes in Europe.

Whilst we profess that we are not prepared to give any opinion on the real merits of Mr. Bray's labours, we award him without hesitation the praise of having cast himself freely and unreservedly into a subject so much neglected and so much feared ; and of having produced a work which cannot fail to be the precursor of very many more useful than his own. We are free to say, that we do not feel the necessity, to obtain clear views on this subject, of going beyond the "new commandment" which is delivered to us in the gospel, and fully believe that, if Mr. Bray had set out from that point, he would have obtained clearer views and a more secure resting-place, besides making far greater progress. His imperfect conception of the Christian system, and his mingling Christianity with the conduct of Christians, draws him frequently into trains of remark highly exceptionable; but their freedom, their severity and boldness are extremely instructive; and Christians should accept the merited reproof, even though blended with misapprehension and error. He characterizes the conduct and teaching of Christians who tell the poor and suffering that all the ills of this life are visitations for sin, chastisements for the discipline of the mind and growth in grace,—who separate religion entirely from any consideration of comfort in this world, and postpone all happiness to the next world,—by saying that, "in place of the good things which God has given so plenteously, and which he intends equally for all his children, they allow liberally to the poor '*post-obit bills on heaven*,'* as a compensation for what the wretched system of society has taken from them here."†

Some works on these subjects may have escaped our attention. Vast numbers of occasional pamphlets have appeared on the various questions involved, many being of signal value and merit. Among these smaller productions, one which is well worthy of notice is—"The Labouring Classes of England, especially those engaged in Agriculture and Manufactures. By an Englishman. Boston, 1847." This was written by an English factory operative, then residing in this country, and contains views and details of the highest interest. Previous to leaving England, he had been employed by a benevolent nobleman to make inquiries respecting the condition of the poor, and thus had facilities for obtaining correct information. Alton Locke and other similar productions must assist in awakening the English mind. The recent exposition of Mr. Mayhew in the Morning Chronicle, which the author is now swelling into a large work, richly illustrated by engravings, has created a sensation and materially assisted in opening the way to a more general comprehension of facts, and to more just views of the rights and wrongs of the poor.

---

* This is a mode of payment adopted by expectant spendthrifts, who, being unable or unwilling to pay, give bills or notes, at enormous interest, payable upon the death of a father, or some one from whom a legacy is expected.

† Philosophy of Necessity, Vol. II. 375.

THE TREATMENT WHICH THE SUBJECTS OF CHARITY, PAUPERISM, AND LABOUR HAVE MET IN FRANCE. FRENCH WORKS ON THESE AND KINDRED TOPICS.

Our author appears not to have been fully aware that the legislation of France, in regard to the poor, for the past three centuries, has many features in common with the English legislation, which he so justly condemns. They are far indeed from being identical, but in France severe epithets and harsh punishments were inflicted for *vagabondage*, as well as in England. Viewed in a merely political light—in the aspect of good police—the public authorities of England and France did not originally greatly differ; but, in the administration and public sentiment which grew out of this legislation, a wide difference arose. The French legislation became, in a great measure, inoperative in its severe features. The English are eminently a law-abiding people; they have shown it as much in the rigid and severe administration of their poor-laws as in any portion of their history. If the law exists, it must be administered: it must not be a dead letter through false sympathy or any mere inefficiency; hence the administration of the poor-laws of England revealed in its progress a scene of brutal hardness of heart, unchristian severity, litigation, and low cunning, disgraceful to human nature and revolting at once to decency and humanity. Such a picture of law-abiding fidelity in a guardian of the poor as that characterized in the extract from *Burns's History of the Poor-laws*, given in a preceding page, (289,) could never find a parallel in France. The English system became, indeed not so much from its actual enactments as its practical working in English hands, the detestation of Europe. It was regarded by many as the climax of inhumanity and the special disgrace of Protestantism. When epithets failed to brand adequately the horrors of this anti-christian treatment of the poor, it was denominated the *English system*.

In our reference to the English works on the subject of the poor, the poor-laws, population, &c., we have seen that, almost without exception, they proceed upon the assumed ground that British institutions, religious and political, were all right, and that of course no part of the mischiefs, irregularities, and misery which occurred under them could be charged to that source. And, of course, the elements of the subject were never touched by those who confined their view to such a narrow range. Before the advent of Malthus, the question was chiefly one of economy. It was simply, How shall we most cheaply feed and clothe these increasing hordes of paupers, so that there shall be no charge upon the nation of having permitted them to perish for want of food, or clothing, or shelter. After the appearance of Malthus, who exalted inhumanity into the highest philosophy, the question became, at least so far as the Malthusian doctrines pervaded English literature, not how to feed, and clothe, and lodge them, but merely how they might be permitted to perish with the least shock to existing prejudices. In France, the English system had some friends and Malthus a few disciples, chiefly among the political economists of the Smith and Say school. A few professed themselves followers of Malthus, like Dr. Chalmers, without considering the whole scope of his philosophy, merely because they agreed with him in some of his positions. Malthus was opposed to a compulsory provision for the poor, and Dr. Chalmers and many more, availing themselves of his authority upon that point, permitted their names to go abroad as endorsers for a man who virtually repudiated all charity, public, private, and religious. In truth, none but the strict political economists, a very small class out of England, ever fully approved the doctrines of Malthus. But even in their pages the Malthusian philosophy carefully hides its most revolting features.

The literature of charity and humanity in France, always far in advance of that of England, is now rapidly swelling into large dimensions. As a whole, it is not merely untinged with the worst aspects of Malthusianism, but it partakes scarcely at all of that hard, dry, calculating, spirit of economy, which regarded poorer classes as an odious burden, and pauperism as a positive nuisance, to be endured only because it could not be abated. It is not in this spirit that the subject of humanity, the science of social well-being, has been treated in France. Whatever may be some of the special faults of this department of French literature, it is so superior in tone, in taste, and in method to the equivalent branch of English literature, that it would be impossible to put them in comparison. To any one filled with earnest longings for human welfare, who has explored the English works on the poor, pauperism, and the poor-laws, with the view of finding instruction, helps for charity, or hopes to cheer the suffering classes, the utter disappointment, if not loathing, experienced, will find immediate relief by taking up the volumes in which French writers have so kindly, so earnestly, so wisely discussed questions bearing on human happiness. The connection of the whole subject with Christianity is much more frequently pointed out and explicitly stated, and much more appreciated in France than in England. The mere question of economy in feeding the poor is scarce ever touched in France, and the English mode of considering that question would not be endured in France, where men that labour for a living, however lowly their position, or suffer the severities of famine and nakedness, for want of labour, are regarded as objects of the highest interest, social, political, and religious. They cannot endure in France that the chief question in regard to such men shall be what it may cost to feed and keep them, and whether the job of keeping them alive, or saving appearances if they are suffered to die, shall be undertaken by public authorities at the expense of a forced contribution, or be left to the spontaneous offerings of private charity or to the parish officers of an established church. In France, the whole question is as open as the day, and every topic is brought forward without reserve, and discussed with a freedom unknown in any other country in the world, and with an earnestness and ability equally unsurpassed. It would be impossible to classify the numerous productions of the French press or to point out the various schools to which they belong, as they range from the strictest conservatism through every variety of opinion, down to the wildest and absurdest schemes a diseased fancy or perverted intellect can create. To give some idea of the richness of the field, we furnish a catalogue, from which we shall select a few on the subjects of CHARITY, PAUPERISM, and LABOUR, to be specially mentioned and their contents noted as specimens of this literature, and as indicating to those inclined to such studies where they may find a rich and profitable field of study.

A CATALOGUE OF FRENCH WORKS ON CHRISTIAN CHARITY, PUBLIC
AND PRIVATE CHARITY, PAUPERISM, POPULATION, AND LABOUR.

Belly, Jehan de. Œuvres de Miséricorde envers les Pauvres, ... Paris, 1572
Exhortation to the People of France touching works of Mercy to the
Poor.

Le Maistre, Ant. L'Aumosne Chrestienne, 2 vols. 12mo. 1651
Christian Alms, or the Tradition of the Church touching Charity to
the Poor, collected from the Holy Scriptures and the Greek and
Latin Fathers.

Thiers, J. B. L'Avocat des Pauvres, 12mo. 1679
The Advocate of the Poor, showing the Obligations of the Church
Authorities to make a good use of the Church Funds in aid of
the Poor.

Vernage et Paccori. Abrégé de la Loi Nouvelle, 12mo.········, ········· 1713
    Summary of the whole Law—the love of God and of our Neighbour,
    with a Treatise upon Charity according to St. Paul.
Saint Pierre, Abbé de. Memoire sur les Pauvres, 8vo.················· 1721
    A Memoir upon the Begging Poor and the Means of Relieving them.
Morin, Henri. Histoire Critique de la Pauvreté. ······················ 1723
    Critical History of Poverty.
Forbonnais. Memoir upon Beggary.··································· 1722
Maugras, J. F. Lettres sur l'Aumône, 12mo.·························· 1726
    A Consultation upon Alms, in which is established the Necessity of
    Alms and Rules for Giving, with a Refutation of the Pretexts for
    Refusing them.
Duguet, J. J. Charité, 12mo. ······················· ··············· 1728
    Explanation of the Characteristics of Charity as given by St. Paul.
Le Pelletier, C. Traité de la Charité, 12mo.························· 1729
    Love to our Neighbour, and its True Character.
Pallu, M. De la Charité, 12mo.······································ 1742
    Love of our Neighbour; its Motives, its Duties, and its Opposite Defects.
Morrice, D. Proposition pour Secours des Pauvres···················· 1753
    Proposition for Efficaciously Aiding the Poor.
De la Morandiere. Police sur les Mendiants, 12mo. ·················· 1764
    Police for Beggars and Vagabonds.
Faiguet, J. L'Ami des Pauvres, 12mo.······························ 1768
    The Friend of the Poor, or Political Economy.
Beaudeau, N. Idées d'un Citoyen, &c., 2 vols. 8vo.············· ······· 1765
    Opinions of a Citizen upon the Wants, the Rights, and the Duties of
    the Poor.
Mery de la Canorgue, Abbé. L'Ami de ceux qui n'en ont point ········ 1767
    The Friend of the Friendless.
Moheau. Considerations sur la Population de la France, 8vo.·········· 1778
Malvaux. Mendicité en France, &c., 8vo.···························· 1780
    A Mode of Stopping Beggary in France, by making the beggars use-
    ful to the public without making them unhappy.

The title of this work was the subject proposed for a prize by the Academy of Sciences in 1777. A large volume of the essays, offered in this competition, was published in 1799.

Percy et Willaume. Memoire, &c. ····································· 1780

A memoir crowned by the Academy of Sciences, of Macon, upon this question : "The Ancients—had they public establishments for aid of indigent, of orphans, or foundlings, the sick, the wounded; and if not, what had they in their place?"

Reymond, Abbé H. Droit des Pauvres, 8vo. ························· 1781
    The Rights of the Poor.

Dupont de Nemours. Idées sur les Secours, 8vo. 1786
   Ideas upon the Succour to be given to the Poor in Large Towns.
Clochar. Mendicitè, 8vo. 1790
   Method of Stopping Beggary.
Montaignac. Reflexions sur la Mendicitè, 12mo. 1790
Bussy de Henrion. De la Destruction de la Mendicitè, 8vo. 1790
Volland. Memoire sur les Moyens de detruire la Mendicitè en France, 4to. 1790
Desmousseaux. De la Bienfaisance Nationale ....
Brogiran. Memoire sur les Moyens de bannir Mendicitè, 8vo. 1791
Bannefroy. Memoires sur la Mendicitè, 12mo. 1791
Bonnefoy. Memoire sur la Mendicitè, 4to. 1791
La Rochefoucauld, Liancourt. Plan pour l'Extinction de la Mendi-
   citè, 8vo. 1790
   Plan for the Extinction of Mendicity, presented to the National As-
   sembly, and Report of the Committee of Mendicity upon the
   Hospital of Paris.
Dillon. Memoires sur les Etablissements de Bienfaisance, 12mo.
   Memoirs upon Public Houses of Charity, of Labour, of Correction, in
   a political and commercial aspect.
Vasco. Memoires sur les Causes de Mendicitè et les Moyens de sup-
   primer. 1799
Bosc. Essai sur les Moyens de detruire Mendicitè, 8vo. 1800
Friedlander. Histoire des Etablissements relatifs aux Pauvres, ... 1821
   Reprinted in Paris in 1822, with a catalogue of works published in
   Germany upon the Poor.
Doé. Traité sur l'Indigence, 8vo. 1805
   A Treatise upon Indigence, its principal Causes and the Means of
   arresting it.
Prestot. Memoire sur l'Indigence, 12mo. 1805
   Upon Indigence, the Means of Curing it without a return of Beggary.
Guignon, Laourens. Des Dépôts de Mendicitè, 8vo. 1814
   Houses for the Poor, and their Influence on Public Welfare.
Aubert de Vitry. Recherches sur les Vrais Causes de la Misère, 8vo. .. 1815
   Researches upon the Real Causes of Misery and of Happiness.
Mansion, H. Essai sur l'Extinction de la Mendicitè en France, 12mo. .. 1820
Gerando, De. Le Visiteur du Pauvre, 8vo. 1820
Bonnefons, C. R. P. Le Chretien Charitable, 18mo.
   The Charitable Christian who visits the Poor, those who are in prison,
   and those who are sick.
Dupin, Baron. Histoire de l'Administration des Secours Publics, 8vo. .. 1821
Poliniere, A. P. Memoire sur la Question suivante, 8vo. 1821
   Memoir upon this Question: "What are the respective advantages
   and disadvantages of Public Hospitals for the indigent sick, and of
   aid at their domicile; and what ameliorations may be properly in-
   troduced in this respect?"
Soviche, J. Des Hôpitaux et des Secours a Domicile, 8vo. 1822

Fodèré, F. E. Essai Historique sur la Pauvreté des Nations, 8vo........ 1825
    Essay, Historical and Moral, upon the Poverty of Nations, Popula-
    tion, Mendicity, and Foundlings.
Ducpetiaux. Traité des Moyens de soulager et de prevenir l'Indigence, 8vo. 1832
Morogues, De. Du Pauperisme, 8vo................................. 1834
    Pauperism and Mendicity, and the Means of preventing their Dread-
    ful Effects.
Sismondi, De. Du Sort des Ouvriers dans les Manufactures,............ 1834
Villeneuve Bargemont, De. De l'Economie Politique Chretienne,
    3 vols. 8vo.. 1834
Bouvier Dumoulin. Des Causes du Malaise.......................... 1834
    The Causes of the Uneasiness of the French Population.
Beres, E. Des Classes Ouvrieres, 8vo................................ 1835
    The Working Classes—the means of ameliorating their lot in point
    of their moral and physical well-being.
Berger. Du Pauperisme dans le Canton de Vaud 1836
Vincens, Emile. De l'Organization Sociale........................... 1836
Duchatel, T. Consideration de l'Economie Politique sur la Bienfai-
    sance, 8vo... 1829
    Considerations upon the Political Economy of Beneficence or Charity,
    in its relation with the moral condition and the well-being of the
    lower classes of society.
Naville, F. M. L. De la Charité Legale, 2 vols. 8vo.................... 1836
    Of Legal Charity, its causes and effects; and particularly of Houses
    of Labour, and of the Prevention of Begging.
    This author was a minister of the gospel at Geneva.

Schmidt. Recherches sur la Population, les Salaries, Pauperisme 1836
Pignot. Projets concernant la Salubrité Publique, 8vo................ 1837
    Projects in reference to Public Health and the actual Extinction of
    Mendicity.
Esterno, D'. De la Misère, de ses Causes, de ses Effets, de ses Remè-
    des, 8vo.. 1842
Du Puynode, G. Des Lois du Travail, &c., 8vo.
    Of the Laws of Labour, and of the Working Classes.
Labourt. Recherches sur l'Intemperance, 8vo.
    Researches, Historical and Statistical, upon the Intemperance of the
    Working Classes, and upon Foundlings.
Guyard, Robert. Essai sur l'Etat du Pauperisme en France, et sur les
    Moyens d'y remedier, 8vo.
Chirat, Abbé. Guide de la Charité, 12mo.
    The Way of being Merciful with Advantage.
Naudet. Des Secours Publics chez les Romains 1838
D..... Mémoire couronné par l'Athénée de Paris.................... 1838
    Upon this question—"What should be the organization of labour
    the best fitted to augment the happiness of the Working Classes?"

Fregier. *Des Classes Dangereuses,* 2 vols. 8vo. 1839
    Of the Dangerous Classes of the Population, and the means of making
    them better.

Gerando, De. De la *Bienfaisance Publique,* 4 vols. 8vo. 1839
    A Treatise upon Public Charity, with a full view of Indigence in its
    relations with social economy, containing the history and statistics
    of charitable establishments in France and in other countries.

Desvaux. De l'Amelioration du Sort de la Classe Pauvre, 8vo. 1839
    The Amelioration of the Lot of the Poor; or, of Charity in its Prin-
    ciple, its Application, and its Influence.

Cochut, A. Du Sort des Classes Souffrantes.

Cerfbeer, A. E. Rapport au Ministre de l' Interieur, 4to. 1840
    Report upon the different hospitals, *hospices,* establishments and
    societies of beneficence, and upon mendicity, in the States of Sar-
    dinia, Lombardy, Venice, Rome, Parma, Placentia, and Modena.

Villerme. Tableaux de l'Etat Physique et Moral des Ouvriers, 2 vols. 8vo. 1840
    Picture of the Moral and Physical Condition of the Workmen em-
    ployed in the Cotton, Woollen, and Silk Manufactories.

Buret, E. De la Misère, 2 vols. 8vo. 1841
    Of the Misery of the Working Classes in France and England.

Tarbe, Prosper. Travail et Salaire, 8vo. 1841
    Labour and Wages.

Chamborant, De. Du Pauperisme, 8vo. 1842
    Of Pauperism as it was in antiquity and as it is now : of the Remedies
    which have been applied, and those proper to be applied at the
    present day.

Loudon, Ch. Solution du Probleme de la Population et des Subsist-
    ances, 8vo. 1842

Dutouquet. De la Condition des Classes Pauvres à la Campagne, 8vo.

Monaco, Le Prince de. Du Pauperisme en France, et des Moyens de la
    detruire, 8vo. 1043

Watteville, A. de. La Legislation Charitable, 8vo. 1843
    "   Statistiques des Etablissements de Bienfaisance, ... 1843

Napoleon, Le Prince Louis. (The President of France.) De l'Extinction
    du Pauperisme, ... 1844

D. S., Le Prince. Aperçu sur la Condition des Classes Ouvrières 1844

Lamothe, L. Etudes sur la Legislation Charitable, 8vo. 1845
    Remarks upon Reforms, financial and administrative, in Establish-
    ments of Charity.

Lamothe, L. Nouvelles Etudes sur la Legislation Charitable, 8vo. 1850

A very thorough and able work upon the administration of Public
Charity.

Annales de la Charité. A monthly journal, commenced in 1850.

Debrie, J. Des Proletaires, 8vo. 1845
    The Poor, and the Amelioration of their Condition.

Marchand, D'A. Du Pauperisme, 8vo. ································· 1845
Marbeau. Etudes sur L'Economie Sociale, 8vo. ······················ 1845
Fix, Theodore. Observations sur l'Etat des Classes Ouvrières ······ ····· 1846
Garnier, J. Sur l'Association, l'Economie Politique, et la Misère ······· 1846
Gougenot des Mousseaux. Des Proletaires ···· ························· 1846
    The Necessity and Means of Relieving the Poor.
Clement, A. Recherches sur les Causes de l'Indigence, 8vó. ······ ···· 1846
Gasparin, Comtesse Agenor de. Il y a des Pauvres à Paris—et ailleurs.
    There are Poor in Paris—and elsewhere.

The authoress is a protestant lady, well known for her benevolence and intelligence. The count is equally well and favourably known.

Du Pont White. Essai sur les Relations du Travail et du Capital, 8vo. 1846
Vivens, Le Vicompte. Lettre sur la Mendicità, addressée à la Reine, 8vo. 1846
Fayet, P. Progres de la Charité en France ··························· 1846
Lourde, Th. Essai sur l'Extinction de la Mendicità ···················· 1847
Dufau, P. F. Lettres à une Dame sur la Charité, 8vo. ········· ······· 1847
Paulmier, Ch. De la Misère et de la Mendicità.
Marbeau, F. Du Pauperisme en France ····························· 1847
    Pauperism in France, and the Remedies; or, the Principles of Chari-
    table Economy.
Egron, A. Le Livre du Pauvre, 18mo. ······························· 1847
    The Book of the Poor.
Farelle, F. de la. Du Progres Social, 2 vols. 8vo. ····················· 1839
    Social Progress, with a view to the advantage of the intermediate
    classes of society, not the rich nor the indigent.
"   "   Plan d'une Reorganization Disciplinaire, &c., 8vo. ········ 1847
    Plan for a Disciplinary Arrangement of the Working Classes in
    France.

These are together in one volume, in the edition of 1847.

Gerando, De. Des Progres de l'Industrie, 18mo. ····················· 1847
    The Progress of Industry in relation to the physical and moral well-
    being of the Working Classes.
Chevalier, M. Lettres sur l'Organization du Travail ················· 1848
    Letters upon the Organization of Labour, upon the Chief Causes of
    Misery, and upon the Remedies proposed.
Du Puynode, G. Lettres sur le Proletariat, 12mo. ····················· 1848
Doisy, Martin. Histoire de la Charité, 8vo. ························· 1848
    History of Charity during the first four centuries of the Christian
    Era, to serve as an introduction to the history of Public Charity
    in modern times.
Tailhaud. Histoire Philosophique de la Bienfaisance, 8vo. ············· 1848
Pelletier. Solution du Probleme de la Misère, ······················· 1848
Faucher, Lèon. Droit au Travail ································ ···· 1848
    The Right to Labour.

Moreau, Christophe. Du Droit a l'Oisiveté, 8vo. 1849
   Of the Right to Idleness, and the Organization of Slave-Labour in
   Greece and Rome.
Rollet et Saint Genez. De l'Assistance Publique, 8vo. 1849
Cador, L. Subsistances et Population, 8vo. 1850
Blanqui, Ainé. Des Classes Ouvrieres en France in 1848, 2 vols. 18mo.
Villerme. Des Associations Ouvrieres, ... 1849
Melun, A. De l'Intervention de la Société pour Prevenir et Soulager
   la Misère 1849
Girardin. Le Droit au Travail 1849
Garnier. Le Droit au Travail 1849
Le Bastier, J. De l'Organization de l'Assistance Publique 1849
Watteville, A de. Le Patrimoine des Pauvres.
Assemblée Nationale. Droit au Travail, 8vo. 1850
   A Debate of many days, in which the most enlightened men of
   France, of all shades of opinion, participated.
Chevallier, M. Question des Travailleurs, 18mo. 1848
   The Amelioration of the Lot of Labourers, Wages, and Organization
   of Labour.
Wolowski. De l'Organization du Travail, 8vo.
Montaigu. Organization du Travail, 8vo. 1848
Garnier, J. Etudes sur les Profits et les Salaires.
Clement, A. Des Nouvelles Idées de Reformes Industrielles, with re-
   marks upon Louis Blanc's work on the Organization of Labour .. 1848
Gratiot, A. Organisez le Travail, ne le Desorganisez pas. 1848
Lamothe. Des Moyens d'Ameliorer le Sort de la Classe Ouvriere.
   By a continued development of charitable institutions.
Daussigny. De l'Organization du Travail.
   Manufacturing Associations.
Cousin, V. Justice et Charité, 18mo. 1848
   The Limits of Justice and Charity, the right to labour, and the mutual
   rights and duties of individuals.
Jandeau, F. Amelioration du Sort des Travailleurs, 8vo.
   Organic Laws of Labour.
Aimé, Berthe-Pommery. Petit Ecrit sur une Grande Question, 12mo.
   The Amelioration of the Condition of the Working Classes.
Barsalon, G. Etudes sur le Passé et l'Avenir, 16mo.
   Of the Industrial Operatives.
Suther, A. Essai sur l'Amelioration du Sort des Classes Laborieuses.
   Indication of a Better System of Rural Economy.
Merson, E. De la Situation des Classes Ouvrieres en France, 12mo.
Druhen, J. Des Causes de l'Indigence, et des Moyens d'y Remedier, 8vo. 1850
Nesmond, P. C. Essai sur les Rapports, &c., 12mo.
   The Relations which exist between Property, Labour, Credit, and
   Misery, and upon the important consequences to be deduced from
   a knowledge of these relations.

Grancoin, Ch. Des Subsistances, et des Moyens de les mettre en Equi-
libre avec la Population. 8vo. ······································· 1850
Audiganne, A. Les Ouvriers en Famille, 18mo.
Conversations upon the duties and rights of the labourer in the dif-
ferent relations of his laborious life.
——————— De l'Organization du Travail, 12mo. ·················· 1844
Leclaire. De la Misère, et des Moyens à Employer pour la faire cesser, 8vo. 1850
Girardin, E. de. L'Abolition de la Misère par l'Elevation des Salaires.
Bernard. Plan d' Organization du Travail·························· 1851
Addressed to the friends of true order, justice, and family, of pro-
perty and religion; in a word, of the Republic; by labourers and
merchants.
Moreau, Christophe. Du Probleme de la Misère, 3 vols. 8vo.······ ——· 1851
Of the Problem of Misery, and its Solution, among people ancient
and modern. The first volume is devoted to paganism, the second
to the Mosaic period and the Christian dispensation of the Middle
Ages, the third to the principal states of Europe, and specially to
France.
Fregier. Solution Nouvelle du Probleme de la Misère, 12mo.·········· 1851
A Practical Method of Ameliorating the Condition of the Operatives
in our Manufactories.
Mohler, E. Sur l'Amelioration du Sort des Travailleurs.
Of the Association of Workmen. The Necessity of a new Industrial
Inquest, and a Model of an Institution of Succour and Retreat.
Cenac-Moncaut, M. J. Elements d'Economie Sociale et d'Organization
du Travail, 12mo.·· 1848
Depasse, E. Considerations, &c., 12mo.
Considerations upon Asylums, and their Influence upon the Future
Condition of the Poor.
Allard, M. Des Moyens d'Ameliorer le Sort des Travailleurs··········· 1848
The Means of Improving the Condition of Labourers, manufacturing
and agricultural, with a *Projet* for a Declaration of their Rights
and Duties and a *Projet* of a Law for the Amelioration of their
Condition.
Luro, V. Du Travail et de l'Organization des Industries dans Liberté,
18mo. ·· 1848
De Bausset-Roquefort. Devoirs, Droits, Assistance, 12mo ·············· 1849
Duties, Rights, Assistance in the light of Christianity, Liberty, and
Education.
Ducellier, F. Essais sur quelques Questions Sociales, 12mo.··········· 1848
Garcin, A. L'Assistance Publique, 18mo.···························· 1849
Public Assistance—what it is, what it ought to be; with a Manual for
Visitors of the Poor and those who exercise Private Charity.
Leclerc, L. Caisse d'Epargne et de Prevoyance, 18mo.
Letters to a Young Labourer upon the subjects of Indigence, In-
dustry, and Savings.

Marchal, L. Question des Subsistances, 12mo. 1849
    To this little volume was awarded a gold medal, as a prize for the
best essay on this subject, by a charitable association. The subject
is treated in its bearing on the interests of the poor.

Scribe, P. A. A. Question du Travail, Moyens, Pratique Sociaux, 18mo.
———————— De la Question du Travail, 12mo. 1848
    A Solution, proposed by a Labourer without Work.
———————— De la Richesse et des Imports, ou Usure et Travail,
    18mo. 1850
———————— De la Liberté en general, 8vo. 1849
    Of Liberty in general, of the Liberty of Labour, and the means of
    assuring the physical and moral well-being of the Working Classes.
Ramon, De la Sagra. Organization du Travail, 8vo. 1848
    Questions preliminary to the examination of that problem.
———————— Le Probleme de l'Organization du Travail, 8vo. ·· 1848
Bijleveld, J. C. De l'Organization du Travail par un meilleur systéme.
    A better system of the Organization of Labour.
O'Connor, A. C. Le Monopole Cause de tous les Maux.
    Monopoly the cause of all the distress.

    This work, published in Paris in 1849, in 3 large volumes, 8vo, by a
General of Division in the French Army, is devoted to the interests of
the poor. It is specially severe upon the *English* system.

Sauriac, X. Un Systéme d'Organization Sociale, 8vo., Paris 1850
Barrau, Th. H. Conseils aux Ouvriers, 12mo., Paris 1850
    Counsels to Workmen on the means of being happy.
Dupin, G. Enseignement et Sort des Ouvriers, 18mo., Paris 1848
    Instruction and fate of labourers.
Marbeau, F. De l' Indigence el des Secours, 18mo., Paris 1850
    Indigence and its succour.
De Cormenin, M. Des Salles d'Asile en Italie, 18mo., Paris 1848
Vee, M. Du Pauperisme et des Secours Publics, 18mo., Paris 1849
Glade, P.-V. De l' Indemnité des Pauvres, 8vo., Paris .... 1850 .
    Of the Indemnity of the Poor in France.
Beziat, G. Organization de l'Epargne du Travailleur, 12mo., Paris 1848
Du Travail et du Pain, 18mo., Paris 1849
    Of Labour and of Bread.
De la Liberté du Travail, 8vo., Paris 1849
    Of the Liberty of Labour, and the means of assuring the material
    and moral well-being of the labouring classes.
Merson, E. Du Droit au Travail, 18mo., Paris 1848
Jollivet. De la Philanthropie Anglaise, 8vo., Paris 1842

DEGERANDO ON CHARITY; OTHER FRENCH WORKS ON LABOUR, THE
POOR, AND CHARITY, SPECIALLY NOTICED.

WE trust the catalogue of French works, furnished above, may go far
to give the desired impression of the fulness, the frankness, and the
thoroughness with which the topics which they discuss have been met
and treated.   If the interested reader has not received as strong an
impression as it is fitted to give, we almost despair, in the limits which
are left us, of carrying his interest to the desired point by the rapid
survey we may now take of some of these admirable volumes.   These
works may be classified by their subjects; as works on charity, beneficence, humanity; on the poor, indigence, pauperism, misery; on labour,—its proper organization and its just rewards; on the history of
the working classes in all ages and stages of society; on Christian political economy; and on special subjects, such as the history of prostitu-
tion, and full accounts of all existing hospitals, asylums, and benevolent institutions.   To these may be added, able histories of the various
reforms and reformers of ancient and modern times.   These subjects
branch and spread over so wide a field, that the classification, like the
catalogue, fails to give an idea of the width of the harvest opened to
the reader.   But these volumes may be also arranged according to the
character, posifion, and opinions of the writers.   We have, then, political economists, philanthropists, catholics, protestants, statesmen, philosophers.   It is, perhaps, most curious and most instructive to regard
this matter under the point of view of the parties from whom the
respective opinions emanated.   We can, however, follow up neither
classification in what we further submit, and only merely indicate a
few of the more remarkable books, making a few quotations and extracts.   For many years the Academy of Moral and Political Sciences
has distinguished itself in the career of discussions touching social interests, physical and moral well-being.   This society offered a prize of
5000 francs for the best memoir on the subject of—" Misery, in what
it consists; what are its manifestations in different countries; and what
are its causes."   This is only one of very many prizes offered for memoirs on kindred topics by this society during the last twenty-five
years.   Very many valuable works have appeared in that period, in
response to the questions thus propounded.

   But this society, having its seat at Paris, was not the only as ocia-
tion which gave earnest heed to these subjects; several others, in dif-

ferent parts of France, had brought forward the condition of the suffering classes. As early as 1777, the Academy of Chalons-sur-Marne received a hundred memoirs in reply to questions upon mendicancy. A summary of these papers was published, and furnishes a vast mine of materials and thought for inquirers. There is, indeed, abundant evidence that the literary and scientific associations of France have not been forgetful of those whom poverty had denied, not only the advantages enjoyed by them, but even the smallest comforts beyond a bare existence.

The most meritorious work, perhaps, which has appeared in France on this subject, is that by the Baron Degerando, entitled, " DE LA BIENFAISANCE PUBLIQUE," published at Paris in 1838, in four volumes, 8vo. The author had previously published the *Visiteur du Pauvre*, in which he had turned the attention of his readers to the condition and claims of the poor, and furnished directions and motives for a constant and zealous attention to their wants.*

This work of Degerando may be fairly considered as having presented the most complete view of public charity which had appeared at the date of its publication, and, though a flood of light has since been shed on its various topics, yet no single production has surpassed it in variety, fulness, method, and the very spirit of kindness. In dedicating it to *his friends*, he prays that " He who is the source of all good, all consolation, and all light, may shed his blessing upon the imperfect attempt, and that his effort may contribute somewhat to the solace of humanity and the progress of good morals." The introduction contains an ample survey of the English, German, and French literature upon the subject of his labours. This exhibits great learning, industry, and discrimination, and furnishes proof how fully he was prepared for his task. In regard to the German writers, we are informed that the number who have taken up this subject is so considerable as to have led to the publication of special catalogues and bibliographical compilations. He indicates a considerable number of the principal works, and furnishes an appreciation of their contents. We cannot better give the spirit of the whole work than from the first portion of the rather prolonged introduction.

" The noble studies of which the interests of humanity are the object, and

---

* This excellent little volume has been translated and published in Boston, with a valuable introduction, written at the instance of the lady who made the translation, by the Rev. Joseph Tuckerman, 1832.

which affect elevated minds with such profound sympathies, are associated by
very intimate relations. Tending to a common end and based upon the same
elements, they afford mutual light and demand mutual support."

"Among their number, that which relates to the ills of suffering humanity,—
to the means of preventing and solacing them,—bears, more than any, close
relations to all the others. It is the centre of the system. . . . . We cannot in-
vestigate the painful phenomena of poverty without penetrating the constituent
elements of society itself, and without entertaining grave considerations upon
the distinction of classes, and the organization of property and labour. The
causes and effects of poverty touch, in many points, upon the subjects of crimi-
nal and civil legislation. In seeking preservatives and remedies, we enter, frequently, upon the most important problems of political economy. All that
regards public health comes under contribution in the consideration of public
succour. The torch of morals casts upon the origin and development of indigence light which we are far from having appreciated in its whole extent. . . . .
Philosophy, also, contributes to the study of beneficence; and these contributions are more important than is generally perceived. Religion, finally, which
rules ever at the summit of human affairs,—as including at once the higher
mysteries and the highest laws, appears, full of warning and wisdom, but
abounding in consolation, upon the scene where so many sufferings are displayed and so many victims sigh; it reveals knowledge, succours, and hopes of
inestimable value; it works wonders which manifest its power and claim the
admiration and the gratitude of the whole human family."

"The study of the ills of humanity mingles intimately with all the interests
of social order. Statesmen who have heretofore disdained this inquiry, discover
now, not without apprehension, that in this study are questions upon which
depend the repose of nations and the destiny of peoples. Governments learn
that, in the tears of the poor, there are for them instruction and duties. Of
all conditions of people, the wretched are, without doubt, those who have the
most right to our cares and anxieties; but we know their interests are connected with the other classes of society by a union which may be violated but
cannot be obliterated."

"If the general happiness, if the improvement of the great human family,
is the object of all the social sciences, that inquiry which concerns the suffering
classes must be preliminary to all others. Must it not contribute to all? Does
it not receive from all? Is it not, in many respects, one of the most vast, one
of the most necessary? Is it not, alas! also one of the practical sciences?"

"To be solid and instructive, such a study ought to be extended to its utmost
compass. It presents many phases, it is complicated in many ways. It must
be regarded as a whole, if the sacred cause of humanity is to be efficiently
served. The different branches of aid cannot be well appreciated but by their
coincidence in a common system, and by their relation with the evils they propose to cure. In considering these evils, we ask, whilst soothing them, if they
could have been prevented; we find ourselves inquiring their origin; we are
led over the whole path of human life,—observing the accidents which menace
it, the helps which sustain it; we regard misfortune in its sad and numberless

forms, in its connection with riches, in its relations with the whole of society, which acts upon it in many ways, and upon which it in turn reacts."

He remarks, that those who visit the abodes of destitution and the establishments for relief " cannot fail to be profoundly affected, to be attracted to the holy cause of humanity, and to be strongly inclined to devote themselves wholly to it."

The treatment of the subject of charity by the Christian fathers is noticed, showing how they "successively vindicate the rights of the poor; how warmly they exhort to the duty of alms-giving, and how, especially, they show that the duties of charity devolve upon the ministers of religion." It seems that the obligations of the clergy in regard to the poor have, in modern times, engaged the attention of the public more in Germany than elsewhere. In 1787, Julius, Bishop of Wurtzburgh, proposed as the subject of a prize essay, " The duties of ecclesiastics and those who have the care of souls, relatively to the well-being of those under their charge, and especially the poor." Twenty-five essays were sent in response, and many of them were published, "breathing the pure spirit of Christianity."

" The principles which establish the rights of the poor and the obligations of the rich have greatly occupied the attention of theologians, moralists, and jurisconsults of Germany. Wagenseilius, in 1700; Muller in 1749; Pfaff in 1771; Count Spaur, in 1802, have made them the subject of elaborate works. Various German and Swiss societies have proposed questions upon these topics; and altogether, in Germany and Switzerland, the subject has been more worthily handled and illustrated by examples than elsewhere."

Degerando notices the Malthusian controversy, and furnishes proof enough, whilst he gives him due credit for ability, that he has no sympathy with the leading doctrines of Malthus. Among the followers of Malthus, he distinguishes Dr. Chalmers, clearly with the intention of explaining why such a man should be found in such company.

" Among the writers who are ranged under the banner of Malthus, are some who have more or less modified his positions and corrected his errors. At the head of these is the respectable Dr. Chalmers. Casting over the whole field of philanthropic studies a *coup-d'œil* at once vast and profound, he perceived the divorce which was separating political economy from Christian charity. He undertook the reconciliation of these two classes of doctrines; he has shown the need they have of each other, and the inevitable mischief of the separation; he pointed out the principles which are common to them, and thus at once served the interests of society and humanity. Beholding, under a new aspect, the influence of Christianity upon the institutions of beneficence, he has shown in his life, not less than in his writings, that ecclesiastical establishments are the appropriate channels of benevolence. A minister himself of Christian worship, he justly appreciated the present state of society and the moral wants it experiences."

*   *   *   *   *   *

"Frequently prolix, but giving a special value to every detail by the spirit of observation which he displays, and by the practical utility at which he aims; with what skill does he not set forth all the springs of the organization suitable for carrying out the actions he recommends! With what authority of reason and experience does he not demonstrate the necessity of localizing, specializing, individualizing the different modes of succour! How admirably he reveals the immense advantages which flow from the relations of good-will which an active and intelligent charity establishes between the rich and indigent classes, and the means of increasing this touching sympathy."

After signalizing at some length and with great discrimination the course of authorship on these subjects, Degerando closes his introductory essay by some remarks upon what remains undone. He notes the " great divergence of opinion among writers, and the confusion in the minds of many, which in some begets discouragement, and in others distrust. The art of beneficence, at first glance so simple in its principles, so easy in its application, has given rise to problems the most complicated. In proportion as we remount to first principles, these problems become even more difficult. Religious and political differences have mingled in these discussions, and thus increased the difficulty by turning inquirers from the unbiassed pursuit of truth. The very foundations of our present social organizations have been drawn in question; the war of the poor against the rich has at some periods appeared imminent; and thus an agitation of mind has arisen which renders the whole of these studies more important for the interests of humanity. Painful anticipations have crept into the minds of good people—a dark cloud lies in their horizon, which seems to be fraught with tempests. They fear to see the scourge of pauperism sweeping over the land, and a feeling of dread takes possession of the thoughtful."

Upon comparing the views of the different parties to this great discussion, he ranges himself on the side of the hopeful, believing that the very discussion itself justifies our expecting the triumph of truth.

"We believe firmly in this triumph. We thus believe, after having partaken of the grievous doubts which arise from such opposite opinions,—after having weighed and compared these contradictions with a conscientious impartiality. Long reflection and continued investigation have produced the deepest convictions, which we shall express with as much sincerity as they were formed. We have faith in the marvellous power of beneficence guided by wisdom. We are persuaded that this holy virtue is not a thing of hazard, or vague or random instinct. It has rules, although difficult, founded upon positive principles. We do not partake of the terror felt by some in the present day on the subject of *pauperism*. We are not alarmed at the increase of population, nor at the flight of industry, nor at the growth of great cities, nor at the inequality of condition; but we think that the new social circumstances begot by the progress of industry, of wealth, of the advance of civilization, have given birth to new necessities, and impose on society new obligations. We are alarmed at dangers more real in our view, and because, perhaps, less known, more dangerous. If our new social duties are neglected, the danger will become more imminent; we need, therefore, a system of public beneficence, worked out with the most liberal and enlightened views, as the greatest of ameliorations in the condition of the suffering. Social ties are now becoming loosened; the spirit of calculation has invaded every thing; individuality feels a conscious triumph; attacks, always imprudent, often culpable, awaken between the different classes of society distrust and discord, if not dreadful hostility. In the very bosom of prosperity, inquietude begins to grow and spread." . . . . . ('All must concur in the restoration of harmony. We shall insist upon this duty, in all its extent and in all its strictness. The result for the rich, will be the enlightened and benevolent patronage of the poor; for the poor, the spirit of labour, of order, and good conduct; for society in general, measures of protection, of prevention, and of solace for misfortune." . . . . .

"A great and principal truth springs up here to our view:—to morals belongs the grand privilege of founding, preserving, and perfecting human institutions; to morals belongs eminently the prevention of the causes of indigence, and the solace of sufferings, and, above all, the establishment of such relations between rich and poor as may be equally useful and happy for both. Public morals are the soul of social beneficence, as virtue is the inspiration of private charity. The august alliance of morals and beneficence is, in our view, the thought which comprehends and governs the whole subject; it has guided our labours, animated our zeal, sustained our strength, and is the foundation of our hopes."

"The well-being of the labouring classes is a subject of immense interest for society, and cannot be purchased at a price too high. To ascertain the means of promoting that well-being; to emancipate this numerous and interesting class from the evils which threaten them, or, at least, to mitigate the sufferings which are inevitable, is the ardent desire of all generous minds. We unite with such with all our soul; we are devoted to this effort with all the zeal and all the perseverance of which we are capable. But to serve this great cause the more perfectly, we are, above all, devoted to the truth; we refuse to indulge in illusions which may defeat our progress by carrying us too far. We have not merely kept in view that which is desirable, but that which is practicable."

We have drawn largely from this introductory essay; but those who will read the whole will find that our extracts have failed to furnish any adequate idea of its merit. It was by far the best statement of the subject, as it then stood, which had ever appeared. No doubt it contributed not a little to awaken men's minds to the pressing importance of questions the discussion of which could not be much longer delayed. It is true, that great delusions prevail on these topics in France, but there is also a large and enlightened body which clings to the sober but earnest humanity of Degerando. In real knowledge of this subject the French are an age in advance of their English neighbours; and if they are more annoyed by those who hold extravagant and impracticable theories, they have weapons to contend with them which must finally conquer. In England, these extravagant and dangerous doctrines are repressed, not refuted. When they prevail in England to an equal extent as in France, they will be more dangerous, because there only brute force will be opposed to them.

We have yet to point out the arrangement and the special topics of the work before us.

THE FIRST PART.—*Book First* treats of indigence in its relations with social economy, as being the object of public beneficence. Indigence classified, absolute or relative; its degrees, and herein of wages. The indigent strong and weak, male and female, skilled and unskilled, by their own fault, temporary and permanent; circumstances, prognostics, and effects of indigence. Statistics of poverty in the various countries of Europe and in the United States of America.

Book Second.—Of social riches, and herein of the total wealth of a country and its special apportionment, of the inequality of conditions, of the lower classes and of the prospects of the extinction of indigence: of industry in its relations with the causes of indigence, and of the labourer under the double aspect of producer and consumer, and herein of the rewards of labour, the relations of the employers with the employed, the rate of wages, and the prices of articles of consumption; raw materials, great enterprises, influences of commerce, vicissitudes of industry, effect of profuse expenditure or luxury in the higher classes upon the labourer, the labour of children, labour as a means of instruction; of population in its relations with indigence. Questions raised upon this subject, of the increase of population, mortality, births, marriages, manners and morals, vices, crimes, influence of towns, influence of higher classes; of social, institutions and their influence upon poverty, institutions political and social of communities, corporations of arts and trades, laws of property and laws as to persons, penal and fiscal laws, public expenditure, taxes, lotteries, corn-laws, customs, military service; how the errors of beneficence multiply the indigent, distinguishing the true poor from the pretended; the grounds of apprehension from the increase of pauperism.

Third Book.—Of the rights of indigence as arising from civilization, their nature and extent, limits, duties of the poor, injuries, distinction between legal charity and public beneficence, of the duties and power of private and public charity.

SECOND PART.—*Book First.*—Institutions for the education of the poor, aiding mothers, placing them at nurse, schools and asylums for infants, their management and economy; orphans, institutions for their care, ancient and modern, in Europe; orphans in England and the United States, France and Belgium, regulations; foundlings, their treatment anciently and now; foundling hospitals, their history in every country of Europe, questions, doubts, and discussions as to foundlings, abandonment of children.

The subject of foundlings is treated at great length in every aspect of the subject, but with a constant inclination to the propriety and necessity of providing fully for the support and education of all foundlings as well as orphans. There is clearly no infusion of Malthus in the twelve chapters of Degerando's work devoted to the interests of little children. The 11th and 12th of these chapters relate specially to schools for foundlings and orphans, to train their minds in knowledge and their hands to useful employment.

Second Book.—Institutions for loans to the poor throughout Europe, their history and utility; of societies for mutual assistance, their origin in Greece and Rome, history; life insurance; savings' banks, their character and history in Europe.

Third Book.—Of the means of preventing indigence by changes in social economy, of measures touching the apportionment of property, of co-operative societies, of the organization of labour, the necessity of it at present, the conditions to be fulfilled, country labour, city labour, the various kinds of trades, large manufactories, public service, special institutions to provide labour, domestic economy of the labourer, public health, instruction of the working classes, prizes for special acts of virtue, the family, contentment of the labouring classes, popular amusements, morals, police, labour as a means of education, houses of refuge for females, temperance societies, morals of criminals in confinement, penitentiary systems, and aid for those who are set at liberty; of religion, as a part of popular education, as the protectress of the suffering, the special power of Christianity for the amelioration of popular morals, the ills of false religious instruction, exterior worship; of the means of strengthening religious influences upon popular manners.

THIRD PART.—*Book First.*—Of the means of procuring useful occupation for the poor, employment with individuals and for the public, labour at the domicil, Hamburg Institute, shops for sale of products of labour of the poor; workhouses throughout Europe, reform of English poor-laws; discussions which have arisen as to workhouses, of their organization, economy, discipline; of workhouses where the labour is forced, their history; of receptacles for mendicants, and their history in Europe, of their utility, objections and replies; of the labour most suitable for the poor, in respect to their capacity, to their management, or to their working by the piece or job, the effect of their labour on the general interests of industry, of the public works, charity-shops, farm-labour, distribution of lands to the poor; *colonization of the poor*, their fitness for colonists, colonies interior, foreign, various experiments, Switzerland, Holland, Belgium, agricultural colonies as a means of beneficence for the poor, objections and replies; of *emigration*, researches on the subject, various emigrations of Europe, interior and foreign.

Book Second.—Assistance at the domicil, origin and first forms of, and specially in Great Britain, organization, succour to the able-bodied, to the weak, results of such assistance, charitable associations affording the mode of relief in England, assistance at domicil in various countries of Europe, and in the United States, of the best methods of giving this succour, visiting the poor, of giving money; of distributions at reduced prices of food, clothing, fuel, to the aged and incurable, to women and children, casualties, burial, succour extraordinary in great public calamities, as famine, fire, and flood, of aid to those who are so timid as not to make known their wants.

Third Book.—Of houses of entertainment for the poor among the ancients, in the middle ages, and at the present day, establishments in France since 1750; *of hospitals,* their utility, objections answered, their constitution, conditions of admission, a great variety of particulars in relation to administration; hospitals for children, for chronic affections, and lying-in hospitals; of houses for the old and the infirm; *of houses for the insane,* their constitution, history, and condition in Europe, in the United States, and in the East.

FOURTH PART.—*First Book.*—Of poor-laws, of the origin of legislation for the poor, legislation of the Egyptians, Hebrews, Greeks, Romans—republican and imperial, legislation of Modern Europe for the poor, requisites in legislation for the poor.

Book Second.—*Of the administration of poor-laws,* unity of system, centralization, union of public and religious charity, officers, associations, and of females in the work of charity; ameliorations desirable in the administration of relief.

If Degerando could, with his wide survey of the subject, with his unprejudiced and frank statement of the truth, have carried with him the Christian fervour, experience, and knowledge of Dr. Chalmers, the work we have just noticed would have been one of the most effective and useful which ever came from the press. The student of humanity should therefore carry to the study of Degerando the Christianity and zeal of Chalmers. Whoever reads the *"Visiteur du Pauvre"* and *"De la Bienfaisance Publique,"* in the strong Christian aspect of the subjects, will find a range of topics open to his vision which will make him lament that at least two-thirds of the volumes which now crowd the shelves of theological libraries had not been devoted to the interests of men, temporal and eternal, instead of being of so little practical value that they might be all destroyed any day without detriment to human welfare. The "Word was made flesh" and dwelt with us in a blended divinity and humanity : let the *word* of our religious instruction be ever so continued to us, that while God is always held up to our view, man is never hidden from our sight.

The History of Charity during the First Four Centuries of the Christian Era, by MARTIN DOISY, which appeared immediately after the Revolution of 1848, is well-conceived, exhibits much research, and, although the whole work is from an earnest Catholic, abounds in considerations of great and instructive interest. The subject is regarded as one clearly belonging to Christianity, and the devotion of the Romish Church to its duties is treated as one of her highest titles to favour. But while it is thus viewed, it is apparent that the chief design of the author is to promote the well-being of the suffering classes.

" No one can accuse us of having erred as to the time of bringing forward a work, of which the suffering classes are the subject and charity the foundation. Politics, social economy, the legislative hall, and the periodical press, history and romance, present us, at every turn, with the subject of the masses. At this moment, history is being recast and rewritten for the benefit of the people." . . . . . " The object of France is the people—it is the progressive amelioration of the lot of the suffering multitudes; that is, the present ameliorated by the education of men; the future assured by the education of the children."

Quoting from Lamartine, who is addressing a proprietor, he says :—

" Keep thy property, for in spite of visions of community of goods, property is the *sine qua non* of society : without it we can have neither family, nor labour, nor civilization."

But he says also :—

"Forget not, that property is not instituted for thee merely, but for all humanity : thou shalt possess it, but upon the conditions of justice, social utility, and an open hand : thou shalt furnish to thy brethren, out of thy superfluity, the means and elements of labour necessary for them, that they, in their turn, may become helpers of others : thou shalt recognise a right above the right of property—the *right of humanity*."

He quotes from Guizot, who speaks thus :—

" It is impossible to regard without profound compassion so many human beings bearing from the cradle to the tomb so heavy a burden, and even then scarcely maintaining a miserable existence. That is a grievous thought, and yet it is a thought never to be dismissed ; to forget it would be a grave and perilous error."

The work before us is not a mere work of theology : its object is to show how the duties of Christian charity bear upon the condition and prospects of the suffering working-classes. He shows us the advent of charity at the appearing of Christ, and sets forth at large his mission of mercy, his humble ministry of kindness, as that which it should be

the aim of his followers to imitate. He recounts the hospitality of
ancient Christians and the charity of the apostolic times; he develops
the doctrines of human fraternity, and, especially, the doctrine of
charity as taught by Christ. Although the Catholic Church is greatly
lauded by this writer, we do not hesitate to recommend his work to
Protestants, as calculated to humble their spiritual pride, and possibly
goad them into paths of charity hitherto little trodden by their feet.

We have *A Philosophical History of Beneficence*, from the pen of M.
TAILHAND, in 1847. It has considerable merit, and is also written
expressly with reference to the sufferings of the labouring classes.
His introduction commences thus:—

"The human race is, in its earthly dwelling, afflicted with so many evils, that
it might be deemed man was a mere abortion upon the earth. The thrill of
joy runs rarely to his heart, and even then it is rarely unmingled with sad-
ness. Infirmities are the portion of his physical nature, and make him a man
of grief." ..... "In the midst of this scene of suffering and disorder which is
displayed around us, there is one bright object which delights us and justifies
the course of Providence to our race; that is beneficence—that is the man of
charity. His deeds are, in my view, rays of the Divinity piercing the night
of this world,—demonstrative evidence of that Providence which never with-
draws its overwatching care. I could never have believed that man was made
in the image of his Creator, if I had not seen him smitten with tenderness and
compassion for the suffering; and now I perceive him to be intrusted with a
special mission of love and mercy to his fellow-creatures. If I inquire whence
comes this charity, the ways of God are unveiled to my eyes in a manner still
more striking; for I find the motives of beneficence in the heart and in the
conscience." ..... "To prove that conscience is the main, the most faithful,
and the most energetic principle of charity, is the object of this work."

Mr. Tailhand, who subscribes himself a *Priest without charge*, gives
a solution to this inquiry which is truly Romish. He makes every act
of charity expiatory, and thus shows the interest of all men to be charitable. Every act of self-sacrifice, in which men sacrifice their own
interests to those of others, goes in part satisfaction of their sins.
Whatever may be thought of this author's theology, he presents powerful motives to those of his faith to abound in charity. Overlooking its
religious tenets, this volume contains useful details, interesting views,
strong exhortations upon the whole subject of beneficence, which do
credit both to his head and heart. His work, like that of Martin Doisy,
is mainly historical, and brings in review beneficence under the patri-
archs, among the Jews, among the pagans, during the first six centuries of Christianity, in the middle ages, and in modern times.

In 1829, M. T. DUCHATEL published at Paris, *Charity in its relations with the morals and the well-being of the lower classes of society.* Speaking, in his preface, of statesmen, he says they too frequently "look upon nations as collective beings, and neglect to extend their regards to the lower classes of society, who, however, include the greater part of the human family; they overlook these classes in their theories as they disregard them in their histories. It appears to us, they ought to have part in the general movement—in the march of civilization; and that progress for the better ought to be sought for them as well as for those classes who are greater favourites of fortune. Such is the spirit in which this work is conceived." After a rapid sketch of the condition of the lower classes, from their original slavery until their gradual attainment of freedom of person and freedom of industry, he proceeds:—

"Since this change has been accomplished, the destiny of the working classes has been regarded in two special aspects. Some, preoccupied with certain theories of political economy, not perceiving any other source of power and wealth for a nation than what is derived from the sale of domestic products to foreign nations, have sacrificed to that object the interests of labourers. This foreign sale proceeds more freely in proportion as merchandise is lower in price; and prices are lower in proportion as wages are lower. It follows that, for the prosperity of this foreign trade, wages should be low. .... It is in this point of view that men, the producers of the articles which enter into this foreign trade, are regarded as mere machines."

He remarks that such is the policy of England, and thanks God that this chimerical system, which sacrifices the well-being of the population to the interests of commerce, has few partisans left. The author, who is now a distinguished public man and friend of the Orleans family, has lived to see the friends of this system greater in number and stronger in influence than ever, under the banner of free-trade. "Others, more humane," our author proceeds, "are animated with an earnest desire for the good of the producing classes: they love their fellow-men. They do not hesitate at sacrifices for the comfort of the indigent; but their philanthropy, not sufficiently enlightened, regards the actual condition of the suffering which requires aid as inevitable and fixed. They think only of helping the poor by means derived from the rich, and by deeds of charity." ..... "Thus, while the interests of the poor are sacrificed by some to false systems of political economy, they are sacrificed by others to a false system of charity." ..... "But," referring to the system last mentioned, he asks, "Is this true charity? Does it not overlook all that the future promises for the amelioration of the lot of workmen? Ought not our efforts to be directed to increasing the income of workingmen? Ought we not to rescue them from the condition of dependence upon charity, by giving them the full reward of their labour?" As a philosophical work, this is far superior to the two last mentioned: it is calm and forcible; it displays ability, varied knowledge, and deep sympathy. He discusses the following topics:—*The necessity of charity, and the rules for its exercise; the causes of misery; the laws which determine the increase of population among the inferior classes; formation of capital; inequality of wealth; employment of machines; influence of government; remedies; public relief; famines; interruption of labour; hospitals; beggary; private charity; political economy and morals; prospects of labourers in the future.* Although we may differ from some of his conclusions, and desire to qualify some of his positions, we commend the work of M. Duchatel to all the students of humanity. One of his chief mistakes is, that there is a perfect accordance between political economy and sound morals: as he conceived the subject, there may be; but the political economy of the great writers and doctors of the so-called science discard all relations with morals and humanity. When political economy is developed from its only proper starting-point, human well-being, it will be found in accordance with strict morals and pure religion. At present, if its advocates dare follow it so far, a strict logic would carry political economy into sheer infidelity.

The next work we specially bring to the notice of the reader, is that of a Protestant minister of the gospel in Geneva, published at Paris in 1836, in two volumes, 8vo.,—*Of Legal Charity, its effects and causes.* Its motto, quoted from the *Monthly Journal of Political Economy*, of 1834, is, "The agitation and uneasiness, now apparent in all quarters, announce that the time has come when we must meet these high and difficult questions." It was written in competition for a prize, proposed by the French Academy, upon the following subject:—"Of charity, considered in its principles, in its applications, and in its influence upon manners and upon social organization." One-third of the prize was awarded to the author, the Rev. F. M. L. NAVILLE, and a very complete report and analysis of this work was made to the Academy by its secretary. In his introduction, the author, after having stated briefly some of the causes of indigence, proceeds:—

"Thence springs a misery of which the spectacle wounds the heart, and produces frequently an excessively importunate beggary, at times even menacing the general security. Humanity, religion, the interests of social order, and public well-being exact an effort to diminish it,—an effort to relieve the wretched whose existence is rendered so painful,—to protect society from the dangers to which it is exposed,—to put an end to the fatiguing importunities of which it is the pretext."

The spirit of this extract makes a slight approach to the English view of the subject. Naville, like Dr. Chalmers, is strongly opposed to a legal provision for the poor; but, while his work is greatly superior to that of the Scottish divine in method and in breadth of view, he falls far below him in conception of the relations of the subject with Christianity. Their united efforts blended would have presented the best work which has yet appeared; and their different conclusions blended would, even yet, form the safest solution of the problems in question. Chalmers committed the care of the poor, as a religious duty, to the officers of the parish church: Naville refers this care to private charity, under the enlightened considerations and cautions which he suggests, stimulated by Christian sympathy. The argument of Naville against *legal charity* is of signal ability and power, with a method at once logical and clear, and fortified by a large array of facts and authorities, derived from all the countries of Europe, and from the legislation of many of our States. Besides the sketch he gives of the various countries, he considers specially the effect of public relief upon the morals and ultimate welfare of the relieved, the effect upon those who are refused, and the effect of collecting the poor-rates upon those who pay them. The plan of succour at the domicile is also fully considered and condemned: so, also, the various plans of hospitals, asylums, private and public labour for the special benefit of the poor. He traces the use of legal charity, or a compulsory provision for the poor, and furnishes a sketch of public opinion on the subject in Europe.

In proposing *private charity* as the only effectual and safe mode of relieving indigence and suffering, he lays down six principles as a guide, which may be briefly stated thus :—1. Pity must be indulged, but caution not forgotten. 2. We must bear in mind that the poor man is a moral being. 3. We must not disregard the social nor the family relations of the poor. 4. We must not only relieve misery, but prevent it. 5. While private charity does the work, it should be able to derive, and employ properly, aid drawn from the public. 6. Whatever organization be given to this public aid, it should be of a nature to encourage and stimulate private charity, by using the agency of

those whose active charities bring them continually in contact with
the poor.

If these principles, as well as much more which Naville has written
on the subject of private charity, had a larger infusion of Christian
light and sympathy, they would be unexceptionable. Chalmers wrote
upon the subject under the influence of a constant glow of Christian
feeling. Naville philosophizes calmly and kindly, reserving the Christian aspect of the subject for a separate chapter, from which, by way
of vindicating him, we proceed to make a few extracts.

"If all men have the same origin; if the same joys are promised to all, and the
same punishments are denounced against all beyond the tomb; if their goods
are but deposites, for the use of which they must render an account to God who
gave them; if the life of the founder of the Christian religion was a scene of
mercies, and his death an act of self-devotion; if, to partake of his glory, it is
needful to walk in his footsteps; if the chief characteristic of his disciples is,
that they love one another; if, in celebrating his memory, they partake of the
same bread and drink of the same cup,—are not these facts, truths, symbols
eminently fitted to inspire charity, to enforce its exercise, and to justify
the general opinion, which regards charity and Christianity as synonymous
terms?"

In this connection, he speaks with commendable impartiality of the
devoted kindness to the suffering of the *Brethren de Saint-Jean de Dieu,*
a Catholic institution in France, and insists that no motive but those of
the Christian could induce such devotion as is visible in these brethren
and in many others who give themselves to works of charity.

"We may not flatter ourselves that any plan of private charity, however enlightened, can ever succeed, if the easy classes, from whom the resources must
come, and among whom also must be found the men to do the work, are not
animated by the vivifying spirit of Christianity."

"We do not mean here that pretended Christianity which consists in mere
faith or in mere deeds." .... "The Christianity we have in view is the religion
of Him who reduced the whole law to the precepts of love to God and our
neighbour, and who, in the parable of the good Samaritan, has taught us who
is that neighbour whom we are to love as ourselves; it is the religion which
feeds the poor, consoles the afflicted, upholds the weak, protects the widow and
the orphan,—which is the hope and refuge of all the unhappy,—which, by its
abounding good works, has exhibited to all people a God of all goodness and
a Saviour who commenced the reign of love on earth. It matters little to
what sect those belong who profess it; it is not by the opinions which divide
them, but by the love which unites them, that the title of Christians is merited."—*Naville,* vol. 2, p. 264.

In 1850, L. LAMOTHE published, at Paris, *New Studies upon Charitable Legislation.* It is a summary, with additions, of previous pro-

ductions on the subject. He is inclined to Malthus upon some points, being, with him, opposed to compulsory provision for the poor, and believing that population gains upon food, without acceding to the mathematical formula in which Malthus states his position. But in his general treatment of the subject, he is far from Malthusian. Himself engaged in the administration of charities, a large experience aided his investigations. "In all my studies and writings upon the subject," he remarks,* "it will be easily seen that one thought runs through the whole,—the amelioration of the condition of the humbler classes." He believes the time has come when the application of the principles of charity which the Scriptures lay down for the direction of individuals, may be also demanded of society at large. He believes, with Messrs. Dufaure, Coquerel, Victor Hugo, Faucher, and Thiers, that Christianity, which has renovated the face of the world during the last eighteen centuries, ought to become the base of every administrative code,—that society should, within the measure of its resources, and within the limits which wisdom dictates, come to the succour of individual misfortune,—that individual foresight and prudence should not exclude that of the community,—that in matter of aid, the public should do all that is possible, and attempt all that is probable. The author who expresses such sentiments may be forgiven if, out of sympathy for the school of rank political economists with whom he is in amicable relations, he declares some accordance with Malthus. We have an additional guarantee for the soundness of our author's views in the evident regard he entertains for the labours of Edmond de Pressensé, a Protestant pastor in Paris, who published in 1849,—*Conferences upon Christianity in its Application to Social Questions,*—a very profound work, which we shall bring more specially to the notice of our readers. We subjoin a portion of the quotations made from its pages by M. Lamothe :

"We reject the division so frequently made of morals, into two kinds: the one of universal application; the other for the guidance of individuals merely. There is but one principle of morals; its applications may vary; it cannot vary itself. If that principle is justice, absolute and exclusive, it can be obeyed by society alone. But if we recognise charity as lying at the base of morals, we cannot conceive any reason why we should not realize its benefits in our social institutions. Is it so that God having foreborne to visit us with justice, we are the less inclined to exercise alike mercy to our fellow-creatures?"

* Preface.

"If the principle of charity is the basis of morals, then the doctrine of pure justice is no more applicable to the sphere of the state than in private life. You are apprehensive, you say, that you will diminish the occasions of individual charity. Be not afraid: ample opportunities will remain for benevolent action, even if the monopoly is taken away from individuals. For, as we say, the applications of charity differ; but one mode does not exclude others. It is to be well considered what is the special application to be made by the state; and to ascertain this, we must inquire what is the providential mission assigned to the state, for within this limit only must the principle of charity be applied." .... "According to the socialists, the state is charged with our moral development—it ought to accomplish this for us, by removing all obstacles and all temptations. That is the paternal government renewed. According to the political economists, the state is merely the medium in which we live: it should hold itself apart, regarding only our crimes, and disregarding wholly our miseries. There is a *juste milieu* between these theories. The state cannot assume the care of our moral development, for that is an affair of conscience and liberty; neither ought it to be simply a power of suppression or punishment."

"The state is the sphere of our moral development." .... "Social life, while it stimulates our activity, might also destroy it, if not under the restrictions of law; if interests and passions were without due restraint; if law was not substituted for the hazards of violence and force. Such is the sublime mission of the state. It is the high social object of saving to every one the right of fulfilling his destiny. Law, in this aspect, is the channel of the possibility of duty. The state is not only the sphere, it is one of the conditions of our moral development; and it is from this high point, we ought to take all our departures, in seeking the providential ends of this great institution. Let the principle of charity once be declared predominant in society, and it is clear that we can no longer content ourselves with attributing to the state solely a negative mission, as would be that of protecting individuals one from another, and merely puting out of the way whatever is injurious to the moral development: we may then demand that this object be directly promoted." .... "The state should render moral development possible to all,—nothing more, nothing less; and it ought to be accomplished by the beneficial operation of our social institutions as a whole. A state constituted upon the principle of charity, would enable every man to fulfil all the duties of his position,—his proper destiny: that is, while it respected his personal liberty more than at present, it would cover him with the buckler of law from undue injury of any kind. Without liberty, there is no moral development, not even if the restraint is accompanied with large benefits: this indeed, instead of a help, is an obstacle to improvement."

"But there are physical sufferings, dreadful privations, and growing inquietudes, which break down and materialize the soul. The raging appetites of privation are as dangerous as the indulgences of luxury. Very well! A well ordered state ought, by the completeness of its adjustments, to prevent these perverting miseries. It ought to furnish food, by proper elementary instruction, for the mind, without which it becomes barren; and food for the body, without which the finest systems of laws upon paper are but illusions and treachery. In this way alone can the state be the condition of our moral development; and thus far, we repeat, it should go, and no farther."—*Conferences, &c., par Edm. Pressensé*, p. 296, &c.

In the first chapter of his work, Lamothe brings into review some of the principal writers on the subject, from which review we take a few extracts.

"Malthus, Chalmers, Duchatel, Naville,—these are the heads of that school, improperly enough called the Protestant, but which, in our opinion, had been more fitly named the rationalist school. Its distinctive character consists in imposing silence upon the language of the heart, and proceeding exclusively by the light of reason and the facts.* Its services are acknowledged by its adversaries; it has laid bare the true principles, taught us to recognise them and to strip off the accessories which lead so many from the reality."

Speaking of Malthus, he says :—

"Is it not he who has best perceived the relations and limits which exist between the prudence which foresees misery and the charity which relieves it,— the relation between wages and the increase of population ?"

He complains of Blanqui for having, in his History of Political Economy, condemned the doctrines of Malthus, and made the epithet *Malthusian* one of reproach, without, however, substituting for his doctrines something better. It is strange that Lamothe could not see the relations of Christianity with the subject, and the solutions it offers. He and others do Christianity the honour of a conspicuous mention, but they draw no solution from Revelation, and are as far from walking in its light as the Protestants whom he calls rationalists. He mentions, next, a work we had designed for special examination in these notes,—*Christian Political Economy, or Researches into the nature and causes of Pauperism*,—the author of which is thus introduced to his readers by Lamothe:—

"In face of these writers, in the opposite camp, M. le Vicomte Alban de Villeneuve-Bargemont presents himself. He is an apostle of the gospel, who sees no remedy for the evils of society but in a strict observance of the teachings of Christ." .... "Christian charity, carried into public policy, into the laws, into the institutions and the manners of a country, can alone preserve social

---

* We may doubt whether Dr. Chalmers would have been flattered by being placed thus in the school of rationalists. Whatever else may justify this classification, he cannot justly be accused of silencing the language of the heart.

30

order from the frightful dangers which threaten it. Without this element,
there is nothing but deceit and illusion."—*Nouvelles Etudes*, p. 3.*

This important work of Villeneuve-Bargemont (in 3 vols. 8vo.) was
the fruit of long-continued and patient study of the whole subject, and
of great experience in the highest offices of departmental administration in France. The author is a zealous Catholic, but not to the extent
of exalting *the church* above Christianity.* The subject seemed to be
of the very highest interest to him, and he pursues it with the ardour
of a true friend of the human family. His preface gives a frank history of the changes which his mind had to undergo in his investigations. We can only transfer a few points.

"That which has chiefly struck me in my studies, is the dreadful influence
which the industrial and political system of England has exercised over France,
Europe, and other portions of the world. That system, based upon insatiable
selfishness and upon a profound contempt of human nature, has been displayed
to my eyes with the effect of exalting my sentiment of nationality to the highest
point, as will be visible in this work; but I have tried to be faithful to truth,
and not to injure or exaggerate."

"In effect, real pauperism, that general distress or destitution, permanent
and progressive, of the population, had its birth in England, and it is thence
the contagion has spread. For three hundred years this power has not ceased
to excite the love of wealth, luxury, material enjoyments; a ruling aristocracy,
a clergy enriched with the spoils of Catholicism, speculators, skilful and
prompt, occupying stations of power, controlling capital, property, and industry,
have not ceased to accumulate lands, and the advantages of commerce and
navigation;—a monstrous centralization of fortune and the despotism of riches
continually employed in extending its power and possessions;—such has been
the incessant advance of this proud and greedy class, in their ascendency over
the population. It is thus they everywhere employ and use the human race;
and, whilst they are distinguished for improving the breeds of other animals,
they are ever engaged in overworking and injuring the race and constitution
of their working classes. It was not enough to swallow all the wealth of Great
Britain—this insatiable cupidity reaches forth to every portion of the earth.
At any price it must be satisfied—violence, inhumanity, corruption, all this
and more have in turn been employed in ministering to this appetite."

"For a long period the opulence of England has dazzled all eyes, and her
example has seduced many other nations; but at last time and experience are

---

* Accompanying this work of Lamothe is an extended bibliography of charity
and the kindred topics, of great value to the student of philosophy and social
science.

† He names among his most intimate friends, with whom he consulted on
these topics, a Protestant professor of theology at Montauban.—Vol. i. p. 9.

removing the veil which conceals the frightful misery of a population,* oppressed, famished, and pushed to the borders of despair."

" Publicity has revealed the excess of production; the manufacturing struggle, under the impulse of unregulated competition, is reacting with vigour. It is plain the colossus is shaken; an abyss is being dug beneath its feet.", . . .

" The English system reposes upon the concentration of capital, of commerce, of lands, of industry, of indefinite production, of universal competition, upon the reduction of wages, and, finally, upon the moral degradation of man."

"Let us found our French system upon a just and wise distribution of the products of industry; upon the equitable remuneration of labour; upon the development of agriculture; upon our industry, applied to the products of our own soil; upon the religious regeneration of man; and, finally, upon the great principle of charity."—*Econ. Pol. Chret.* preface, vol. i. p. 22.

The motto of the *introduction* is quoted from *Droz*, and runs thus:—

" In reading certain economists, one might be led to think that the products of industry were not made for man, but that man was made for the products."

The first lines of the *introduction* are as follow :—

"Individual poverty, that is privation more or less absolute of the necessaries of life, is a position so painful, that the natural sympathy between man and his fellow compels us to yield our compassion; it is, in the eyes of religion, a suffering of which Heaven enjoins upon us the solace, wherever it exists; it is a physical and moral degradation, for which the interests of society require a remedy."

He distinguishes between that isolated and transient poverty arising from the very nature of man, the relative inferiority of physical strength and of intelligence, the inequality of social position, and other inevitable evils incident to the differences between men, and that "indigence which passes under the new and sadly energetic name of pauperism, which invades entire classes of the population, and tends to increase at the rate of the industrial production." "If this," he remarks, "is not an accident of society, but a condition of life forced upon large portions of the community, it cannot be a mistake to find in these symptoms of suffering, thus diffused in the body politic, a disease, deep-seated, and menacing the approach of severe and perhaps fatal disturbance to the whole social system thus affected."—Vol. i. p. 27.

It would be interesting, as well as profitable to the heart and to the understanding, to follow this truly humane and Christian writer

---

* A population worked for the benefit of foreign, not domestic trade; for the benefit of merchants, not of the producers; for foreign, not home consumption; for cheap production, that foreigners may purchase; but at the lowest wages, that the producers may not consume.—[*Editor.*]

through all the volumes of a work conceived in a spirit so charitable,
making extracts as we proceed; but we must forbear, and merely indicate an outline of his topics.

The first volume treats of *the religious view of indigence; the inequality of men; theories of civilization; of progress; of the principle of population; celibacy of priesthood; of labour; of the production, distribution, and consumption of riches; profits and wages;
agricultural industry; manufacturing industry; machinery; the new
feudal system; commercial industry; St. Simonism; taxes; luxury;
ignorance and immorality of the working classes; political revolutions.*

The second volume treats of *the condition and number of the indigent and of beggars in Europe; of charity and its application, private
and public; of legislation in regard to the indigent.*

The third volume is devoted to *charitable institutions; the revision
of the poor-laws; and to agriculture, considered as a means of relieving and preventing indigence.*

He takes leave of his readers on the last page by saying, whilst
lamenting the deficiencies of his work,—

"Our intentions, however, will be understood and our efforts appreciated by
those who have studied the moral causes and effects of misery, and reflected
upon the means of prevention. Besides, our ambition will be satisfied if we
shall awaken the attention of any of the governments of Europe to questions
so vital to the present epoch; if we shall have aided in disseminating useful
truths; and above all, if we shall have excited a spirit of charity in some
Christian hearts."

"May that which we have been able merely to indicate, be completed and
perfected by abler hands. The age is ripe to comprehend that social order
must be based on laws, and confined within limits traced by an Almighty
hand. To acknowledge this eternal truth, to return to our obedience to its dictates, that is the progress which ought to characterize our day, and for which
we shall not cease to pray whilst we desire to promote human happiness."—
Vol. iii. p. 584.

We should gladly extend our notices to other French works upon
charity which are lying round us, making such extracts as might
characterize them, but it would far exceed our limits.

There is another class of productions of great interest which we
must pass over, devoted exclusively to the topics of *pauperism*, the
poor, the *wretched*, the *dangerous*, the *disinherited classes*, the *misery
of the working classes*, &c.: the titles of many of these, of great merit
and breathing the very soul of humanity, and not unfrequently, also,
the very spirit of Christianity, will be found in the preceding catalogue.

We must not, however, omit all mention of those which go to show that, while humanity and Christian sympathies are so intelligently excited in France in favor of the suffering, efforts are not wanting in the direction of a more enlarged treatment of the whole subject, and in the way of prevention of evils, as well as their cure. A discussion has been actively proceeding in France for many years, which, until very recently, could not be touched, much less endured, in England nor in the United States. The fact that the labouring classes—the great mass of producers, to whose industry we are chiefly indebted for our material comforts—do not receive a just remuneration of their labour, and do not enjoy their proper share of the blessings which social institutions should afford, is freely admitted in France, and the best minds of that country are devoting their energies and acumen to the solution of the great problem involved in the just reward of labour. They no longer meet this great question with the estoppels, that the poor will always be with us, and that inequalities of condition are inevitable: they feel the necessity, having granted the truth of these propositions, of inquiring, nevertheless, what can be done to diminish the number of the poor, and to render inevitable inequalities as tolerable as possible. They admit the necessity of seeking the clue to the true and just organization of labour, so that he who toils to earn a subsistence by the sweat of his brow may have some assurance that an undue portion of the avails of his labour shall not go to those who do not labour at all. It would require large space to bring before our readers even a slight indication of what has been written on this subject. It is well known that French authors have led the way in a change of historical writing, which is not only highly popular, but eminently philosophical and instructive—that of giving the history of people and their condition in past times, as well as the history of wars, of kings, of nobles, and of generals. This historical research has been applied specially to the subject of labour and labourers, with a constant view to the best interests of humanity. We might show what has been done by Thierry, Michelet, Guizot, and others, but their productions are sufficiently known and appreciated. We shall mention a few less known, but whose efforts have been exclusively applied to the subject. We refer with pleasure, among them, to one of signal ability and learning—*The History of the Working Classes and the Town's People, by Adolphe Granier de Cassagnac*, published in 1837. It was apparently intended as an introduction to a more extended work, but we have met with no continuation. It forms in its present state, a

30*

very appropriate introduction to the history of the world, especially of the European world, and those countries of antiquity from
which European civilization and institutions were derived. After
pointing out the deficiencies of history in regard to the masses, the
author enters upon his task of a brief, strong, and bold outline of the
changes of condition which these masses have passed through in
various stages of the progress of humanity. His sketch includes, of
course, the history of slavery before the advent of Christianity, before which time, he says, the justice of the relation was never seriously
questioned; and also after Christianity, the progress of which for several centuries was marked by the emancipation of immense multitudes
of slaves, although neither Christ nor his apostles denounced it as inconsistent with their teachings. These enfranchisements, made with
more kindness than prudence, he shows to have been the fruitful
source of crime, misery, and degradation, among those who were freed
from compulsory service, but not admitted to the full level of freemen,
nor placed in a position where their labour would command a just remuneration. He shows that the worst of the European population are
descendants of emancipated slaves, who, as a body, have sunk below
the level of slavery, and have never been able to emerge into a better
situation under European institutions. The crimes of slaves in the
Roman Empire were far fewer than in the same number of the lower
classes of modern Europe. Freedom from personal servitude in
Christian Europe does not raise the masses to the level of slaves in
the Roman Empire. This is illustrated and shown by a vast number
of references and proofs, which make a strong impression of his cor-
rectness. We must add, as the result of our own investigations, that
the feudal slaves liberated in England in the 15th and 16th centuries,
sank after their liberation to the condition of paupers, from which, as
a body, they have never emerged. Something more than liberty is
due from the master to the slave, from the community to its poor,
and from man to his neighbour. Our author dwells upon the rise of
the *commune*, the isolated castles of the nobles, the cities, villages,
and walled towns of the people, the history of property, and the history of the peasantry, so completely forgotten by historians. But we
cannot enumerate the topics of a work so condensed. It is rich in allusion to the Bible, of which the author had an enlightened comprehension, rich in classical allusion, in Greek and Roman antiquities, in
knowledge of the civil law, in church history, and in the history of
European civilization.

The History of the Working Class, from the Slave to the Proletaire of our Day, a work in four super-royal octavo volumes, by ROBERT (DU VAR,) Paris, 1847, is a production evidently dictated by an extreme regard for the best interests of the class of whom it treats. The first words of the author are :—

"The increasing diffusion of knowledge, by awakening the sentiment of justice in souls the most withered, is extending daily the discovery of what is painful and grievous in the situation of the labouring classes. God forbid that any should be hereafter astonished that those who produce so much and consume so little should insist, by all possible arguments, upon the amelioration of their condition! This general feeling is to the thinking man a prophecy. It is the solemn guarantee of the early emancipation of labour."

After enlarging upon the importance of the history proposed, he proceeds :—

"The very idea raises grave and capital questions : we inquire at once, by what great and terrible deviation from justice, human society has become so disturbed and so badly adjusted as to produce, for some only, wealth, leisure, liberty, and comfort, while leaving to the greater number only labour, misery, and all the ills of slavery? Whence springs this disinherited class?"

Robert does not accord to slavery so high an antiquity as Granier de Cassagnac, but believes "there was a time when man was not the servant of man ; when every one, living for himself, made his own wants his master, and gathered without hindrance the fruits of his own industry ;" but he traces the poverty and misery of the masses at this day to ancient slavery.

"We have looked upon the toil of the slave of antiquity, the serf of the middle ages, and the labourers of modern times, and have set forth their reward in each period. We have lifted the veil at each epoch which conceals the misery of the working classes; we have not feared to descend to those minutiæ which, however apparently unimportant, are the real index of their condition; we have inquired, along the progress of ages, how they were nourished, lodged, and clothed, whose industry produced the food, built the houses, and manufactured the clothing."

"But the labourer, although a labourer, is yet a man in the fullest extent of the word, and as such he exists in the presence of the body politic. Citizen or not, the state, by the fact of his existence, is obliged to recognise his presence—to pronounce upon him ;—hence the historian must take account of this legislation. From the definition of slavery by pagan laws to the legislation of the present day, by which the working-men are excluded from all voice in the direction of their own interests, and completely exiled from the path of power, we have noticed and numbered the charges which legislation has brought against them, the penalties it has inflicted, and the thousand chains in which it has held them bound."

"Of course, we have followed step by step the intellectua. compression to which they have been so long subjected, their consequent ignorance, and their dangerous prejudices : to give these facts full relief, we have disclosed the different methods of education and training successively applied to the masses."

" Consolation is not wanting !—as we advance to modern times, humanity, pushed on by the invincible cravings of its nature, appears to comprehend its old error. The revolts of the ancient slaves against their masters, those of the serfs of the middle ages against their lords, had for their chief motive anger, vengeance, and other hateful passions. Modern labourers begin to call to their aid philosophy and science ; the organization of industry and the application of the principle of human brotherhood are the ideal which now stimulates the working classes. After having revolved for ages in the fatal circle of individualism, of war and contention, a necessity for harmony begins to be felt where irritation would be most excusable—order and peace begin to be sought in the arena of the interests of all."

These extracts are from the introduction. The field surveyed in this work is so extensive that we cannot even enumerate the topics. His notice of the influence of Christianity in procuring the enfranchisement of slaves is interesting :—

" Certainly, that influence was remarkable. To pass from paganism to Christianity was to pass from slavery to liberty."—Vol. i. p. 247.

He examines the effects of slavery upon the habits and history of the enfranchised, and concedes that the blessing of liberty was far from an unmingled benefit. His details upon this head are of great interest, but his views of the whole subject are less broad than those of Granier de Cassagnac.

In the progress of his work he details, with evident satisfaction, the career of the great reformer Wickliffe, who attacked the Romish hierarchy with so much boldness and vigour; he tells us, that reformer disputed the theory of property, which was prevailing then in England, and insisted that the great wealth of the clergy was wholly inconsistent with their character, and that those who would be ministers of Christ must follow his example of poverty and personal kindness to the poor. He claims Wickliffe as an apostle of humanity, holding views in accordance with those of modern reformers, and then proceeds to show at length that John Huss followed him closely in these views. (Vol. iii. p. 356 and 386.)

Our author takes a wide distinction between the Protestant Reformation of Luther and his colleagues, and the reforms proposed by Wickliffe and Huss. The reforms of the former were merely aimed at the abuses of the Romish Church, while the latter contemplated also social amelioration. The noblesse and the rich could readily coalesce with Luther's principles; but they would have been slow to sustain those of the two earlier reformers, who contemplated measures for the temporal benefit of the masses. He shows the bearing of the wars of the peasants, which followed the teachings of Huss and the doctrines of the Anabaptists, on social questions.

This work has great value as a history, and for the details it furnishes upon subjects yet very far from being exhausted; its leanings are, however, plainly to some form of socialism. This proclivity does not often mar the course of the history, and is only made clear in the fourth volume, in which he reviews the plans of various schools of socialists. He insists that, whatever may be their errors and their want of agreement among themselves, they have rendered the cause of humanity essential services. He avers that they only have rightly framed the problem of social amendment, which, alone, is a long step towards a correct solution. He evidently believes the solution will come from the side of the socialists, and that the strongest guarantee of the success of social reform is the prevalence of modified views upon the subject.*

The great problem of adjusting the relations of human labour to human well-being has been met in France, with more or less zeal, by all schools of politicians, philosophers, and writers: all are not equally enlightened, nor equally liberal, but all admit the urgency of the inquiry, and all contribute some aid to the solution. The political economists have shown great activity of the pen, perceiving that their craft was in danger from any direct inquiry into what would most promote human welfare. They have yielded to the pressure of the time whatever they can surrender without destruction of their theory of the *wealth of nations.*

It might be as profitable as agreeable to enter into an examination of the large number of works published in France, within the last twenty years, on the subject of *labour, the liberty of labour, the organization of labour, the right of labour, the laws of labour;* but the

---

* We are absolutely compelled to refrain from extending these notices by the space they are consuming, thus leaving unnoticed the productions of many writers of great power and research. As the discussion proceeds, it is instructive to watch the advance which the later writers are making under the advantages and the light derived from their predecessors. But we must forego the profit as well as the pleasure of such an examination.

greatness of the task and the narrowness of our limits forbid.* The phrases thus employed and made the subjects of elaborate and profound inquiry, are ridiculed in England, and even in this country, as implying impossibilities, or nonsense, or socialism. In France, humanity is placed, in importance, above human institutions and laws; or it is acknowledged as their object. In Great Britain and in the United States, it is assumed that our 'institutions and laws are perfect, or so nearly perfect that any consideration of mere humanity, or beneficence, which interferes with them, or calls for their amendment, is regarded as the puling conception of a visionary. Such a man, in the estimation of men of the world, is unacquainted with the stern and inevitable realities of life; he is a labourer at that which is impracticable, and is rather to be pitied for his ignorance than encouraged in his investigations. Such, in the main, is the language of the Protestant ministry and the religious press, who very promptly extinguish all such inquiries as belonging to the domain of socialism or communism, for which the horror exceeds that which is felt for mere infidelity. For, certainly, German infidelity is tolerated in many libraries for the sake of its learning, where works of socialism would not be admitted for the sake of humanity.

---

* We refer to the following, as well deserving the attention of the inquirer:—

The Liberty of Labour; an exposition of the conditions under which human powers are exerted with the most effect. By Charles Dunoyer. 3 vols. 8vo., Paris, 1845.

Essay upon the Organization of Labour, and the Future of the Working Classes. By Theo. Morin. 1 vol. 8vo., Paris, 1845.

The Laws of Labour. By Gustavus Dupuynode. 1 vol. 8vo., Paris, 1845.

The Right of Labour. A complete collection of the speeches made at the National Assembly on that subject. 1 vol. 8vo., Paris, 1848.

Essay upon the Relations of Labour to Capital. By Ch. Dupont White. 1 vol. 8vo., Paris, 1846.

SOCIALISM.

THIS word, in its commonly misapplied signification, may denote sufficiently the subject of the following remarks. If we have not already brought forward the writings of French socialists, it is not because we have overlooked them, nor because we regard them as devoid of interest and instruction. We belong not to that school which regards with a seemingly pious scorn all that passes under the name of socialism,—we are afraid to say even to the socialist, "Stand by, for I am holier than thou." We look upon the whole socialist movement as one of the greatest events of this age. We believe no man can understand the progress of humanity or its present tendencies who does not make himself, to some extent, acquainted with the teachings of socialism, and does not watch its movements. It is regarded by many, and especially by Protestant divines, as a war upon Christianity. This betrays ignorance, not only of socialism, but of human nature, and a sad misconception of Christianity itself. It is true, that a large mass of the socialists of France are not Christians, and that many of them openly express their disbelief; and it is just as true that many among us are not Christians who never scoff; and many more live in open and direct violation of Christ's injunctions of love and mercy, who make the loudest professions of Christianity. It is true enough that socialists are in error in many material or vital points, but they are earnestly seeking truth according to their opportunities and light. We hesitate not to aver that, in other material points, the Protestant communities of Great Britain and the United States, under the fuller light of the gospel, hold to errors as fatal in their final issue.

Let us inquire a little into the origin and nature of this socialist movement. Every one knows the condition of the human family under Grecian and Roman domination. It may be expressed, for our present purpose, in two words, SLAVERY and WAR. Christianity greatly ameliorated the operation of these evils of humanity. But this amelioration was incomplete when Christianity was swallowed up by a combination of priestcraft and paganism, and a long night of superstition, with slavery of body and mind, fell upon all Christendom. There was no relief for the masses, until the Reformation came and placed the Bible in the hands of the laity. The Reformation itself ended in mere Protestantism, in which the chief advantage left to the people was the possession of the sacred volume. Darkness still brooded over the people of Europe, for part remained steeped in the errors of the Papacy, and part were stuffed with the dry husks of Protestant theology. But the light of the gospel continued to brighten, until something of its power was seen in Great Britain, and a more dazzling display was exhibited in the United States. However far short these exemplifications came of the requirements of the gospel, they attracted the attention of the world. Those who were suffering every manner of evil, under institutions framed by priestly cunning, unholy ambition, and political misrule, when the benign precepts of the Saviour began by degrees to reach them, when they began to realize, from the examples of Great Britain and the United States, that men might think for themselves and estimate their own rights, perceived very soon that they were unjustly treated, that they were not admitted to their proper position in the scale of humanity, and that they were not permitted to make their own industry as available for their own benefit and comfort as justice required. Resentment against their supposed oppressors was not slow in following this view of their condition; priests, kings, rulers, and institutions became alike the objects of a hatred which became indiscriminate in proportion as it became violent. As the Papal priesthood assumed to have all Christianity in their hands, religion itself came in for a share of its dislike; for these people cried out, What has religion done for us? They had bitter experience that the dignitaries of the church were as greedy of money, and of power, as the functionaries of civil authority. It is not very surprising that they began a vigorous opposition against all that, in their view, was inimical to their interests. They could not acquiesce in doctrines, moral, political, or religious under colour of which humanity suffered such inflictions: they resisted the religion, the law, and the philosophy which gave birth to such doctrines and practices. They entered the field of theory and speculation, to find if by investigation they could deduce laws for their protection and guidance more in consonance with humanity. Being wholly unembarrassed with prejudices in favour of antiquity, or indeed in favour of any existing institution, they entered with sharp appetites upon the discussion of all abuses of power, religious and political; they held a sharp and unswerving knife as they proceeded to the dissection of Papal and civil institutions, against which they held a grudge so serious; they subjected modern society, with its accumulations of errors, to a scrutiny far more severe and searching than it had ever encountered. A great diversity of conclusions resulted from this spirit of inquiry—this active and unsparing investigation; and this army of social philosophers became separated into many camps. They quarrelled with those around them, and especially with those above them; but they were also far from agreeing among themselves. They received, finally, the name of socialists, a term intended to convey a characteristic of the whole. Properly explained, it is sufficiently significant:—they are a body of men who deem themselves injured; they point to the causes of their sufferings in the church and state, and demand a remedy; they insist that society is bound to amend their social position. They insist that no institutions can be wise or just which encourage or permit oppression—which fail of giving fair scope to industry and knowledge—which do not, as far as practicable, secure to labour its proper reward, and to knowledge and enterprise an open field and due defence. It is true that those upon whom these doctrines have brought the epithet of socialists, have run into wild errors and mistaken theories, and many of them, perhaps, into absurd and crazy conceptions. But the mistakes of some, or all, by no means set aside or nullify the irrefutable truths they have announced. It is sheer nonsense to attempt to crush these truths by the cry of socialism; it is worse than nonsense not to know and appreciate truths which have already spread far and wide beyond the ranks of the socialists. It is a pitiable ignorance which chooses to remain blind to light which is guiding great multitudes as they pass before you. It is a stubborn and wicked conservatism which is rooted to one spot in this world of evil, refusing to believe in any thing better, scouting humanity as a dream, not conceding to Christianity the triumphs which are assured by its own promises, offering to Christ this present world as now exhibited, or none,—not perceiving that the social, political, and commercial institutions of the present day, founded upon and sustained by a selfishness heretofore unequalled, are the great barriers to the progress of Christianity. The works of the socialists have exposed this hideous skeleton of selfishness—they have pursued it with unfaltering hatred; and this constitutes our main obligation to them. Our language to them should not be that of scorn or denunciation; it should be that of sympathy in their desire of truth, and compassion for their sufferings and their errors. They do desire to learn: to them every question is open: they have burst away from the chains of superstition, false morals, and false social science. Who is able or prepared to instruct them? Will not Christians step forward and show

31

them that the equality and the brotherhood and mutual kindness which they seek are all embraced in that very Christianity, which they have rejected, because they never knew it.   Do not the teachings of Christ contain all, and far, far more of the benefits they seek than their highest wishes ever reached?   It cannot for a moment be denied that if Christians,—all who are called such, made even a fair approach to the precepts of Christ in their lives and conversation, the abuses of which socialists complain and the sufferings to which the poor are subjected could no longer disgrace Christianity and outrage humanity.

While we lament that the socialists have injured their cause by indulging in vagaries at once absurd and wicked, we lament still more that those who assume to know so much better,—those who do know better,—those who have read the benign injunctions of Christ,—should have so far erred in life and teaching as not to have exhibited to the socialists a living exemplification of that kindness, that mercy, that charity, that justice, that equality, that brotherhood for which they sigh.   Can any one doubt that such examples would attract the eyes and the admiration of all the socialists and well-wishers of humanity in the world?   Can any one doubt that such an example would correct the theories and repress and set right the erroneous speculations, now on all sides so rife, in regard to social progress?   Such an argument would go farther to reclaim the socialists who are opposed to religion, than all the works on theology extant.   It does not meet the objections which they offer, when the Catholic priesthood say to them that they must not oppose the authority of the church, that the church will take care of them, that she will make up in alms what may be wanting for their sustenance from the avails of industry.   Nor is the case made better when they are told by Protestants that their position is the one assigned them in the order of Providence, which cannot be changed nor resisted without fatal consequences; that their misery and sufferings are the natural results of that depravity inherent in our nature and inherited from our first parents, and that we can no more banish wretchedness and poverty than we can eradicate original sin.   Neither do the political economists meet the case by urging that the laws of trade are founded upon the very nature of things, and, if some men suffer apparently under the operation of these laws, the evil is inevitable, and that these laws cannot be altered because their working may not be equally favourable to all; if some be less happy, others will be more; if some are starving now, others will have plenty elsewhere or hereafter, and thus the average will be fair; if many die, there will be more for those who remain; and if men are deprived of labour in one department of industry, they can turn to another; and if they die in the transition, it is because they were not needed. So, neither is the complaint of socialists met by statesmen, who tell them their demands cannot possibly be conceded without the greatest injustice to vested interests, without disturbing society to its foundations, without such a radical change of political institutions as would wholly change the existing order of things, and thus revolutionize our present social system; to the ruin of those who now hold wealth and power, advantages not to be surrendered without a struggle. No such responses as these can allay the excitement or stem the progress of socialism, the very object of which is to remove the barriers to progress, to open the career of industry to poverty-stricken multitudes, who now, when they labour at all, labour for the advantage of others more than for their own; who insist upon the solution of the problem, —What will best promote the interests of the whole number of any community?

Although we totally dissent from the plans of reforming political institutions which the socialists have proposed, we cheerfully concede their having rendered a great service to social science by demonstrating the justice and necessity of reform. Their strong sympathy for human suffering throws an interest over many of their writings, very much in contrast with much of the theology, political economy, and politics of the present day. It would be a useful task to glance over pages thus in contrast, and entertain our readers with socialists pleading the cause of humanity, and Christians taking the part of wealth and power. If much cause of humiliation should be found in this comparison, it would not be the only lesson of that kind which might be administered to those who profess to be the followers of Him who, when he took upon himself the form of humanity, became also its champion and friend.

Whatever may be said or thought by those who regard socialism as synonymous with infidelity, it is very certain that many of them are not only Christians, but derive their strongest assurances of the final success of their reforms from the universal prevalence of Christianity. It will be new to many, that one of the most noted of the socialists, the author of *Icaria*, and the leader of the French colony now settled at Nauvoo, M. CABET, is the writer of a work with the title, *True Christianity as it came by Jesus Christ*, (Paris, 18mo., 635 pages,) in which is an exposition of the Christian system as delivered by the Saviour to his disciples, in not a few respects superior to any in our Protestant libraries. He sketches the Jewish dispensation, the law, ritual and moral, the types, the prophecies, the promises of a coming Saviour, his appearing in the fulness of time, and his divine mission: he receives Him as a Divinity, as the Son of God and the Saviour of sinners, as having given a new commandment and introduced a new dispensation, intended to open up the way of life for lost transgressors, and wisely designed to amend their condition in this world. But the distinguishing excellence of this work is the exposition it gives of the life, miracles, and teachings of Christ, precisely the department in which Protestant writers come short of what is due to their great Teacher, the author and finisher of their faith. We commend this volume, which is not free from serious defects, to those whose duty it is to produce, as far as human ability will permit, something worthy of the subject. Let us have an exposition of Christianity as it came from the lips of its Author, a full development of his doctrines and precepts, as the best and only appropriate introduction to the expositions and teachings of the apostles.

LATER INDICATIONS IN GREAT BRITAIN.

WHILST the preceding pages were going to the press, we have gathered fresh evidence that the subject of human well-being is receiving in Great Britain increasing attention. Not all the interests of rank or wealth, nor the influence of the church, nor the prejudices of education, nor the immovableness of conservatism, have sufficed to keep down the topic. Socialism can no longer be kept out of sight, and the subjects it involves can no longer be overlooked. That is the real triumph of socialism—it has raised the questions and forced on the discussion. The French mind has been fully employed upon all aspects of social science; in Great Britain they are preparing to follow. They begin to admit the subject may be openly treated, and that there may be something for consideration. We have referred to some of the pioneers in this path of thought. We now notice some of later date.

We find an article in No. 22 of the *North British Review*, for August, 1849, devoted to the subject of German and French socialism, which displays some knowledge of the various writers included in the survey. The writer treats them with unsparing, and, for the most part, just criticism: he perceives their weak points, their mutual variance, and the absurdity of their conclusions; but never once touches the question which such an examination should have presented to the mind of a thinking man. Another article in the same Review, No. 30, for August, 1851, enters so far into the subject as to concede there may be room for discussion,—there may be a necessity of examining theories of human welfare,—there may be a social science. Speaking of Newman's (Political Economy) depreciating socialism, the writer remarks:—

"Among the many merits of Mr. Newman's volume, we cannot rank, however, his unexcepting depreciation of the political force of the socialist movement. No movement occupying so large a space in history could possibly be so devoid of positive worth of any kind as he represents socialism to be. In this respect, Mr. Mill, who anticipates much from socialism, seems to entertain the more just and philosophic view."

But the writer is far too deeply steeped in political economy, and too deeply convinced of the perfection of British institutions as they

31*

are, to be able to conceive the importance or breadth of the subject
which lay before him. His glimpse of the truth, however, obliges
him to say—

  " Followed out to the utmost, indeed, the spirit of political economy leads to
the fatal conclusion—that the conduct of the social life should be left entirely
to the spontaneous operation of those laws which have the seat of action in
the minds of individuals, without any attempt on the part of society, as such,
to exert a controlling influence; in other words, without allowing to the state,
or institutions for general government, any higher function than that of protecting individual freedom. And it is in this respect that political economy
has called forth the antagonistic doctrine of socialism. Viewed historically,
socialism has certainly some of the marks of a genuine step in the progressive
development of the human mind." . . . . . " The influence of socialism, however, on social science, properly so called, has consisted less in the addition of
positive doctrines of any substantial value, than in the general impulse it has
given to social speculation. As opposed to political economy, its effect has been
to vindicate the right of other laws than those concerned in the acquisition of
wealth to a recognition in the social constitution; and also, to reassert, in a
new and higher form, the necessity of general government—that is, the scientific superiority of the will of society as such, to that of all its members individually."*

  This is a large concession from that quarter, and a long step in advance of the article on socialism, in the number for August, 1849.
It is far from explicit, but it clearly reveals the transition state into
which the writer has passed. He begins to perceive that there was
something in socialism which he did not see, and that there may possibly be some deficiencies in political economy which he did not conceive. He had not yet perceived that political economy, strictly
so called, is as much opposed to the spirit of Christianity as it is antagonistic to socialism; or, in other words, that there is far more in
common between socialism and Christianity, than there is between
the latter and political economy. We make only one more remark,—
that this Review, being the organ of one of the most orthodox and
enlightened of the Protestant sects, it is hopeful to find its door opening for the discussion of social science on its merits, and that the
interests of humanity may yet find a place in Scotch theology.

  The *Edinburgh Review* has long been known for its strict devotion
to political economy. This might be exemplified in a way very little
to its credit as the friend of humanity. But the light which has burst

---

  * North British Review, No. 30, August, 1851. Article 1.

into the Protestantism of the North British, has reached, also, the interior of the Edinburgh. In the first article of the number for
January, 1851, we find the following:—

"It does seem as if the time were come for genius to find a new field for its
development and display; and there are many hopeful indications that the
same glorious faculty which has reaped harvests of enduring laurels in most
other departments, is about to take up the case of man himself. The time is
come for the leading spirits to devote themselves, heart and soul, to the solution
of those perilous enigmas of life which have so long formed our perplexity and
our despair, and to the cure of those social anomalies which darken the fair
face of the modern world, and make us feel, sadly and humbly, how imperfect
and partial is the civilization we exult in. It cannot be that the same intellect
which has wrung from nature her most hidden secrets, which has tri-
umphed over the most gigantic material obstructions, ... should not,
when fairly applied to social and administrative science, be competent to rec-
tify our errors and to smooth our path; unless, indeed, society take refuge in
the dreary creed, which never shall be ours, that the problem before us is in-
soluble, and the wretchedness around us inherent and incurable."

These are words of grand promise from a periodical so conservative
and influential as the Edinburgh Review. Clearly, the question of
human well-being is becoming an open one in Great Britain: it has
forced itself upon the attention of the enlightened, in such manner
that neither shutting eyes nor stopping ears has sufficed to keep it
away; neither ridicule, nor scorn, nor denunciation has been able to
repress its swelling vigour. The subject must be considered fairly,
openly, thoroughly: if met candidly and earnestly, by men in power
and men of wealth, it will involve no revolution, but a more faithful
performance of Christian duties.

In 1850, appeared *The Method of the Divine Government, Physical
and Moral*, by Rev. JAMES McCOSH, a Scottish divine, a large and
elaborate work, the merits of which were at once admitted, and placed
the author in a high rank as a profound thinker and able writer. He
could not, however, traverse the whole field of the providence of God,
as had been the habit of the theologians aforetime, without touching,
in several points, the growing topic of human welfare:

"Ever since the days of Adam Smith, we have been seeking to promote a
great abstraction, which we call national wealth; and in looking to it, we forget that to which it should be a mere stepping-stone—national happiness and
national virtue. A traveller is filled with admiration of our large factories," &c.
. . . . . "But has he entered the houses in which the workmen live?—has he
sitten at their boards and viewed their domestic arrangements?—has he inquired

into the character of woman, as affected by the state of society, or her work, which takes her from her family, or renders her unfit for the management of it?—has he inquired into the training of the rising generation?—has he visited those humble and humbling abodes, to which the poor and outcast are driven by crime or misfortune?—has he visited those crowded lanes of our cities, whose physical is not so polluted as their moral atmosphere, but in which the heart—larger than even the imagination—of Dr. Chalmers used to feel a livelier interest than in the gorgeous scenes of nature he so much admired? If he has done this, he will be ready to doubt whether any country, in any age, has produced a more demoralized or debauched population than the masses to be found in our large cities, (and not a few of our agricultural labourers are no better,) possessing, as they do, little of civilization but its vices, and the knowledge and wealth of the classes above them producing in them only discontent and jealousy."—Pages 263, 264, Am. Ed.

"It does look as if our earth were waiting for something greater or better than has ever yet been realized." .... "Does it not appear as if these great and beauteous works of God were preserved for a grander purpose than they have ever yet served?—that this air is yet to be breathed by, and the light of these heavenly bodies to shine upon, beings as pure as themselves are?"

"How universal, too, the restlessness, how deep the groanings and travailings of the human race! This world is not now and never has been what its inhabitants wish it to be. Hence the constant endeavours to improve it. Whether taken individually or collectively, human kind do not feel themselves to be at ease." ..... "What never ending schemes for the improvement of mankind, all proceeding on the principle that mankind need to be improved!" .....

"Can we suppose such universal desires and expectations would be excited without a deep reason? Do not the universality and the fundamental depth of the desires seem to indicate that they may be gratified?"

"Let it be frankly admitted that there is progress in the world. There is progress in agriculture, there is progress in all the arts and in all the sciences." ..... "But is there to be a physical and intellectual, and no moral progress? Is the less to advance and the greater to remain stationary?" ..... "Some of these considerations may be regarded as brought from a distance; yet by their collection and clustering, they seem to us to form a pleasant belt of light—a kind of milky way, hung over our world, in this its dark night, to give light to the traveller who has set out in search of truth."—Pages 467-469.

These extracts exhibit either the efforts of a deep thinker groping his way in a subject with which he was not yet familiar, or of one who, understanding the subject, was feeling the pulse of his readers, to know how far he might go in aspirations for human progress. In either case, the inquiry arises, how Christian men, believers in the Scriptures, can so wholly overlook the four Gospels as not to perceive the ample light they shed upon these dark problems and deep imaginings? He must either have been labouring in the mists of theology, or have been afraid to speak out his sentiments in an atmosphere of theology. Few Scottish divines could have ventured upon the career of Dr. Chalmers; and even with his courage, few could venture upon a subject, the paths of which were so hedged in by the prejudices of education.

Among the works placed in our hands since we commenced these notes, is *The Theory of Human Progression and Natural Probability of a Reign of Justice*, (8vo., London and Edinburgh, 1850,) which we regard as a striking evidence of the advance of social science in Great Britain.

We can only commend it to the reader's notice, as a volume of more than ordinary ability. It is the offspring of a profound thinker, but of one who has not sufficiently explored the whole ground of social science to be an equally safe guide in all places. His chief position is that *knowledge is reform*—that the increase of knowledge must be the basis of all human progression. He regards Divine revelation as an indispensable accompaniment of all other knowledge, which must ever be kept within Christian limits and inspired with Christian aims. The author does not believe that pauperism comes from God:

"It is man's doing, and man's doing alone. God has abundantly supplied man with all the means of support; and where he cannot find support, we must not look to the arrangements of the Almighty, but to those of men, and to the mode in which they have portioned out the earth. To charge the poverty of man on God, is to blaspheme the Creator, instead of bowing down in reverent thankfulness for the profusion of his goodness. *He* has given enough, abundance, more than sufficient; and if man has not enough, we must look to the mode in which God's gifts have been distributed. There *is* enough, enough for all, abundantly enough; and all that is requisite, is freedom to labour on the soil and extract from it the produce that God intended for man's support." . . . . . "If we find, at one end of society, a few thousand individuals with enormous wealth, for which they work not, and never have worked, and on the other end of society, millions born on the same soil, with barely the necessaries of life, and too often in abject destitution, there is no other possible conclusion than that this poverty arises from man's arrangements." . . . . . "If Englishmen discover that pauperism and wretchedness are unnecessary; that the Divine Being never intended such things; that the degradation of the labouring population, their moral degradation consequent on poverty, is the curse of the laws, and not of nature, does any man suppose that Englishmen would not be justified in abolishing such laws, or that they will not abolish them?"—Page 313–315.

This writer is a vehement opponent of the whole theory of political

economy, as now held by the chiefs of that school. He states his
objections strongly, and, we think, convincingly. They are so well
founded, that we may wonder why he did not take the *welfare of man,*
which he avers to be the true object of political economy, as the subject
of his volume. It would have formed a much clearer radiating point
for his inquiries than the indefinite term *knowledge.* He thus com-
mits the very error, and indulges in the very same kind of fallacy
which lead astray the writers of political economy : he exalts the
means above the end. Knowledge is a means of human progression,
an indispensable means ; but human welfare is only to be achieved by
a variety of means—knowledge among the rest. So industry, wealth,
and commerce are means of human welfare, and can only be properly
treated in that aspect. The attempt to construct a science out of the
facts of industry, wealth, and commerce, without any regard to human well-being, or to any moral considerations, is as baseless as
knowledge, apart from men *to know.* The leading imperfection of this
very creditable performance may be traced to this erroneous starting-
point.

A work which attracts much attention, appeared a few months since
in London, with the title, *Social Statics,* by *Herbert Spencer.* It is
apparently an attempt to consecrate some of the more refined of the
Malthusian doctrines, by placing them on more specious grounds, and
assuming new data and a more popular line of argument : it comes to
the aid of the political economists, by offering them a basis for their
whole fabric different from that which they ever claimed. It comes
to the aid of the English institutions, not only by assuming a theory
of society which adopts the views of the few who hold the power and
the wealth of the country, but by starting from the present distribution of power, rank and wealth, with the position that the perfection
of society consists in the perfect liberty of every individual to do
what he pleases, provided he infringes not the liberty or rights of
others. That is, the present distribution of the good things of this
world must not be changed in the United Kingdom ; but that being
conceded, the man of power and the man without, the man of wealth
and the pauper, should each have the largest and most perfect liberty
consistent with their not touching each other. This is the highest and
most ingenious sublimation of English political philosophy which has
yet been given to the world ; and it is given forth under the plausible
colours of the largest liberty. It forbids the thought of charity or
brotherhood or sacrifice ; it consecrates selfishness and individual-

ism as the prime feature of society. It forbids all deliberation for the common good—all legislation for the present good of the greatest number. Its principle is, the least possible restriction, the fewest possible enactments—the weak must be left to their weakness, the strong must be trusted with their strength, the unprotected must not look for favour, and government must resolve itself into the lowest possible agent of non-intervention.

It may be hoped this is the last specimen we shall see of that philosophy which aims to exalt the present institutions of society into the first principles of social science. This volume of Mr. Spencer is characterized by clearness and severe logic, and the ability of the writer increases the regret that it is not employed in the service of humanity. When a logical mind like his shall, in a survey of *social statics*, set his compass from the point of human welfare, we shall see him developing a very different system from that which we have noticed. It will be a system in which public good will be pursued with a view to individual welfare; in which politics, political economy, and Christianity will be found blending their efforts and interests in the sole consideration of social happiness; in which selfishness will not be consecrated, under the name of the largest individual liberty, as a fundamental principle of society, but self-denial and mutual kindness taken as the basis of human society.

The following works, omitted in the catalogue at page 294, are worthy of being consulted :—

Essays on the Principles of Charitable Institutions, 8vo., London,········ 1836
The Wrongs of Man, by Wm. Manning, 8vo., London, ················· 1838
The Claims of Labour—Duties of Employers and Employed, 12mo.,
    London, ·· 1845
The Elevation of the People, Moral, Instructional, and Social, by Rev.
    Th. Milnor, 8vo., London, ····································· 1846
Over-population and its Remedy, by Wm. Thomas Thornton, 8vo., London, 1846
An Analysis of the Occupations of the People of Great Britain, Wm. F.
    Spackman, 8vo. London,·· 1847
The Organization of Industry, by T. C. Banfield, 8vo., London,········· 1848

PROTESTANTISM.

WHATEVER advantages many sects may enjoy in point of orthodoxy, purity of doctrine, and knowledge of revelation, the mass of Protestants have no special grounds of complacency. In proportion to their light, their privileges, and their mental freedom, their advances in pure Christianity are by no means so creditable as generally assumed. There is more ground for recent assertions of Catholic authorities, that Protestantism is declining, than is admitted. The Catholics did nôt perceive that true religion was gaining even where Protestantism was crumbling, nor did they perceive, when they made this boast, that Christianity would become for them a far more formidable adversary than Protestantism. When Christianity has made all the conquests which belong to its career, the Christian will look back upon Protestant history with grief and mortification, that so much light and so many privileges were so long abused under cover of a hard and unprofitable theology. We might multiply quotations to this effect, from other sources than Papal writers, but restrict ourselves to a very few. We have already referred to (ante 347) *Conferences upon Christianity in its Application to Social Questions*, by the Rev. ED. DE PRESSENSE, *a Protestant and evangelical pastor in Paris.* From this volume, which deserves the profound study of Protestants in other quarters of Christendom, we offer another passage :—

"But the social question is nothing else at this day than the degree of predominance to be allowed to charity in our institutions. It was this principle of charity which should have been graven upon men's consciences, and we now know why the Protestant dogma could not do it."

"If we are willing to be convinced of the insufficiency of Protestantism to direct society in the transformations it is now undergoing, we have only to look at the attitude it assumes in regard to the social questions of the day. It has shown itself indifferent or hostile to this movement: in Germany, France, England, and Switzerland, the real Protestants have refused to entertain this question; and in their just opposition to socialism, they have smothered the very legitimate question of which socialism has usurped the place. This is specially to be remarked in England; for, if there is one country more than another where a question touching the interests of humanity should have been favourably regarded, that was England. Close to the magnificent residences of the aristocracy, the manufacturing towns conceal more miseries than we can conceive; and Ireland, suffering the tortures of famishing poverty, continually stares her in the face." . . . . . "If England, then, displays such a hideous exhibition of poverty, we must infer that there is not in the religious spirit which rules there, an inspiration strong enough to lift the public mind into the career of wise social reform."

"We have very strong proof that the weakness of Protestantism cannot be attributed to second causes, but must be laid at its own door—it is everywhere crumbling."*

"In England it seems to preserve intact its ancient form, because the revolutions which have shaken the continent have not penetrated there; but from the day it shall penetrate, wherever the heated wave strikes, that ancient form must yield." . . . . . . "In Germany, where social and political questions have long been largely discussed, Protestantism is routed."

"In France, Protestantism wields so little power, that many are disposed to inquire where it is concealed; and it does well to hide its miserably degraded condition. It cannot assume here the name of a church. Weak and small, yet so divided that we cannot return a united response to any question. Sad state! proving that Protestantism in France, as elsewhere, has had its day."—Page 214.

M. Pressensé insists that the Catholics annihilate the principle of charity by their system, which exhibits God as only granting his pardon to our good works; that is, paying us the wages of our labour. It implies no love, no compassion in the Deity.

The Protestant system is, he alleges, scarcely less erroneous. It exhibits the sovereignty of God so nakedly and so constantly in its teachings, that those revelations of his word showing him to be a God of Love, as well as of Infinite Power and Justice, blending his attributes into that perfection of Judgment and Mercy which we adore, are lost from sight. Charity expires under a theology so ungenial to its nature. (Page 202.)

In reference to Protestant theology, we are reminded that it is important not only to hold to right doctrines, but to keep them in the right place, assigning to each their due prominence. We must wear our garments in their proper order, if we would be perfectly clothed. The Christian who dwells only upon God's sovereignty, and speaks only of God's immutable decrees, cannot but lose the harmony which should reign in Christian life and demeanour.

For an article containing some wholesome truths for Protestants, we commend to the reader the *Battle of the Churches*, in the Westminster Review, No. 108, for January, 1851. It is well at times to be taught by

* Since 1849, the date of M. Pressensé's publication, English Protestantism has been shaken to its basis, and is certainly in danger, if not already crumbling.

our enemies, and the extract in that article, from Mr. Newman, who writes under all the rancour of a fresh family quarrel, giving unmistakeable evidence of his willingness to point out Protestant failings without mercy and without compunction, may furnish food for thought and motives for self-examination, if not grounds for profound humiliation.

We know there is a vast deal of complacency and pride among us Protestants, and if any thing can justify such a feeling, there may be many grounds for this self-satisfaction. Our minds are free from the bondage of Romanism, we perceive clearly the iniquities of priestcraft, we have the Scriptures, read them freely, and exalt them to the skies as divine in their origin and teachings, we build imposing and costly temples for the worship of God, we punctually attend upon that worship at the summons of the church-going bell, long lines of well-clad, decently behaved, genteel people crowd the walks and roads which lead to the house of God; luxurious seats are weekly filled with these order-loving people, attending upon the regular preaching of the word, and giving ear to the strains of the organ or the efforts of the choir; the weekly meeting for prayer sends up its stated supplications, the Sunday-school gathers in multitudes of children, the regular agents of the church and its religious and benevolent institutions are yearly enriched with large contributions. But in all this, however much there is to admire and love, there may be none, and very often is very little true Christianity. Many true Christians mingle in this external pageant of religion, as doubtless do many in the Papal churches, but in neither case is the external exhibition any essential part of religion. It may not be all wrong—it may be all right—it may be a means of grace, but it should never be mistaken, as it is extensively, for Christianity. It is the foreground of a picture, in which there is much to delight the eye and gratify the taste, a beautiful blending of colours and fine outlines: but there is a dark, unregarded background in the depths of the picture. When an individual of one of the forsaken classes in London was asked what his class thought of religion, the reply showed he had seen the picture:—"Religion is not for the likes of us; it's for the great and rich people." In this deep, deep background are the masses of humanity, far outnumbering those in the front: there is poverty, pauperism, misery; there is ignorance, envy, hatred, and crime; there are willing hands and nothing for them to do; there is unrequited labour; there is famine, disease, and premature death.

Protestants have not invited this neglected multitude to the entertainment of Christianity; it has not gone into the streets and highways to bring in the poor to the house of feasting; the courts and lanes and alleys have not been visited, to constrain the wretched to come in and fill up the vacant seats in Protestant churches. How differently would the picture strike the beholder if suddenly transformed in a perfect representation of Christianity! The stately temples would fade away, and whole masses of suffering humanity would rise to view: instead of the long lines of orderly people in the path to church, we should see hosts of good Samaritans hurrying through crowds of the poor, pouring in oil and wine, and speaking everywhere words of life and comfort, in the name of Christ; and while myriads of hands were eagerly thrust out for the cup of cold water, as many would eagerly extend it to parched lips. Praise would no longer go up merely from this mountain or that, but from every heart, in every place. The gospel would be preached to the poor, and the disciples would be as well known by their loving one another, as they are now distinguished by strife, bigotry, and estrangement.

Protestantism has a fearful account to render for abused privileges and wilful blindness, for exalting theology above charity, for leading children to theology instead of to Christ, and thus giving them a stone in place of bread, for discarding humanity, for abjuring the brotherhood of man and substituting sectarian exclusiveness and bitterness. It would be easy to prolong this accusation—but it is enough to excite reflection. Let it not be thought that these charges bear with as much force against individual Christians as against Protestantism and its sects. A crime of society is often the accumulation of centuries. Such evils are felt by many who are powerless to remedy them. How many lament the effects on their minds of a religious education encumbered by superstitions or fettered by a useless theology! They find themselves cooped up in the frame-work of a system they can neither escape nor modify nor overthrow. Christian men are not acting freely; their paths of active duty are not marked out by the precepts of Christ, but according to the arrangements of man. They cannot oppose the church without scandal: they cannot obey Christ without being eccentric. Fetters of man's invention are now restraining the movements of thousands of intelligent Christians, who long for the liberty of the gospel, — to be free in Christ. They are restrained by the consideration that they must not so use their liberty as to offend weak brethren, or by the prejudices of their own education. These are truly orthodox, evangelical Christians, whose great desire is to place Christian charity at the head of Christian graces, where it belongs.

There are multitudes, on the other hand, whose only mode of showing their zeal for religion is a rigid observance of the established usages of their church, a prompt appeal to its standards in cases of doubt. To such a degree of assurance does this narrowness of the mind arrive, that men, while indulging a spirit at war with the very essence of Christianity, look upon many around them with the condescension of pity or the unconcern of conscious superiority. Love for the human family is a sentiment to which they are utter strangers: they can rise no higher in their efforts for it, than contributions or labours to bring converts to their particular denomination. These are the Pharisees of modern times. Their faults are the result of their education. They are men who, under proper training, would have been real benefactors of their race; but their theology, which is perhaps sound, has smothered the heart, instead of reforming and guiding it, and has absorbed instead of having sanctified their affections.

It is a serious mistake to claim infallibility for Protestantism: we take the Scriptures, which are unerring, for our guide, but our fallibility is displayed at every step, not only in interpretation of what is doubtful, but in our imperfect compliance with what is perfectly plain. We must not forget that human nature is as prone to evil among us as among others; and that the ENEMY is as active among us as he is in the Papal camp. We must not be surprised, indeed, if his greatest feats of cunning and power are directed against us. It was indeed a masterly stroke of policy to win a signal advantage, in the very hour of his overthrow at the Reformation. The Reformers were bent on extricating the truth from the mass of papal rubbish, and on erecting a structure of sound theology: they were resolved upon having the Bible in their own hands, to decide for themselves. Theological controversies without limit furnished them full employment for their time and full use for their Bibles: mounted on their own hobby, the Reformers rode hard, and they rode far. They had the Scriptures, but the enemy carefully hid from their sight, in the excitement of controversy, the precepts, the parables, the sermons of Christ—these were of no use in theological polemics, and very inopportune in a period when strife raged and all the evil passions were in full exercise. The Scriptures were used freely and constantly in this warfare upon matters of faith, to vindicate the truth; but they were little heeded in their instructions as to conduct and conversation. Spiritual perception was wide awake in matters of controversy, but asleep in those of charity. These controversies even yet continue, and theology is yet enlarging its boundaries. The Scriptures for three centuries have been chiefly thus applied. If the heat of the contest has abated, and if interest in theology has diminished—if the cries of humanity are coming up in our ears from all Christendom, and we are compelled to search the Scriptures anew, to discover whether there is any thing there applicable to the demands of poverty, oppression, and misery—we find this long forgotten and unused life of Christ, his precepts, sermons, and parables, whose instructions cover the whole ground and meet the whole case. But, unfortunately, our standards, creeds, confessions of faith, catechisms, and manuals of devotion were drawn up by men more versed in polemics, more engaged in the heat of religious controversy, than versed in the principles of peace, mercy, kindness, and charity; unfortunately our whole Protestant literature, our whole religious education has all come from the same mint. The life and precepts of Christ are not incorporated in our religious ideas. We cannot, therefore, instantly apply them. We require time to cast the old skin and come out clothed in new garments of love, mercy, and peace. It was, indeed, worthy the cunning of our great spiritual enemy, thus to cheat the Reformation of half its truth and half its energy; but his skill has been not less manifested in later times, by giving to all the sayings and doings of the Reformers the sanction of age and the bulwark of conservatism: having emasculated Protestantism at its birth, he now rallies all the sober, substantial, conservative clergy, and all the rich, substantial, satisfied laymen, in defence of the noble band of Reformers who so valiantly fought the battles of the Reformation. To desert them, it is urged, would be to desert Christianity. It is virtually admitted that the Scriptures are insufficient without the explanations of these men of battle and storm; and that our theology, born in the heat of religious controversy, is our only safeguard, even at this day. The Jews fastened their traditions upon the Old Testament Scriptures, the Papists concealed the whole Bible in the machinery of their church, and the Protestants cannot escape the charge of overlaying the Scriptures with a mass of theology, in the shape of creeds, articles, catechisms, standards, platforms, confessions of faith, and manuals of devotion. Let these formularies be examined simply in the light of Christ's teachings, and their coldness, dryness, and inconsistency with the true spirit of Christianity will be manifest.

They breathe none of the spirit of kindness, mercy, and charity of Him whose ministry was among the poor, and whose miraculous powers were chiefly exerted to feed the hungry and heal the diseased. Christ's life and teachings were not deemed available in the contests of the Reformation, and were, therefore, not incorporated into the systems of that day. And now they are to be deemed inadmissible, because they come too late—the divines of that day and a century or so later having settled the whole frame-work of our Protestant religion. Taking as a sample of these compends of theology, one of the latest and most admired specimens, one that is, perhaps, the most faithfully taught and the most highly venerated by the denominations who receive it as their *vade mecum*, the *Shorter Catechism* drawn up by the Westminster Assembly of Divines, we ask a moment's attention to its main features. This catechism, framed with singular aptness, precision, and vigour of expression, is placed by several large denominations of Christians in the hands of children of the tenderest years: it is pressed upon their attention and memories as the best religious instruction which can be given them, as the very marrow and essence of Christianity. It teaches the doctrines of the Trinity, of the decrees of God, of Providence, of original sin, or the fall of man with Adam; the covenant of works, the covenant of grace, election, eternal Sonship, Christ made man, the offices of Christ as Prophet, Priest, and King; his humiliation, exaltation, and death; of justification, adoption, sanctification; of the resurrection, of the obligation of the ten commandments, of eternal punishment, of faith in Christ, of repentance, of the sacraments of baptism and the Lord's Supper; concluding with a few questions on the Lord's Prayer. And this is the milk with which their babes are fed—this is the fountain to which good people carry their children. Christ said, "Suffer little children to come unto me;" and, although these people have Christ in the Gospels, his very words intelligible to children, abounding in the most simple and touching lessons, in a form the most interesting for the tender mind of children, and containing injunctions suited to every age and every walk in life, these are all made to give way to this compend of mere theology.*

Is this bringing children to Christ? Is this honouring his instruc-

---

* We have just noticed a work on charity, by the great Jonathan Edwards, advertised as now in the press. It is rather a remarkable fact, and somewhat indicative of the Protestant estimation of that subject, that such a work should have been permitted to sleep a century, during which time not a volume on that topic was extant in the English language.

tions? But how does it look, in an epitome of Christianity, to pass unnoticed the comprehensive precepts of Christ, reaching so deep into the heart and stretching so wide into human obligations, substituting the decalogue and applying all possible power of enlargement to make it reach the ground so explicitly covered by the very searching injunctions of Christ? Let any unprejudiced man compare this enlargement with the special sermons of Christ, and he must inquire, with amazement, what could have been the motive for the substitution? The words of Christ extend to our whole outward and inward duty, and need no paraphrase. They should be impressed upon the minds of children from infancy upwards. They constitute a practical guide for our duty to God and to man, and are, therefore, of daily and incessant application. They refer to our conduct, and direct our Christian life and conversation—therefore, perhaps, they have been left out. The framers were far more concerned about faith than works, and they passed over all of Christ except his offices, if we except the Lord's prayer, which is specially distinguished. The Reformers, and the successors to their vocation and spirit, always inculcated prayer. They could not rise to the conception of charity, and mercy, and peace, but they could pray devoutly, and loud, and long. They were willing to talk with God, but they could not preach the gospel to the poor. They could stand up and make long prayers—they could pray in secret, and with earnestness, but the kindness of brotherly love was almost a stranger to their bosoms. In the judgment of charity, there have been hosts of such men who were true Christians, not according to the measure of their own estimation, but according to the grace of Christ, which perceives a spark of faith far less than a "grain of mustard-seed."

Whatever may have been the number and value of the children of the Reformation, Charity is yet to be born. We may rejoice that Christendom is now in labour. If Christians can now be brought to know and do what is right, charity will be the fruit of these throes, and the world will be gladdened to see the brightest and loveliest offspring of Christianity.

A CASE SUPPOSED UPON THE SUBJECT OF VARIOUS INTERPRETATIONS OF THE BIBLE.

LET us suppose that an ardent friend of the truth has found in his missionary tours a large number of people who are strangers to the Bible and its contents. The good messenger of the gospel hastens to place in their hands the holy volume which points out the way of eternal blessedness, and by his earnest exhortation and amiable deportment obtains assurance that the good book shall be carefully read. In due time the missionary invites his beneficiaries of the Bible to communicate their impressions. He finds their views differing with every different mind, from the closest adherence to the letter to the widest limit of liberal construction—he finds opinions corresponding, in greater or less degree, to all the sects of Christendom. Some profess their confidence and full faith in the whole volume, some in portions; some cling to the letter, others to the spirit; some announce it as a spirit of eternal life, but clothed in earthly habiliments; some receive it as a veritable and entire revelation from heaven; others as only containing heavenly truths mingled with human statements—as containing a mass from which we may select the important declarations which convey the message of eternal life; some admire the history of the Old Testament, and the morals of the New; some, the poetic portions of the Old Testament and the benign precepts of the New; some find the Trinity clearly taught; others, while they receive the Bible as the word of God, Christ as their Saviour, and the Holy Spirit as their Sanctifier, cannot receive the doctrine of the Trinity; some find warrant for believing in a great mysterious mystical body, called the church, while others believe that Christ enjoins no form of organization upon his followers, leaving them to adopt such, in all circumstances, as they may deem most effective, most suited to peculiar cases—that the organization and the form of the ministry may be unfolded and gradually shaped by the piety of the people, and not that this piety can be dependent upon any form of church government or ecclesiastical arrangement—that no other creed or confession or manual of piety is required than the New Testament itself.

A much greater variety of opinion was manifested by these students of the Bible, among which were many who could perceive no beauty nor truth in its pages, and some who were disposed to regard the whole as an invention of impostors.

Our missionary replied to this candid expression of the views of his Bible readers, that he had much reason to be gratified by the evident attention which had been given to the holy book he had placed in their hands, and thus continued :—" I am not surprised to find a wide diversity of opinion among you. It could not be otherwise, as God has constituted the human mind : if we judge for ourselves, our judgments must be different, for our minds are no more cast in the same mould than our faces. Diversity is a characteristic of the world and its creatures. There is even much diversity in each one of us at different times. God could easily have given us his word in such a form that no shadow of doubt could have rested upon any passage, and no room have been left for inquiry, or thought, or weighing of conclusions. He has not done so. The course of His providence, as well as the nature of his revelation, shows that his mode of dealing with men is, to place before them, constantly, that which must exercise all their mental and moral powers. As by bodily exercise the muscles are developed in size and improved in strength and facility of motion, so, in the order of God's laws, the powers of the soul expand with exercise and attain increasing energy and activity. You differ widely in your construction of God's word, because you vary in mind, in knowledge, in judgment, in mental habits, and because there are varieties also in your moral constitution. If you were all willing to be guided implicitly by me, giving up your conclusions for mine, it could not benefit you, because God knows your real opinions, and, in His view, acquiescence is not faith, and sincerity is better than mere profession. According to my understanding of the Scriptures, some of you have seized the whole truth and have found the way of life, and some of you have found a Saviour, who have not perceived the whole truth; some of you have a very clear view of the letter of the word without having attained, perhaps, to the spiritual meaning; there is a line, seen only by the eye of God, between those of you, whether wholly right or not, who believe unto salvation, and those who come fatally short. No human hand can trace that line. I beseech you all to strive that you may not at last come short of a saving knowledge. You have merely begun the study of the Scriptures ; a long life will not exhaust their lessons of wisdom. But stop not, as too many do, in their mere learning and exposition, study rather their spiritual meaning and their general scope. Let every step you make in the knowledge of the

Scriptures be exemplified in your life. I have not the least doubt, that the highest attainments in God's word are only made by those who exemplify strictly what they learn. It is only when Christian experience accompanies Christian wisdom that the spiritual understanding is opened. To such only is it given to understand the truths which lie hidden from those who, having eyes, see not, and having ears hear not, the truths of the gospel. I cannot point out the line of fatal error which runs between you, but I can, with some certainty, by your future lives, tell who is travelling heavenward. I shall entertain strong hopes of all who cling to this book as their rule of life, even though they may, in my estimation, err greatly in its interpretation. To those who are alarmed at the doctrine of eternal decrees and God's foreknowledge, let me say there is nothing more difficult in that than in the existence of such a world as this with such people in it. If we cannot reconcile our free will with God's decrees, he has removed all practical difficulty out of our way, by making our wills free and making us responsible for our acts. It cannot be otherwise, according to the clear tenor of the Scriptures, than that we are free to choose between eternal life and death; and it cannot be otherwise than that God foreknows whatsoever is to come to pass. This is enough for us. But there remains a class of you to whom I must say a word :—You who perceive no truth in the Scriptures and do not regard them as a message from God. I am sorry, most sorry, but I do not despair: I have known many entertaining the same views to change them. Let me exhort you to keep in mind, that if you are in error, it is a fatal error, one which entails eternal and unavailing repentance. You should be very sure before you adopt such opinions. I shall not cease to pray for you, hope for you, and do all I can to aid you.

"I might regard you all as the representatives of the various churches or sects to whose opinions you respectively make the nearest approach; and you who put no faith in the Bible, I might range with the unbelievers of the world. But I prefer to have all look at the subject from a different point of view. There is much less diversity in what, as Christians, we have to do, than in what we may believe. The mind is able to traverse far more ground than the body; a greater arena is therefore given for its exercises. I wish you to agree in what is to be done for your fellow-men and yourselves, and leave you, while in harmony of action, a wide divergency of belief. I ask you to keep the Bible in your hands, striving to realize the spirit and main object of its instructions. I know there must be a diversity of interpretation; but whilst you are unable to agree in many points of doctrine, you all agree that your chief duties are to love God and be a brother and a helper to your fellow-man; on this broad platform you may all travel heavenward in harmony, making your differences of opinion in other matters continual occasion for the exercise of charity and forbearance; not forgetting, however, that the great use of these differences is to stimulate and strengthen the mind to increased efforts after truth. While we, therefore, sharpen our perceptions and quicken our pursuit of the truth, let all undue struggle and collision be moderated by labours of love and mercy. If our theology—our divinity be not blended with humanity it cannot be genuine. Our Saviour was not only the Son of God; he was also the Son of man.

The case here supposed, has occurred in part. The Bible has been scattered broadcast for half a century; it has been sent forth without paraphrase or explanations. Its truths are diffused among the nations of the earth. The result is various, and may be readily seen by close observers. The most remarkable is that which is seen in the universal movement in favour of human well-being. Never, since the world began, was such a voice raised in behalf of humanity. It is daily growing in force and in extent. Can any one imagine any fountain from which all this charity could have flowed, but the Gospels? There is no human source which could have furnished the opinions which are now proclaimed, or excited the feelings of human sympathy now prevalent. Let us then welcome back the bread which was thrown upon the waters, even though it may have gathered impurities from exposure and improper contact. Let us hear the report from all who come with the Bible in their hands, and let us treat them kindly, aid them when we can, and, if need be, let us be humble enough to receive instruction from those who have had the Bible free from all the trammels of prejudice, early education, and systematic theology. It is possible that these new students may bring up truths, or applications of truths, which have escaped those who preceded them. It is very certain that those whose minds have not passed through the theology of the Reformation, almost always fasten upon the life and instructions of Christ as the most interesting and precious portion of the volume. These have passed from mouth to mouth, and are now throughout Europe beginning to leaven the whole mass of the population, and thence the general cry for the amelioration of the condition of the inferior classes.

THE END.